ADVANCE PRAISE FOR

PUTIN'S RUSSIA

"Lilia Shevtsova is in a class by herself as an analyst and explicator of Russian politics, and her mastery is fully on display in *Putin's Russia*. She combines investigative skills with hardheaded judgment and narrative verve. Her portraits of the main actors are textured and convincing. Not only is this a superb book by a powerful author, it has an additional significance in the context of Russia's evolution as a normal modern country: As recently as fifteen years ago, this sort of gimlet-eyed look at what goes on in and around the Kremlin was available only from dissidents, emigrants, and Western specialists. It's a testament to how far Russia has come from Soviet times—and it augurs well for Russia's future—that someone of Shevtsova's intellectual integrity, independent convictions, and relentless honesty, based at a Moscow think tank, can help all of us understand what's happening—and why—in the leadership of her country."

—**STROBE TALBOTT**, president, Brookings Institution

"Winston Churchill said that Russia is a mystery inside an enigma. Having been in Russian politics for the past twelve years, I can attest that Lilia Shevtsova in her latest book has brilliantly succeeded in unwrapping the Russian enigma. As for the mystery, it will finally be solved only by history."

—**GRIGORY YAVLINSKY**, head of Russia's Yabloko Party

PUTIN'S RUSSIA

OTHER BOOKS BY
LILIA SHEVTSOVA

YELTSIN'S RUSSIA: Myths and Reality

GORBACHEV, YELTSIN, AND PUTIN: Political Leadership
in Russia's Transition (*edited with Archie Brown*)

---

*To read excerpts and find more information on these and other publications
from the Carnegie Endowment, visit* **www.ceip.org/pubs**

PUTIN'S
RUSSIA

LILIA SHEVTSOVA

CARNEGIE ENDOWMENT FOR INTERNATIONAL PEACE
Washington, D.C.

Carnegie Endowment for International Peace
1779 Massachusetts Avenue, N.W., Washington, D.C. 20036
202-483-7600, Fax 202-483-1840
www.ceip.org

The Carnegie Endowment for International Peace normally does not take institutional positions on public policy issues; the views and recommendations presented in this publication do not necessarily represent the views of the Carnegie Endowment, its officers, staff, or trustees.

To order, contact Carnegie's distributor:
The Brookings Institution Press
Department 029, Washington, D.C. 20042-0029, USA
1-800-275-1447 or 1-202-797-6258
Fax 202-797-2960, E-mail bibooks@brook.edu

Cover photo: Russian president Vladimir Putin at the Kremlin during the three-day hostage siege at a Moscow theater in October 2002 (AP/Wide World Photos).

Interior design by Naylor Design. Composition by Oakland Street Publishing. Manufactured on acid-free, 20% recycled content paper with soy-based inks by Jarboe Printing.

Library of Congress Cataloging-in-Publication Data

Shevëtìsova, Liliëiìa Fedorovna.
    Putin's Russia / Lilia Shevtsova.
        p. cm.
Includes bibliographical references and index.
    ISBN 0-87003-201-1 (pbk. : alk. paper) -- ISBN 0-87003-202-X (cloth : alk. paper)
    1. Russia (Federation)--Politics and government--1991- 2. Putin, Vladimir
Vladimirovich, 1952- I. Title.
DK510.763.S492 2003
947.086--dc21   2003003917

10   09   08   07   06   05   04   5   4   3   2   1   1st Printing 2003

CONTENTS

FOREWORD

R ussia continues to matter. Major world challenges—the war on international terrorism; confronting Islamic fundamentalism; preserving European and world security; stabilizing volatile emerging markets; fighting the proliferation of weapons of mass destruction; the diversification of energy supplies; dealing with regional conflicts, including the Middle Eastern quagmire; and counterbalancing potential new powers, first of all China—cannot be met without Russia's constructive participation. To secure Russia's integration into the international community is becoming one of the most ambitious challenges for the West in the twenty-first century.

It is true that Russian leader Vladimir Putin has made a pro-Western shift since the terrorist attacks of September 11, 2001. Russia became a U.S. ally in the antiterrorist campaign without asking for any reciprocity and without the usual horse trading Soviet leaders demanded for any concession to the West. There are times when history makes leaders. In the fall of 2001, the attacks transformed a hitherto cautious and tentative politician into a leader who surprised the world by proposing a new role for Russia, one almost unprecedented in history: unconditional support for the West.

Yet, as events after 1945 remind us, a wartime alliance will survive the end of war only if it embodies shared interests and values. Are both the West and Russia prepared to grow from their current antiterrorist alliance into a constructive strategic partnership, including Russia's full-fledged integration into the West? The answer depends first of all on domestic developments in Putin's Russia, on how soon Russian elites and Russian society embrace liberal democratic rules of the game.

So far, Russia remains an area of ambiguity. Both optimists and pessimists can find arguments to support their views. On the one hand, one can see that Putin has restarted economic reforms that had stalled under his predecessor Boris Yeltsin and has led a foreign policy revolution in opening Russia to the West. He has introduced a new type of political leadership—pragmatic, rational, with a more predictable type of governance.

On the other hand, the Russian leader has demonstrated a profound mistrust of the key elements of liberal democracy: political pluralism, an independent opposition, and free media. He has attempted to base his rule on a mix—economic liberalism, pragmatic authoritarianism, and a pro-Western orientation. This mix may have been enough to modernize a peasant country. But it hardly can help Russia deal with the challenges of the postindustrial era. Sooner or later, the limitations of one-man rule—even in a more pragmatic wrapping—will become clear.

The question therefore remains open: When and how will Russia be ready for its major breakthrough: dismantling personified power and establishing independent institutions and the rule of law? Only then can the new Russia become a real partner of the West. The future of Russia's transformation depends on whether its ruling class can understand that the status quo could end with stagnation and degeneration; whether its leader can realize that accumulating all resources in his hands will not make him omnipotent; and whether society can learn that it has to create its own destiny, not wait for a decision from the top. Furthermore, Russia's shift toward the West needs a strategy for integrating Russia on the part of Western powers.

Putin's Russia is the first comprehensive account of Russia's new leadership, puzzles of transformation, and relations with the West. Its author, Lilia Shevtsova, a senior associate in the Carnegie Endowment's Russian and Eurasian Program, has long been a keen observer of Russia's politics, dividing her time between Moscow and Washington. She is one of the most respected political analysts in Russia and the West who are following the postcommunist transformation of Russia. Her previous landmark study, *Yeltsin's Russia*, was also published by the Endowment.

We are grateful for the support provided to the Endowment's Russian and Eurasian Program by the Carnegie Corporation of New York, the Starr Foundation, and the Charles Stewart Mott Foundation.

Jessica T. Mathews
President
Carnegie Endowment for International Peace

ACKNOWLEDGMENTS

This political diary would have never appeared in print without the support and friendship of a terrific group of people. It would not have been published without the constant support and encouragement of Jessica Mathews, the president of the Carnegie Endowment. Both vice presidents of the Endowment, Paul Balaran and Thomas Carothers, are also partially responsible for this story about Putin's Russia. Paul created the warm atmosphere that has always surrounded me in Moscow and Washington. Tom was a good reader, with an ironic eye, who helped me prepare the book for the Western reader.

Special thanks go to Strobe Talbott, who was my first reader, both for his good advice and extensive comments and for the thoughts he generously gave to me.

Andrew Kuchins, the director of the Carnegie Endowment's Russian and Eurasian Program, and Robert Nurick, the director of the Carnegie Moscow Center, read the manuscript and helped me with matters of style and logic.

I am indebted to Nina Bouis, the translator, who found my voice and gave part of herself to the book as well.

I am grateful to Alice Phillips, who edited the manuscript and delicately shaped its final form, making it more accessible to a wider readership.

Alfred Imhoff made final editorial corrections of the manuscript and gave astute comments.

My thanks go to Trish Reynolds, the Carnegie Endowment's director of publications, with whom I have now worked on two books about Russia, and to Sherry Pettie, the Endowment's production manager, who has now coordinated the editorial and production process for three of my books.

Caroline McGregor and Faith Hillis, junior fellows at the Carnegie Endowment, helped me prepare the manuscript for publication.

I am grateful to my friends and colleagues at the Carnegie Endowment and outside the Endowment—in both Moscow and Washington—for being there, grateful that I can see them and argue, agree and disagree, and we still remain friends. They all, perhaps without realizing it, help me keep my political diaries.

And finally, my thanks to my family—mother, husband, and son—for their patience and for understanding that thinking and writing about Russian politics is a habit that can't be kicked.

PUTIN'S RUSSIA

PROLOGUE

On December 31, 1999, Yeltsin's Russia became Putin's Russia. Boris Yeltsin—a political maverick who until the end tried to play the mutually exclusive roles of democrat and tsar, who made revolutionary frenzy and turmoil his way of survival—unexpectedly left the Kremlin and handed over power, like a New Year's gift, to Vladimir Putin, an unknown former intelligence officer who had hardly ever dreamed of becoming a Russian leader.

Yeltsin—tired and sick, disoriented and having lost his stamina—apparently understood that he could no longer keep power in his fist. It was a painful and dramatic decision for a politician for whom nonstop struggle for power and domination was the substance of life and his main ambition. His failing health and numerous heart attacks, however, were not the main reasons behind his unexpected resignation.

The moment came when Yeltsin could not control the situation much longer and—more important—he did not know how to deal with the new challenges Russia was facing. He had been accustomed to making breakthroughs, to defeating his enemies, to overcoming obstacles. He was not prepared for state building, for the effort of everyday governance, for consensus making, for knitting a new national unity. By nature he was a terminator, not a transformational leader. It was time for him to graciously bow out and hand over power to his successor. And Russia had to live through a time of real suspense while the Kremlin was preparing the transfer of power.

The new Russian leader Vladimir Putin has become a symbol of a staggering mix of continuity and change. For part of Russia, he symbol-

ized a link with Yeltsin's past; for another part, he was a sharp break from
it. The new Kremlin boss has been shrewd enough to let people think
what they want and to see what they long for.

Outwardly, with Putin's ascendancy to power, the style of Russian
leadership has changed dramatically. He is unusually young for a Russian
leader, a 48-year-old dynamic yet ascetic-looking man, such a contrast to
the pathetic Old Boris at the end of his rule. Putin not only has succeeded in taming Russian elites and arrogant tycoons but also has maintained an amazing 70 percent approval rating for several years.

Putin does not even try to play monarch. He wants to be accepted as
a pragmatic manager. He has succeeded—at least outwardly—in achieving order and stability. He has begun a pro-Western revolution in foreign
policy. He has pushed forward economic reforms that had stalled under
Yeltsin. Yet at the same time, he has demonstrated a deep distrust of the
major democratic institutions and an open desire to keep tight control
over society. Unlike Yeltsin, who knew how to survive in an atmosphere
of spontaneity and acquiescence, the new Russian leader prefers subordination and loyalty.

Not only its leader and leadership pattern but Russia itself has suddenly changed, as if someone had closed one chapter and started another. The
country—only recently torn between extremes, anticipating an apocalyp-
tic scenario, in a desperate search for its new self—has drifted into a lull,
dominated by longing for calm private life, by disgust for any great ideas,
and by fear of new shake-ups. President Putin has become an embodiment
of this longing for stability and tranquility. He would have never ascend-
ed to the top if the country had wanted to continue its revolution.

But in Russia the appearance of calm is always deceptive. Too many
questions still remain unanswered: How sustainable is Russian stability? Is
it based on readiness to pursue further transformation or on the desire to
make peace among all political forces? What is the true nature of Putin's
leadership, and how far will he be able to go with a new round of reform?
How can he combine his authoritarian ways with economic liberalism
and pro-Western policy?

Putin's epoch is not over, and both the president and Russia may baf-
fle us with their answers to these questions. Putin's Russia is still an unfinished story.

This book shows how Russia under Vladimir Putin has tried to define its new identity internationally and domestically, moving forward and backward from optimism and hope to anguish and resentment. It is a book on transitional ambiguity. On the one hand, this ambiguity helps to preserve continuity with Yeltsin and the pre-Yeltsin past and acts as a soothing drug for those who want to live in the past—and thus it has become the major stabilizing factor. On the other hand, it prevents Russia from making a more vigorous transformation, with its inevitable new tensions. Every country in transition has been facing its own dilemma between stability and breakthrough. For Russia, this dilemma is complicated by the fact that a radical transformation might trigger developments that Moscow would not be able to control.

This is also a book about the paradoxes of transition. It is intellectually intriguing but politically alarming to watch the holdovers from the past in action—the Communists are fighting for parliamentary democracy, and the liberals are defending authoritarianism and personified rule. It's perplexing to see how former KGB colonel Putin has led Russia's pro-Western shift. And the list of puzzles is not complete. Here is one more paradox: Ordinary Russians are much readier to modernize than are Russian elites, who are dragging their feet, being totally unable to rule democratically.

This is also a book on leadership, which continues to be Russia's major political institution—in fact its only one. Since 2000, leadership has enabled Russia to reenergize itself. Yet the fact that leadership is the only institution makes it the major stumbling block, the key obstacle preventing Russia from becoming a modern state and liberal democracy.

This is not a book for those who are looking for quick and definite answers. It is for those who are ready to look behind the evident, who want to understand the reasons for vacillations, who can imagine how difficult it is to fight depression and dismay, especially when the political class is not up to the dramatic tasks at hand.

This is not simply a book on a country and its leader. It is a story of constant overcoming, of challenges and opportunities, of the ability to learn by losing and making blunders. If I succeed in provoking your interest in trying to solve Russian puzzles, my mission will be fulfilled.

Chapter 1

THE KREMLIN'S POWER PLAY

Yeltsin on the wane. The Primakov formula. Who runs Russia?
The Kremlin seeks an heir. The Bank of New York scandal.
Enter Putin. Russia wants order. The uses of war.

It is Moscow in the spring of 2000, less than half a year since Vladimir Putin emerged in the Kremlin as the new leader of Russia. Oligarchs, once arrogant and bullying but now living in fear of a visit from secret police in black masks, have already moved their money and their families abroad and are keeping a low profile.[1] Only notorious tycoon Boris Berezovsky, one of those who orchestrated Putin's ascent, desperately tries to build an opposition to challenge the new Kremlin boss; but no one will dare to join him. Russia's governors and other regional lords, many of whom ran almost independent fiefs under Putin's predecessor, Boris Yeltsin, now look to Moscow in servile fashion. The corridors of the Kremlin are full of people with a military bearing and nondescript faces.

Women, particularly middle-aged ones, swoon over President Putin, lifted from obscurity and named prime minister, victor in the March presidential election, champion of the "strong hand" in Chechnya and of "verticality of authority" (a term coined by Russian elites to describe a top-down system of governance based on subordination and a domineering role for the executive branch). Some declare their love for their slender, athletic leader in television interviews. Putin, with his tireless activity and determined air, baffles observers accustomed to watching a chronically ailing leader and speculating about who rules Russia. This new president stirs anxiety among various groups; after all, no one is sure what is on his mind.

Editors in chief and heads of major television networks censor the mass media, steering clear of any topic that might disturb the new boss in the Kremlin. The intelligentsia returns to the kitchen to berate the authorities over a cup of tea or a glass of vodka, their criticism driven back inside, as in the long-forgotten Brezhnev years. Ordinary Russians just lie low.

Remembering too well Yeltsin's final phases, I keep wanting to pinch myself. Just six months ago, Russia was a different country. By the end of the 1990s, Yeltsin had lost control of it and himself. Berezovsky whispered his plans for Russia into the ear of the president's sweet daughter, and she and a few friends elevated and toppled high officials and made government policy. Oligarchs kicked open the doors of government offices and ran for their own benefit the remnants of the economy, which had been decimated by long-standing weaknesses and the August 1998 financial collapse. Regional leaders ruled over their provinces like little tsars, either paying no attention to the Kremlin or blackmailing the Moscow courtiers and the president himself.

The Russian state eroded, losing its power and the ability to perform elementary functions of government.[2] Russia sank deeper and deeper into social and economic crisis: falling life expectancy (for men, from 64.2 years in 1989 to as low as 57.6 years in 1994); a resurgence of contagious diseases that had been eliminated in the Soviet Union; decaying schools; hundreds of thousands of homeless children; millions of migrants; a shrinking economy that during Yeltsin's tenure contracted in real terms by 40 percent; and finally, rampant lawlessness and corruption that had become a lifestyle passing for "normal." Ordinary people had lost both the past and the future, and the present was confusing for many. But neither the president nor elites seemed to notice—they were busy pretending to rule, struggling for a place at the top, robbing the state.

The newspapers attacked Yeltsin ruthlessly, but ordinary people had wearied of their unprecedented freedom to criticize the government, because it brought about no improvement. The president was regarded with both pity and scorn. The authorities were blamed for everything from failed hopes for a normal life after the fall of communism to people's feelings of helplessness. The Kremlin had totally lost the aura of sacredness and mystery that had surrounded rulers of Russia through the ages, revealing itself as a marketplace where everything could be bought and sold.

In another dispiriting development, the Russian presidency seemed to have reverted to the Soviet pattern of gerontocracy, in which one old man hung on as leader until he died, only to be replaced by another old man. President Yeltsin, once powerful and charming, with an astonishing strength of will that had enabled him to destroy the Communist Party and the Soviet empire, now hid from the world, shuttling between dachas outside Moscow. Few besides his family and physicians had access to him. His physical decline was tortured. It was not only his heart condition—though he later admitted he had had five severe heart attacks. He seemed to have problems with everything, including walking, holding himself erect, concentrating, and even comprehending what he was being asked about. When he was shown to the public, his doctors alone knew the effort it took for him to hold himself together. And he was not that old as we watched him deteriorate; he was still in his late sixties.

Like Yeltsin, the other denizens of the Kremlin were more and more removed from society and its ills. Neither constant charges of corruption nor crushing national problems worried them; they thought only of holding on to their power and perquisites. Those who formed the Kremlin entourage were reckless, sure of themselves and their control of the game. They seemed to have no premonition that the game might end.

At the end of the 1990s, in fact, no one was really running the country. Beginning in 1996, the political class was preoccupied with when Yeltsin would step down and who would rule Russia after him. How did Tsar Boris look today, was he compos mentis or not? How long would he last? Everything else was secondary. Society settled in for what it assumed would be the patriarch's prolonged good-bye, while Russia continued its political and economic decay.

Who then had even heard of Vladimir Putin? Who outside a tiny circle in Moscow knew his name even in early 1999? The few who had met him had trouble later recalling the man or remembering that Yeltsin had made him head of the Federal Security Service (FSB), formerly the KGB. In 1998 or much of 1999, a suggestion that Putin would be the next president of Russia would have elicited bewilderment, if not laughter.

The slow crumbling of governmental authority seemed well-nigh irreversible then, and rapid assertion and consolidation of central control highly unlikely, but very soon those and other expectations would be stood on their heads. It seemed that Yeltsin would never leave office voluntarily, much less before his term was over—that he would sit (or lie) in the Kremlin until he died. It seemed that there would be a vicious struggle among the main "power clans," or interest groups; the heads of some were already imagining their victories and gloating. It seemed clear that the two leading contenders for Yeltsin's throne were Moscow mayor Yuri Luzhkov, who successfully competed with federal authorities for power and money, and recent prime minister Yevgeny Primakov, experienced apparatchik, former head of the Federal Intelligence Service (SVR), and current foreign minister. Finally, whatever the result of the power struggles at the top, many assumed that the Russian people had gotten used to a free and spontaneous life, to constant political bickering, to the unruliness of elites, and would reject any return of the "iron hand." But those who thought so turned out to know little of the Russian soul, or of how panic and fear can suddenly change the political mentality of millions.

As the 1990s drew to a close, economic and social emergencies and the febrile mood they created among the populace were ready to speed up events in Russia. In 1998, Russia moved inexorably toward a financial crash. Russian stocks were plummeting. State bonds were paying 130 to 140 percent. The Central Bank was trying desperately to keep the ruble stable. On August 19, the Ministry of Finance had to cover 34 billion rubles worth ($5.7 billion before devaluation) of GKOs (state short-term bonds). The treasury did not have that kind of money, nor could it borrow it anywhere. The $22 billion International Monetary Fund and World Bank credit granted to Russia—under heavy pressure from U.S. president Bill Clinton—had vanished to parts unknown.

During what for many ordinary people was a painful postcommunist transformation, Russians had become used to labor strikes, hunger strikes, suicide, and self-immolation driven by despair and hopelessness.

But the situation grew more volatile in 1998. Desperate miners from state-owned mines, who had not been paid for months, began blocking railroad tracks. Their representatives came to Moscow and set up a tent city in front of the White House, where the Russian cabinet sits. The miners demanded not only back pay but also Yeltsin's resignation. I remember the men, stripped to the waist in the broiling sun, sitting in the street and rhythmically beating their miners' helmets on the hot cobblestones. I remember their angry looks at officials' limousines with closed and shadowed windows hurtling past. Moscow was suddenly back in the throes of class hatred dredged up from long ago. The hungry Russia of the provinces had come to Moscow to remind the capital of its existence, and the wake-up call was ominous. In the late 1980s, it had been the miners—when they wanted Yeltsin in the Kremlin—who had rattled the throne beneath Gorbachev. Now they wanted him out. The power in the Kremlin was registering seismic movement again.

The miners were left unmolested, however, and mayor Yuri Luzhkov gave orders that they be allowed to demonstrate and even had them fed. As a pretender to the highest Kremlin post, Luzhkov had an interest in keeping the miners in Moscow as long as possible: They could hasten a new distribution of power, and he was the first waiting in line to claim his prize.

Russia cried out for leadership at this critical juncture, but neither the president nor the cabinet nor other political figures had the answers to the country's problems. The doddering Yeltsin had almost disappeared from view, making occasional public appearances only to confirm that he was still alive. "Working on documents," the official explanation for his absences from the Kremlin, drew a skeptical smile from Russians. Even usually sure-of-themselves liberals seemed to have lost their nerve. The 37-year-old prime minister, Sergei Kiriyenko, dubbed by the press "Kindersurpriz" (after a chocolate popular with Russian children), looked perplexed. When elevated to prime minister shortly before, he had brimmed with self-assurance. Now, in an apparent attempt to hide his confusion, he talked nonstop. His words, like persistent, boring rain, meant nothing.

Left to deal with a deepening financial crisis, Kiriyenko didn't have time—much less the ability—to gauge its seriousness. His experience as a Komsomol (Communist Youth League) leader and then a provincial banker in Nizhny Novgorod until coming to Moscow the year before had not prepared him for this. I remember the reaction of officials at international organizations who dealt with Kiriyenko. "My God, how will he cope?" they asked, clutching their heads. "He doesn't even know which buttons to push."

Before the end of 1998, treasury officials had to find 113 billion rubles ($18 billion) to pay the interest on GKOs and OFZs (state loan bonds). Moscow also had to pay salaries and pensions for public-sector workers, and the nonpayments had been accumulating since the beginning of the year. Tax revenues would not exceed 164.6 billion rubles ($22.5 billion). The fragile Russian banking system was on the verge of collapse. The economy was disintegrating. The West could no longer help. Russian citizens were still being patient, but that could end at any moment. And then—no, no one wanted to contemplate what could happen in Russia then.

Some of the members of Yeltsin's team quickly figured out that the financial chaos, with millions of rubles streaming out of the country, presented a unique opportunity for enrichment for people who kept their heads. In any case, everyone in power in 1998 not only survived the crash but continued to do well financially, even better than before. Russian history has shown how much advantage can be extracted from a crisis, especially if you are the one managing it.

After some hesitation, on August 17, 1998, the Kiriyenko government declared Russia bankrupt, deciding to go for default and devaluation at the same time—this after Yeltsin's promise that there would be no devaluation. The small circle that reached the decision on bankruptcy included leading reformers Anatoly Chubais and Yegor Gaidar. The previous day, Kiriyenko and Chubais had flown to Yeltsin's dacha with proposals that the president had been forced to approve, having no other solution. A demoralized Yeltsin had lost control over events.

Acknowledging the influence of the powerful oligarchic clans, Kiriyenko met with their representatives late that night to give them a report on what had happened. Most likely, Yeltsin's oligarchs knew what was coming. Grigory Yavlinsky, the leader of the democratic movement Yabloko, openly accused Kiriyenko of acting on behalf of the tycoons, saying, "The financial collapse was Kiriyenko's fault, because his actions had been ineffective and, most important, favored certain oligarchic groups." In any case, all the tycoons had gotten their money out of the failing banks in time, and soon they established new banks and continued to prosper, while ordinary Russians lost their savings in the collapse and had to start from scratch.

Yet the Kiriyenko government was not fully accountable for the August 1998 financial crisis. The emergency was partly a reaction to the Asian economic meltdown that had begun the year before. Moreover, the pre-conditions had been established in Russia under the government of prime minister Victor Chernomyrdin, who had survived for quite a long while in the time of Yeltsin's permanent cabinet reshuffles. Appointed premier in 1992 after Gaidar's dismissal, he was fired in 1998 only because Yeltsin suspected him of harboring an interest in the president's job—which Chernomyrdin definitely did. (One of the catalysts for his firing was a visit to the United States, during which he met with his old negotiating partner Vice President Al Gore and Gore treated "Cherno" like a future leader of Russia. Yeltsin could not tolerate that.)

What had led to the financial collapse were parliamentary populism and the premier's craven behavior. Instead of fighting for a workable budget, Chernomyrdin chose to create the GKO pyramid—to borrow money at a high rate of interest. As for the parliament, which pumped unsecured rubles into the budget, we know that venting and caving in to populist demands for fiscal irresponsibility are always among the functions of parliaments. In the case of Russia, that populism gets more play because the Duma, the lower house of the parliament, does not form the government and is not responsible for its actions. That was true in Yeltsin's era, and it is still true in Putin's.

Nor was Kiriyenko's government blameless. Kiriyenko had enough financial know-how to have realized he could avert catastrophe by devaluing the ruble gradually, but he did not do so. Either he panicked or he was certain that his luck would hold. Or else he was working in the interests of certain oligarchs, as Yavlinsky suggested.

Russians rushed to save their money, desperately trying to withdraw funds from private banks. But many lost everything. Foreigners lost their money as well. Most of them closed their offices and left the country. The Moscow gold rush seemed to be over for good. After some vacillation, Yeltsin fired the government of Kindersurpriz Kiriyenko and decided to bring back Victor Chernomyrdin, whom he trusted, hoping that that political heavyweight would find a way out. Yeltsin himself remained at his dacha, unable to face his people as their country slid toward the abyss.

Yeltsin's absence during the crisis gave rise to rumors about his stepping down. CBS News in the United States reported that the Russian president had signed a letter to be read after the parliament approved Chernomyrdin's candidacy, in which Yeltsin resigned from office and handed over all power to his successor. Chernomyrdin's close associates assiduously spread that rumor, hoping to push events in that direction. Journalists hurried to update their political obituaries of Yeltsin yet one more time.

Finally, when rumors of his resignation had become the top news story of the day, Yeltsin appeared in public. On August 21, the ailing president made a point of inspecting Russia's Northern Fleet and visiting the nuclear-powered battleship *Peter the Great*. It was a warning—"Don't touch me, I have military might behind me." Yeltsin was accompanied, as Brezhnev had been in his day, by an entire hospital. But even though at that moment he could barely speak, Yeltsin could still create a lot of trouble. The old bear had the power to fire people, to shuffle and reshuffle the cabinet, to use force if necessary. God alone knew what an unpredictable Kremlin boss could do when threatened or feeling depressed or angered, or when at a loss as to what to do.

On August 28, Yeltsin gave a television interview, his first in a long time. Much care must have gone into preparing and editing it. Nevertheless, Yeltsin looked extremely ill and old during the interview; it was hard for him to talk and, it appeared, even harder for him to think. He grew animated just once, when he declared firmly, "And I won't retire." Only then did he come alive, the old stubbornness in his eyes. The interview had been done for the sake of that one phrase, when the president suddenly awoke.

Events took another unpleasant turn for Yeltsin when the parliament rejected Chernomyrdin. The country was without a government and burdened with a collapsing economy. Yeltsin could have insisted and pro-

posed Chernomyrdin again, and yet again, and if the deputies had rejected his candidate for prime minister three times he could have dissolved
the parliament and called new elections. That meant war with the parliament. But the president could no longer operate with any certainty
that society, the power structures (the army and navy, the intelligence
services, and internal affairs—*siloviki*, as they are called in Russia), and
regional elites would support him. Now real panic set in at the Kremlin.
Its inhabitants, so cocky yesterday, were suddenly paralyzed with fear,
unable to cope with the growing disarray.

Television viewers got another look at General Alexander Lebed—
who had long frightened Russians with his dictatorial aspirations—when
he arrived in Moscow with the clear hope of being invited to take
charge. Several years before, Lebed had been one of the most influential
politicians in Russia. In the presidential election of 1996, Lebed came in
third; and as a reward for calling on his supporters to vote for Yeltsin in
the second round, he was given the post of secretary of the Security
Council (the body coordinating the activity of the power structures).
Lebed was the one who signed the Khasavurt peace treaty with
Chechnya that ended the first Chechen war (1994–1996). He could not
quiet his presidential ambitions, and in late 1996 Yeltsin fired him. After
that, the irrepressible general won election as governor of one of Siberia's
richest regions, Krasnoyarski Krai, and became a regional tsar.[3]

The general could not suppress a triumphant grin as he descended the
aircraft's stairs upon arrival. His whole demeanor seemed to say, "Well, it
looks as if I'll have to save this country!" Lebed's appearance in Moscow
was supposed to signal the Kremlin's readiness to use force to hold onto
the power that was draining away from it. But it was a rather desperate
ploy, because the general, as everyone knew, had vast ambitions and had
never been on a leash. He could not be trusted. If Lebed ended up in the
Kremlin as Yeltsin's savior, the best Yeltsin and his team could expect was
to be pensioned off the very next day.

The year 1999, decisive for the future of Russia, showed how far the
country had moved beyond the monolithic, autocratic power traditional

for Russia and yet how much it still lived by it, even when power was transferred to a new leader through democratic mechanisms. It was a strange and disturbing mixture of continuity and change, this fusion of governance à la Old Russia with elements of liberal democracy. The degeneration of Yeltsin's presidency and the crumbling of his power that accelerated after the financial collapse revealed the essence of the regime that Yeltsin had created to be an *elected monarchy*. In fact, Yeltsin, a revolutionary of a sort, who had delivered a fatal blow to the Soviet empire and to communism, helped preserve—without meaning to—aspects of the "Russian System" that had perpetuated itself down through the long centuries, surviving tsarism and the Bolshevik Revolution.

The Russian System is a specific type of governance structure whose characteristics include paternalism, the state domineering over the individual, isolation from the outside world, and ambitions to be a great power. The heart of the system was the all-powerful leader, above the law and a law unto himself, concentrating in his hands all powers, without a balancing accountability, and limiting all other institutions to auxiliary, administrative functions. The Russian System did not need fixed rules of the game; it needed fixers.

Yeltsin's ascent to power through victory in a free and fair election fatally undermined the Russian System, introducing into politics in Russia a new kind of legitimation, which destroys the sacred and irrational character of power and makes power dependent, at least partially, on society. As president, Yeltsin weakened the Russian System by opening society to the West and turning away from at least some of the great-power complexes. But by preserving one-man rule, Russia's first non-communist leader preserved the inertia of the Russian System, not only in the people's mentality but in the style of presidential rule, in the relations between authorities and society.

Russia's experience in the 1990s proved that the one-man regime could function relatively well in a stable environment but could not manage in a crisis, especially when the leader was physically incapable of performing a leader's routine tasks, had no support in society, and could not rely on the army and other instruments of coercion. In the absence of mature institutions, Yeltsin inevitably had to share power with his most trusted and loyal people. Naturally, the most trusted and loyal people turned out to be members of his family and friends of the family.

Yeltsin's political family (known in Russia as "the Family") was a mixed group that included the president's younger daughter Tatyana (Tanya) Dyachenko; her closest pal and, it appeared much later, boyfriend, Valentin Yumashev (they married after Yeltsin resigned); Yeltsin's chief of staff, Alexander Voloshin; and oligarch Roman Abramovich. The infamous oligarch Boris Berezovsky, the master of intrigue, was their leader and the brains of the bunch. These were the people who ruled the Kremlin in the late 1990s, and they continue to exert their influence on Russian politics.

It is a story that has been repeated in many countries in many periods: The strong leader who has worked so long to gather all power into his own hands becomes a hostage of his court as he ages. From inside that trap, he watches his power and his character degrade. Sometimes he understands that he is becoming a weakling and even a laughingstock. Often he doesn't.

It was hard to discern in the shell of a man left by the late 1990s the Boris Yeltsin who had ridden the democratic wave in the late 1980s and the beginning of the 1990s and who could elicit unconditional support from crowds merely by his presence. The leader who had made his mission Russia's return to Europe and its transformation into a flourishing democratic state ended up a politician completely dependent on his Kremlin servants, stooping to primitive intrigue and manipulation to survive.

Yeltsin's every appearance outside the Kremlin threatened to compromise him and his country. Russia and the world knew of his outlandish behavior: Here a drunken Yeltsin conducted a band in Germany; there he crawled out of his airplane, puffy-faced and staggering, after missing an official meeting with the Irish prime minister. We can only guess at scenes the cameras of Western correspondents failed to capture. As Yeltsin grew weaker physically, the ostensibly superpresidential system became obviously disabled, devolving into a half-hearted Impotent Omnipotence.

Yeltsin's primary means of exercising power as his second term wore on was the personnel merry-go-round that never stopped. In the eight years of his presidency, he changed prime minister seven times and prosecutor general six times, went through seven heads of his old agency, the FSB, and had three ministers of foreign affairs. Permanent cadre revolution became his major instrument for holding onto power. Shakeups of his team made it seem for the next week or two as if he were still in control, and created an artificial need for him to play coordinator and arbiter. It was an illusion of governance.

Having lost the reforming impulse, the elected monarchy turned into a source of instability. Under the Russian Constitution that Yeltsin had edited after he dismantled the parliament in 1993, the parties elected to the parliament had no opportunity to form a cabinet, and the rubber-stamp parliament had no real opportunity to affect the policies of the government. Thus the regime procured for Russia an irresponsible parliament with an irresponsible multiparty system. Both the parties and the parliament kept themselves alive by means of constant attacks on the executive branch. The cabinet, formed by the president and subordinate to him, was even less accountable. It consisted almost entirely of representatives of influential groups and existed to serve their interests. Such a regime could not deal successfully with the challenges Russia faced. At best, it could guarantee stagnation.

For Yeltsin personally, the important thing in early 1999 was to find a candidate for the prime minister's job who would be acceptable to the parliament yet pose no threat to himself. Moscow mayor Yuri Luzhkov seemed to think his time had come to ascend the Russian throne. For that, he first had to become prime minister. Under the Russian Constitution, the prime minister's best chance to take over the presidency comes if the president resigns for reasons of health. In such a case, the prime minister organizes new elections—and in Russia, that gives him the resources for organizing his own victory at the polls.

Even some members of Yeltsin's team bet on Luzhkov, indicating a certain defeatism within the ranks. But for Yeltsin—or rather, for his political Family—Luzhkov was unacceptable. Independent and headstrong, Luzhkov ruled Moscow godfather-style. But the biggest headache for the Yeltsin team was the mayor's entourage. Even a dull observer noticed the hostility between the Kremlin court and the Moscow court, which sometimes broke into open warfare.

When foreign minister Yevgeny Primakov's name came up, Yeltsin decided right away that he was his choice for premier. The first to suggest the idea was Grigory Yavlinsky, leader of the democratic party Yabloko. Yavlinsky saw Primakov as a lesser evil than other possible candidates for the job and thought he would not want to go on to be president but would be merely a transitional figure who would help Russia escape coups or political upheaval in any form during the inevitable transfer of power from Yeltsin to his successor.

Primakov was an experienced Soviet apparatchik who knew how to keep up good relations with all important groups. He had managed to get through the collapse of the Soviet Union without alienating either Gorbachev or Yeltsin. He succeeded in simultaneously being friends with Iraqi president Saddam Hussein and U.S. secretary of state Madeleine Albright! Primakov always avoided conflicts and knew how to wait. He also understood how to be loyal without servility. This was a man who could be supported by the most varied groups—a moderate conservative who at the time was the perfect symbol of the stability that the majority of Russians desperately wanted and needed.

Yeltsin offered the prime minister's post to Primakov. "I refused categorically," Primakov wrote in his book *Years in Big-Time Politics.* On leaving Yeltsin's office, however, he ran into the president's younger daughter, Tatyana Dyachenko, and family friend Valentin Yumashev—that is, the people who ruled the Kremlin. They managed to persuade him to accept Yeltsin's job offer. Primakov explained his turnaround this way: "For a moment, reason took a back seat and feelings won out."

Yeltsin, by taking on Primakov as prime minister, obtained a reprieve for himself. And in early 1999 an informal double-rule gradually prevailed in Russia, with political weight shifting to the cabinet. The new prime minister brought in his people and made the cabinet a major decision-making body that did not wait for advice or endorsement from the presidential staff—a development hardly welcome to the Yeltsin Family. A new "ruling party" began to form around Primakov, and interest groups that had not been satisfied with their roles signed on.

It was the second time in a decade in postcommunist Russia that a quest for the redistribution of power in government had begun. The first attempt took place during the clash between the president and parliament in 1991–1993, when the two branches of government contended to see which would be the more powerful. That conflict had ended dramatically, with the dissolution of the parliament and Yeltsin's order to fire on the White House, the former parliament building in Moscow. A peaceful separation of powers had been unlikely then, because both sides wanted a monopoly on power and neither was prepared to impose any limitations on itself.

In 1999, a redistribution of political resources initiated by Primakov began within the executive branch. It included a strengthening of the cabinet, which had never been independent or strong in Russia, and the prime minister's taking over of the economic agenda. The rest of the governance, including security policy and control over the power structures, remained in the hands of Yeltsin's staff. It was an informal re-division of power within the executive, making the split among president, cabinet, and prime minister much more even than it had been. Influential political forces—the Communists, and also major representatives of regional elites—openly supported the idea of constitutional reform that would remove the president's excessive powers and legally endorse the change of rules that Primakov had initiated. The main proposals for reform came down to the idea that Russia must switch to a hybrid premier–presidential regime, under which the president's personal power would be lessened and the parliament and the cabinet would have a larger role.

Russian liberal reformers, especially those close to Gaidar and Chubais, had from the start been against a system of counterbalances to the president, because they believed it could slow economic reform. Their position was understandable, given that the left wing dominated the parliament; strengthening the legislative branch, and especially forming the cabinet on the basis of the majority in the parliament, could mean trouble for reform policies. So for the sake of economic results, the liberal reformers rejected an extremely important principle of liberal democracy: checks and balances, provided by strong institutions.

Russia had fallen into a historical trap. What it boiled down to was that those who called themselves liberals did not trust the representative institutions or society, fearing the unleashing of populism. They preferred to leave governing exclusively in the hands of the leader, making him the sole center of power. The liberals' fears of populism were not unfounded. But rule through a superpresidency did not speed the course of economic transformation in Russia; on the contrary, the reform measures introduced by presidential decree lacked legitimacy and were often boycotted by numerous bureaucrats and by social groups that felt the decrees endangered their interests. Moreover, the president's unusually extensive powers created the temptation at the top to move toward frank and harsher authoritarianism. Yeltsin did not go that way. But his successor might try.

In addition, the weakness of institutions meant that the president was drawn into day-to-day management, which would have been taxing for even a much hardier person than Yeltsin. The existence of a prime minister allowed the president to evade responsibility for the work of his cabinet; when his policy failed, he simply fired cabinet members. Or he fired the prime minister, who in that era was only a presidential appointee with no strong party support in the parliament. So the model of power in the Yeltsin years, during which the cabinet was intentionally weak—and was in fact an extension of the president's staff—created room for the leader's erratic behavior.

In early 1999, Primakov's government, backed by the Duma, put through the most liberal budget in Russia's history, which reduced government spending and made control of inflation a goal. And the most amazing thing was that the Communist Party supported fiscal austerity. It seemed that the left wing, forced to bear responsibility for the government, had to curb its appetite.

The "Primakov formula," however, was not to be incorporated into the Constitution. On May 12, 1999, Primakov was forced to resign, and the experiment with separation of powers in Russia—particularly reapportionment of executive power—failed again. Eighty-one percent of those polled immediately afterward by the Public Opinion Foundation disapproved of the firing, whereas a mere 8 percent approved. Twenty-two percent of those polled said they would vote for Primakov if he ran for president—15 percentage points ahead of Communist Party leader Gennady Zyuganov, 11 ahead of Yavlinsky, and 7 ahead of Luzhkov. It appeared that Primakov had become quite popular and had a good chance to be more than a transitional figure. And that did not fit with the plans of Yeltsin and his entourage.

Naturally, Primakov is not a democrat or a liberal, and never was. He is an adherent of bureaucratic capitalism. He is known to hate personal criticism and to be suspicious of reporters.[4] He would have been unlikely to tolerate freedom of opposition if he had gained power. He also distrusted the West, especially the United States. The former premier was famous for his "Primakov loop"—learning of the March 1999 NATO bombing of Yugoslavia while en route to the United States, Primakov had the pilot turn the plane around and fly back to Moscow. That loop immediately made him a hero in Russia.

But we should not spend much time lamenting Primakov. He might have pushed constitutional changes curbing the enormous power of the Russian president. But bearing in mind the influence of left-wing and centrist forces in the country, such changes could have slowed economic transformation even more. Nor do we have good reason to believe that Primakov would have begun building independent institutions after his ascent to the top Kremlin post. Finally, we might come to the conclusion that Primakov would never have made the pro-Western shift that Putin accomplished in 2001. That by itself allows us not to regret Primakov's exit.

Why didn't the Primakov experiment succeed? It was not simply because Yeltsin could not bear for the prime minister's office to become the hub of government activity. That was certainly a factor, but much more important was that under the Primakov formula the Yeltsin Family's hold on power was not guaranteed. An independent prime minister supported by the Duma and with his own power base within the state apparatus and power ministries would not allow the Yeltsin crowd to name anyone else as Yeltsin's successor. And the Family did not want to see the too powerful, independent Primakov, who was not obligated to the Family, as the heir.

An old Russian tradition came into play as the succession issue loomed: failure to establish the mechanisms for a legitimate and truly constitutional transfer of power. A lack of such mechanisms had condemned Russia to the palace coups under the tsars and the putsches that brought in new general secretaries of the Communist Party. Even the passing of power from Gorbachev to Yeltsin in December 1991 was accompanied by the fall of the state and took the form of a coup run by three republic leaders, one of them Yeltsin. Eight years later, as Yeltsin faded and the shadow network formed around him, the question of how to resolve the succession took a dramatic turn. And the solution must acknowledge yet another challenge: integrating the ruling class's desire for self-perpetuation with the new democratic mechanisms in Russia, particularly elections.

The Yeltsin team wanted not only to receive assurances of future security but also to retain control over the power and property that its members and the tycoons close to them had amassed during Yeltsin's rule. Primakov could guarantee the president's safety. But he was unlikely to promise a peaceful life to the entire Yeltsin entourage—especially because after being appointed prime minister he had dared to proclaim a war on corruption, thus challenging the mighty oligarchs close to the Kremlin. Rumors flew around Moscow that special forces loyal to Primakov had prepared a list of potential victims. At the top of the list, according to the rumors, was the name Boris Berezovsky, friend and adviser of Yeltsin's daughter Tatyana and oligarch extraordinaire. Drawing Berezovsky's hostility was dangerous even for an experienced political wolf like Primakov.

Several other kinds of Yeltsin supporters found Primakov unsettling. The technocrats and bureaucrats who had been winners in Yeltsin's distribution of power and property were as interested as he was in maintaining the shadow networks by which they were able to arrange sweet deals behind the scenes, and as leery of Primakov's anticorruption stance. Primakov also worried the liberal-leaning with his dubious attitude toward political freedoms, especially freedom of the press. The liberals could not forgive his distrust of the West, or even his assertiveness toward the Western powers. Thus Primakov was unable to consolidate the support of Yeltsin voters, who included not only oligarchs and liberals but all those who had benefited from Yeltsin's rule.

But it was Primakov's challenge to Yeltsin's clique that signed his polit-ical death warrant. Yeltsin's entourage could not forgive the prime minis-ter for his accumulation of power or for the threat emanating from him that he would use that power against some members of the Kremlin power clan. It was clear from the way Yeltsin behaved at meetings with his premier that he did not like or trust him. Yeltsin later admitted that he had never planned to give Primakov power and looked on him as a tempo-rary figure. "Yevgeny Maksimovich willy-nilly helped me achieve my main political goal—to bring the country peacefully to 2000 and to the elections. Afterward, as I thought then, we would together find a young and strong politician and hand him the political baton," Yeltsin wrote of Primakov, rather disingenuously, in his book *Presidential Marathon*.[5]

In the last months of Yeltsin's rule, the president and his team became openly hostile toward their independent premier. When the two leaders appeared on television together, Yeltsin looked grim, unable to hide his irritation, and he avoided eye contact with Primakov. The prime minis-ter made an effort to appear calm, but it was obvious how much it cost him. In *Presidential Marathon*, Yeltsin explained his displeasure by saying that Primakov had rallied around himself elites who dreamed of a "return to the old ways." But what Yeltsin found unforgivable was that in the eyes of many Russians, Primakov had become a candidate for successor with-out Yeltsin's approval.

Yeltsin's plans to get rid of Primakov were accelerated by the impeachment vote in the parliament, scheduled by the Communists for May 14, 1999. The Kremlin was afraid that Yeltsin's possible impeachment by the Federation Council—the upper chamber of the parliament, which had grown increasingly hostile toward the president—would empower the second most influential figure in Russia past recall.

The experienced fighter in Yeltsin decided on a preemptive strike. Two days before the impeachment vote by the Federation Council, he fired the prime minister without warning. Seemingly exhausted, weak, and unable to speak coherently, Yeltsin was reanimated by danger. His political sense of smell sharpened at such moments; he was still capable not only of defending himself but also of attacking—especially a rival. Yeltsin couldn't stand to have anyone next to him—he wanted to be completely alone at the top.

Primakov—unlike several other prime ministers and almost all of Yeltsin's other subordinates who had found themselves in similar situations—did not plead with Yeltsin to keep him on. "I accept your decision. You have the right to do so under the Constitution. But I consider it a mistake." That was all Primakov said in farewell to Yeltsin before he left the room. He retired with dignity, not asking anyone for anything.

Primakov's departure did not spark protests in Russia, though the Kremlin was worried about such a reaction. But it was a heavy blow for the entourage that had formed around the prime minister and had dreamed of future positions. Primakov's political Family started looking around for other shelter, and some of its members even tried to get back into Yeltsin's good graces. When the leader is the major source of power and politics, the only survival skill worth having is the ability to see which way the power is flowing. Under such circumstances, it is difficult to remain loyal to people or principles.

The attempt to impeach Yeltsin was a failure. Primakov's firing left the potential opposition to Yeltsin without steam. That helped create a new atmosphere inside the Kremlin, giving the presidential team a new feeling of determination and vigor. They again felt sure of themselves. All their energy was directed toward settling a single issue: finding a political heir loyal to Yeltsin and themselves. In the spring of 1999, Yeltsin seemed to be considering leaving the political area prematurely. His entourage was having more and more trouble controlling his behavior and maintaining the charade that he was in charge.

Yeltsin was a very sick man by that time. He had intervals when he was more like his old self and thought rationally, but one suspected that such periods were created by doctors and medication. Tsar Boris was becoming a ruin. His decay roused both fear and pity. After all, he was formally the leader of a state possessing nuclear weapons. Watching him, you felt that you were seeing the political funeral of a once great and powerful politician. Hardly anyone could have predicted at that time that the first Russian president would ever reemerge on the political scene.

Yeltsin would indeed amaze us—and not only once. But that would happen much later, after he left his post.

As Yeltsin faded, he relied even more on the people around him, most of all on his younger daughter Tatyana, then in her mid-thirties. He admitted in *Presidential Marathon* that Tatyana played a major role in the Kremlin: "Tanya by her humble presence and occasional bit of advice really did help me."

That was too modest an appraisal of his younger daughter's contribution. In actual fact, in the last years of Yeltsin's second term, Tatyana became the virtual ruler of the country. The sweet young woman, practically a girl, with limited life experience, found herself in the thick of political events. In early 1996, when the fight was on to keep Yeltsin for a second term, family friend and journalist Valentin Yumashev had the idea of bringing Tanya into the election campaign to serve as a direct channel between the campaign team and the president. Shy and timid at first, Tanya entered politics as an "information channel" and stayed on.

When Brezhnev was fading, the person who had the most influence on him was his nurse. With Yeltsin, it was his younger daughter, but it could have been a nurse, a driver, or a cook. Before the Family became the main influence on Yeltsin, the gray cardinal of the Kremlin was Yeltsin's bodyguard, Alexander Korzhakov.[6] In a one–man political show, especially in a weak one like Yeltsin's, the absence of independent institutions when the leader goes into decline means that power can fall into other hands most randomly.

After 1996, Tanya gradually took control of all important political appointments. A grimace of dislike on her face was enough to get someone fired, while an approving smile could speed someone else up the ladder of success. All vivid personalities in the Yeltsin entourage were removed, to be replaced by faceless people who preferred to operate behind the scenes, or by out-and-out ruthless individuals who did not even conceal their nature. Yeltsin's last team, the one that prepared the Successor Project, was selected by his daughter and her intimate friends.

Tatyana's friends became heads of government institutions and received huge chunks of state property. Tanya decided when and how the president would be shown to the public and prepared drafts of his speeches. She managed the emotions and eventually the behavior of her father, who grew more helpless every day. Yes, Yeltsin was stubborn and egocentric. But he loved Tatyana and let her do almost whatever she wanted with him; he turned into her puppet. Russian tradition and the weakness of civil society had brought the country to such a pass that it could do nothing but sit back and watch the drama of the collapse of power and the state, and the degradation of the president's personality.

In the late 1990s, Russia entered the era of the political Family: rule by the president's daughter and chums of hers undistinguished by expertise, brains, or talent. The situation with the next ruling team, however, would be even bleaker, which proves that governance based on loyalty and mutual obligations never brings bright and responsible people to the top. The names of Tanya's major associates—Valentin Yumashev, Alexander Voloshin, Roman Abramovich—meant nothing to anyone. Only Berezovsky, Tanya's adviser, the leading intriguer of the tsar's court, was known, and only because he liked being in the spotlight. In the later years of the Yeltsin administration, Berezovsky was crowded out by younger people whom he had introduced to Tatyana and with whom she felt more comfortable—people like Abramovich and Voloshin, with a strange, even dubious, past, implicated in shady dealings.[7] Perhaps these characters who suddenly surfaced and were attracted to the president's daughter were good friends to her, spoke her language, and had the same interests. It is also very likely that they provided various services to the Yeltsin family that tied the family to them.

As the Kremlin brotherhood grew accustomed to armored limousines and official bodyguards, to having every door open for them and no one monitoring their behavior, they lost all sense of limits. They began discrediting potential opponents and economic rivals; as in Soviet times, only the servile survived. It is a good thing that the Family was driven mainly by greed. Its members were not interested in foreign policy or relations in the post-Soviet space. They did not indulge in state building. They were capable of nothing more than moving pieces on the political chessboard. But they achieved perfection in that game. They ran an extended intrigue intended to create the appearance of activity on the part of the president, a sick old man, who in turn, and perhaps unaware, provided cover for them. From their position deep inside the Kremlin, this corrupt cooperative of friends and business comrades-in-arms created a giant vacuum to suck money out of Russia and into their own pockets.

The moment came when the question of a successor was more important to the Kremlin circle and its closest associates than to Yeltsin himself. The weaker the president grew, the more acute became the Family's need to find a successor they could rely on after his departure. Survival and the perpetuation of their power preoccupied the Yeltsin team throughout 1999. The heir had to be prepared, legitimated through service as prime minister, so that the political class would get to know him. Leaping straight onto Yeltsin's throne, the Kremlin's team realized, was hardly possible for their candidate, for even patient Russian society would not tolerate that.

Actually, Yeltsin himself had been giving some thought to his successor for a while. But before 1997, his objectives had been different—then he was apparently interested in finding a leader who would continue his mission, who would pursue his reforms. Starting in 1997, though, he began to look at the people around him, pondering those he might be able to entrust with his political inheritance. For a while, he seemed particularly fond of Boris Nemtsov, governor of Nizhny Novgorod, a young, flamboyant liberal who would become one of the leaders of the Union of Right Forces (SPS). After Nemtsov, Yeltsin closely observed the work of General Nikolai Bordyuzha, for some time his chief of staff.

In many ways, however, Yeltsin's search for a potential heir was a game with Machiavellian overtones. The president was provoking potential pretenders so that he could gauge their attitude toward him. Anyone who dared apply for the role of successor was destroyed. Thus Yeltsin fired Prime Minister Chernomyrdin, who considered himself the heir in 1997 and 1998. The search for a successor was also a search for rivals to be neutralized or, better, erased from the political scene. But by 1999, Yeltsin could not rule, and therefore the succession issue had to be solved.

On May 19, 1999, Sergei Stepashin became the new Russian prime minister.[8] He was a Yeltsin loyalist who had moved from post to post—he had been director of the Federal Counterintelligence Service (predecessor of the FSB), minister of justice, and minister of internal affairs. Stepashin had had a paradoxical career—at one time he had been a democrat, and then in 1994 he had been entrusted with the pacification of Chechnya. Such sharp switches were typical for politicians drafted by Yeltsin. Temperamentally, Stepashin was a cautious man who never tried to play leading roles. That Yeltsin was appointing representatives from the power structures (*siloviki*) to the office of prime minister revealed the thought process of the ruling group. The Kremlin must have believed that the prime minister of a transitional cabinet should be someone who controlled the army or other power structure. He might be needed to defend the Kremlin from rivals.

However, in May 1999 there was no final clarity on the optimal candidate for regent. Yeltsin subsequently said, in *Presidential Marathon*, "Even as I nominated Stepashin, I knew that I would fire him." That Yeltsin's team had not yet decided on the final appointee is the only explanation for the constant presence in the president's inner circle during that period of Victor Aksyonenko, minister of transportation, who was fighting for the position of first loyal subject. In comparison with the crude and rascally Aksyonenko, who had long been suspected of financial machinations, the other candidates to the throne, including foreign minister Igor Ivanov, interior minister Vladimir Rushailo, and Putin, seemed like intellectual giants and models of conscience.

Gradually, Yeltsin and his clique came to prefer Vladimir Vladimirovich Putin. In his memoirs, Yeltsin wrote that as early as 1997, the year Putin moved to Moscow, he had his eye on him. Yeltsin was "amazed by Putin's lightning reflexes." The president had the feeling that "this young . . . man was ready for absolutely anything in life, he would respond to any challenge clearly and distinctly." In this case, Putin's relative youth (he was then 45) seemed to matter to Yeltsin, who must have felt that Russia needed dynamism rather than stabilization. If Yeltsin is to be believed, he did not dare propose the unknown Putin while Primakov retained his influence, and so he used Stepashin as a buffer between Primakov and the real heir. But most likely it was not that complicated—the Kremlin Family was still vacillating over its choice.

In his narrative, Yeltsin paints himself as savvy and sharp, in control of the process, picking out candidates and rejecting others, elaborating on the consequences of his choices. Reality was more pathetic: Yeltsin would never have quit his post and never have looked for an heir if he had been in command.

Stepashin was not fated to be the successor. But he did not know that. He threw himself into his role as prime minister with total sincerity. He even tried to form his cabinet, rejecting advice from the Kremlin. What unforgivable carelessness! He failed to understand that to survive in his position he had to lie low. Even more important, the Kremlin wasn't sure that Stepashin would protect his benefactors. So, on August 9, less than three months after his appointment, Stepashin was sent packing in the most humiliating manner.[9] The Kremlin was in a hurry. The entourage must not have been certain how long Yeltsin would last. It was time to present the real heir to the public. By early August, the main candidate for successor had been selected.[10] The game of prime ministerial poker was drawing to a close.

Vladimir Vladimirovich Putin appeared on the national stage unexpectedly. The political class as well as the public was surprised to see him, but everyone was so exhausted by the moves leading up to this that the new holder of the prime minister's office roused no opposition. He was seen as just one more premier in a long line, most likely an accidental figure. No one realized that this was the true heir. The unlikely choice and Putin's personality lulled suspicions. Many people simply paid no attention to him or considered his appointment something of a joke.

Who was this Mr. Nobody? He was a KGB officer who had served in East Germany. It wasn't clear what he had done there—gathered intelligence or spied on his fellow citizens. Putin retired in the rank of colonel, which meant that he had not had a brilliant career in the KGB. The Fates then made him a close aide of the liberal mayor of Saint Petersburg, Anatoly Sobchak. The trajectory—from the special service to the liberals—was not at all unusual in the early post-Soviet era; Putin's predecessor as prime minister, the short-lived Stepashin, had followed the same course in reverse. During Yeltsin's presidency, many people performed extraordinary somersaults, moving from camp to camp and rising to and falling from power.

Having become Sobchak's shadow, Putin turned into an effective manager. His relationship with his boss is exceptionally significant in understanding his future ascendancy. Putin proved he could be loyal and faithful and showed that allegiance to bosses and friends was extremely important to him. He followed the rules and could be relied on. The latter, we admit, was and still is a rare quality for Russian politicians and managers. Putin behaved decently toward the people with whom he had ties and to whom he was obligated. He quit his job immediately after Sobchak lost the gubernatorial election in July 1996, even though he could have stayed on working for the new governor of Saint Petersburg, Vladimir Yakovlev. After Putin managed to move to Moscow and unexpectedly jumped up the career ladder when Yeltsin appointed him director of the FSB, he demonstrated his loyalty to his former boss one more time. But more about that later.

Outwardly, Putin was an unexpected choice for a leader: hardly good-looking, rather short, with an inexpressive face and an awkward manner in public. He certainly was not charismatic. Next to the tall and powerfully built Yeltsin, he looked like a boy. He did not belong to the Yeltsin entourage—he was merely in its orbit to execute orders. Putin never pushed himself forward, keeping to the sidelines. In the beginning, he appeared shy and withdrawn. He was definitely not a public figure. Even the most sophisticated Kremlinologist was unlikely to see in him the future ruler of Russia. He was faceless and bland, either by nature or by training as an intelligence officer who had been taught not to stand out. There was nothing memorable about him except for his interest in the martial art of judo; that suggested he was not as simple as he seemed but possessed an inner strength and hidden ambitions.

When Yeltsin asked Putin whether he was prepared to become prime minister, he replied at once, according to Yeltsin in *Presidential Marathon*, in the military manner: "I'll work wherever you assign me." The answer pleased Yeltsin. On August 16, 1999, the Duma confirmed Putin as prime minister. The confirmation went smoothly precisely because no one took Putin seriously. Many saw his appointment as a sign that the Kremlin was giving up the power struggle. Luzhkov and Primakov must have been pleased with Yeltsin's choice—inconspicuous and shallow-looking Putin certainly did not seem to be a serious threat to their presidential ambitions. What poor judgment on the part of those old-timers in politics!

In his memoirs, Yeltsin goes on about his affection for his successor. Here is how Yeltsin (or the author who ghostwrote Yeltsin's memoirs) describes Putin: "Putin has very interesting eyes. It seems that they say more than his words. . . . I had the feeling . . . that this man, young by my standards, was absolutely ready for everything in life, and could respond to any challenge." However, the declarations of love in Yeltsin's book, which was published after Putin became president, are more likely an attempt by the Yeltsin Family to keep Putin in their embrace, to explain publicly that he had been their choice, and to impress on him that he owes them for it.

It wasn't Putin's eyes and precise answers that convinced Yeltsin to make him his final choice. Something about the man—in his behavior, in his life experience—encouraged Yeltsin and his closest associates to entrust him not only with the country but with their lives. After a long and tortuous selection process involving the testing of numerous pretenders to the throne, the ruling team saw in Vladimir Vladimirovich something that made it believe he would not sell them out, that they could trust him and be assured of their future. And they had ample reason to worry about the future—because of the allegations of corruption, because they had acquired many enemies, because they were blamed for all the country's ills.

One event in Putin's life could have reassured them significantly in this regard. Putin helped Anatoly Sobchak, his former boss, who was suspected of abuse of power and corruption in Saint Petersburg, to get to Paris secretly. That saved Sobchak from a trial and perhaps from being thoroughly discredited if he had been found guilty of misdeeds. Getting Sobchak into France was a military operation that involved the special services, a chartered plane, and the covering of tracks. In Paris, Sobchak was probably under the protection of Putin's agency. To put it baldly, Putin used his position as head of the FSB to help a witness and potential suspect escape justice. Yeltsin considered that a good deed; he had "great respect" for the man who would do such a thing, he said in his memoirs. Here we have a window into the way both the former and current Russian presidents relate to the law. The Sobchak story must have convinced Yeltsin and his entourage that Putin would not give them up, even if it endangered his career.

Sobchak died unexpectedly on February 1, 2000, after his former assistant had already become the Kremlin boss. Putin attended his funeral and did not hide his tears from the television cameras. One could see that he was not acting; he was sincerely grieving over the death of his boss. Russia saw that the new leader was humane, and his behavior struck a chord in Russians' hearts. In some way that could not have been predicted, Putin succeeded not only in being accepted by the ruling Family but in being liked by society as well.

Putin confirmed his capacity for loyalty in the spring of 1999, when he defended Yeltsin during his conflict with then–prosecutor general Yuri Skuratov. At that time, a great many elites had turned their backs on Yeltsin, and it looked as if the president was about to be toppled. It was then that Putin first appeared in the spotlight, playing the role of Skuratov's exposer in order to defend the president.[11] Putin burned his bridges, taking Yeltsin's side at a time when even Yeltsin's staunchest supporters were distancing themselves from the Kremlin (partly because Yeltsin was playing dirty). The ruling Family saw then that Putin could be trusted, that one could rely on him.

The most important argument in Vladimir Putin's favor as Yeltsin's successor was that he was completely obligated to Yeltsin for his advancement. Putin had nothing of his own—no supporters, no charisma, no ideology, no popularity, no experience—nothing that made him an independent figure. He had been created by the people around Yeltsin; naturally they expected gratitude and allegiance from him.

There may, however, have been other circumstances in Putin's life history that guaranteed his dependence on his creators. We can only speculate about what those could be, but a heftier security deposit than Putin's promises of fidelity must have been required by Yeltsin's people. That, however, is only a guess; there is no proof for it. Though there were obvious cynical reasons for this choice of successor, Yeltsin may still have considered Putin—a man who had a liberal period in his past and who belonged to a younger generation—someone who could carry on his work.

The appointed heir had time to prove his loyalty not only to Yeltsin and his Family but to some of the leading oligarchs as well. Boris Berezovsky recalled later: "Primakov intended to put me in prison. It was my wife's birthday. . . . And quite unexpectedly, Putin came to the party. He came and said, 'I don't care in the least what Primakov will think of me. I feel that this is right at this moment.'" That act of Putin's, when Berezovsky's fate was uncertain, can be seen as evidence either of Putin's human decency—supporting a person he knew who was in trouble—or of his pragmatism—supporting a person who still had enormous influence. Most likely the episode showed that Putin was capable of devotion to people with whom he had been thrown together. Putin came to a party hosted by a man who might have ended up in jail; in other words, Putin clearly was no coward. However, he might have known that Primakov's days were numbered and he could safely visit. If Putin only knew that Berezovsky would soon become his worst enemy!

That Putin had no political ties but did have roots in the power structures was important for the ruling team. It was better, the team reasoned, to have military protection during the volatile period when Yeltsin disengaged and the successor took over. That Putin had no ties to any political group was a plus in the new Russia, for it might mean that no interest group had claims on him. And that the final candidate for the role of successor had no political past at least guaranteed that, as a completely new face, he had not yet bored his audience. The absence of ideological engagement made it possible for the ruling team to shape Putin's image in whatever way they desired. Thus he could be presented as a liberal, a conservative, or a patriot.

However, for the new premier—barely known outside the Moscow Ring Road—to be taken seriously as Russia's leader, there had to be a perceived need among the Russian public that Putin would step in to fill. The need was clear after the financial crash of 1998 and from the moment Primakov took office. Weak Russia needed a strong state and a leader with a tough image who was ready to stop the rot. Ironically, at just the same time, in August 1999, an international scandal broke that gave yet more impetus to Russia's move toward a stronger rule. The Bank of New York was implicated in the alleged laundering of $4.2 billion from Russia.[12] Russian government officials and people close to them allegedly played a role in the money laundering as well. The world press made Russian money and Russian corruption the top story of the day.

The Bank of New York scandal violently upset ruling circles in Russia. It was one thing for law enforcement authorities in tiny Switzerland or even Italy to suspect high officials and members of the Yeltsin Family of laundering money and taking bribes. It was quite another when the secret services of the United Kingdom and the United States fastened on the idea. The scandal widened, leading to hearings in the U.S. Congress, the threat of sanctions against Russian businesses, and the possibility of investigations into the financial dealings of Russian politicians.

The passions and fears loosed by the scandal increased the feeling of vulnerability among Russia's elites.[13] Some elites who had engaged in dubious activities and financial manipulations and who had been involved in illegal deals now realized that they could lose the safe harbors they had prepared in Western countries, to which many of them had already sent their families. Now they were forced to deal with their own survival inside Russia. A strong leader who could defend their interests was what they urgently needed.

At the height of the uproar over money laundering, evidence of fresh scandal created a sensation: the credit cards reportedly provided by the Swiss company Mabetex to Yeltsin and members of his family.[14] The Russian president, who until then had kept silent, called U.S. president Bill Clinton with just one aim: to deny the allegations about his and other family members' "Swiss connections." Evidently, Yeltsin really cared what kind of reputation he had in the West. But why did he and his family need credit cards from Mabetex? They had an enormous country at their disposal.

Meanwhile, the anxiety of the political class was not enough to create a mandate for a "strong-arm" regime in Russia; the masses needed to feel the need for a new and authoritarian rule as well. An occasion quickly arose: the invasion of the Russian republic of Dagestan by separatists from neighboring Chechnya on August 2, 1999. The separatists supposedly took advantage of the confusion in Russian political life to attempt to create a radical Wahhabite Islamic state in Chechnya and adjacent regions. But by a strange coincidence, they attacked Dagestan when preparations were already under way in Moscow for a transfer of power. And why didn't Moscow stop the invasion? Why did the Russian power ministries calmly watch the open massing of armed separatists in border regions? Moreover, a brigade of Interior Ministry troops that had been protecting the border between Chechnya and Dagestan was quickly removed just before the invasion.

Some Russian journalists wrote openly that people close to the Kremlin, primarily Berezovsky, might have pushed the Chechen fighters to attack Dagestan to increase the Russian people's sense of vulnerability and pave the way for a change of rule.[15] "Why did Chechnya happen before Yeltsin's reelection? Why is there now Dagestan before these elections?" asked the magazine *Profil'* on August 30, referring to the parliamentary elections scheduled for December. "Who ordered a war in Dagestan, and why?"[16]

In any other country, such questions would have called for court hearings and a mass firing of officials. But in Russia they were merely shrugged off. Such is the effect of living with continual scandals, and of the still-powerful ingrained fear of the authorities.

The Chechen invasion prompted in Russian citizens the very feelings that are vital for the formation of a new type of order—fear and a sense of vulnerability. The next month, August 1999, several residential buildings in Moscow and other Russian cities were blown up, killing about 300 civilians and sending shock waves throughout the country.[17] The explosions put society in a mood that could be described as demanding a "strong hand." In September, just after the blasts, Russian citizens considered "personal safety" a higher priority (40 versus 28 percent) than "social guarantees"—a major issue after the loss of the Soviet social security net that had previously obsessed them. "Crime" and "instability" topped the list of concerns (47 and 46 percent, respectively). Even before opening an investigation, the Kremlin announced that there was a "Chechen trace" in the crimes. Police began rounding up anyone who looked remotely Chechen. The terrorists, however, were never found, which gave rise to suspicion about the involvement of Russian secret services in the explosions.

The conspiracy theory is too simple an explanation for the watershed change in Russian public opinion. In the confusion that reigned in Russia, with the constant leaks of information from the top, even the secret services would have had difficulty carrying out such an operation without leaving many clues and witnesses behind. In any case, there are no secrets in today's Russia—all that is hidden is revealed sooner or later. But at the same time, we must admit that to this day there are no satisfactory answers to numerous questions stemming from that period. Nor does one sense any desire by the Kremlin to conduct a thorough investigation of the events that would lead to the capture of the perpetrators, thereby putting an end to all the rumors.[18]

The prime minister lost no time showing himself to be a strong and powerful politician. Speaking to the Duma after the explosions, Putin described the challenge facing Russia: "In blowing up the houses of our fellow citizens, the bandits are blowing up the state. They are undermining authority—not of the president, city, or Duma. But of authority per se." He stated that his goal was "to defend the population from bandits." He said what millions of citizens expected of a leader. When he spoke from the podium of the Duma, the Russian audience finally saw what it wanted—a determined, willful face, the springy walk of an athlete, and . . . very cold eyes. Many decided that a man with eyes like that had to be strong. And a majority of Russians wanted a strong man in the Kremlin. They were tired of watching Yeltsin fall apart.

Having done nothing yet except declare his determination, Putin received mass support from the main forces in Russian society. The accumulated fears, the disarray, the feeling of being in danger, and the very real Russian "Weimar syndrome" all pushed people toward a longing for order and a new face in the Kremlin. The sociologist Yuri Levada wrote in the last edition of *Moskovskie novosti* of 1999: "No researchers had ever seen Russian society in this state. . . . All the fears and passions that had been biding their time came to the surface and the hidden layer of our consciousness was exposed."

All the feelings that had been stored away in people's minds during the years of Yeltsin's administration now surged up as disillusionment and yet also hope for change. But that hope was reflected mainly in the search for a new leader, not in a demand to break the pattern of personalistic rule. In their mass longing for security and order, it seemed that Russians would have supported any new face as long as it appeared confident and was not that of a human wreck. Youth and dynamism were what Russians wanted in a president, and that in itself was a positive break with the tradition of declining and impotent leaders.

The blasts in Russian cities were the final straw that rendered retaliatory action in Chechnya inevitable. On September 30, 1999, federal troops entered Chechnya. Large-scale war began. It was a civil war where victory is impossible and what is considered victory can easily turn to defeat. Because the military actions were labeled "antiterrorist operations," no approval from the upper chamber of the parliament, the Federation Council, or declaration of a state of emergency in Chechnya was required. Thus the war was conducted outside the framework of legality. Whatever political expediency demanded could be done unhampered in Chechnya.

Whereas in early 1999 only a madman would have contemplated a new war in the Northern Caucasus, by autumn the second Chechen war had helped unite Russian society, soothing Russians' vulnerability complex. The operation against Chechnya had been prepared under Primakov and Stepashin, but as a limited action against Chechen terrorists and criminal elements. The plan was to move the army to the Terek River to create a buffer zone between the pro-Russian and separatist regions of Chechnya, and also to mount surgical strikes on terrorist bases.

Why did Russian troops cross the Terek and go into the territory beyond? Why did the military begin mass bombing in Chechnya, leading to thousands of casualties among civilians and the creation of tens of thousands of refugees? We know that Russian generals wanted revenge for their humiliation at the hands of a small number of poorly armed fighters in the first Chechen war. Perhaps they managed to convince Putin to pursue the war to its end and were certain of victory. Perhaps Putin himself wanted that. What is known is that the prime minister himself proposed the initiative of the "antiterrorist operation." He did not hide it. Reporters once asked him, "Then the entire responsibility (for Chechnya) is yours?" He replied: "To a great degree that is so. I told myself: I have a certain amount of time—two, three, four months—to shatter those bandits. And then, they can fire me."[19] But did he know what the operation in Chechnya would be like? Once it began, it was too late to change his decision; he was hostage to the new war and the generals' ambitions.

The majority of Russians considered the first Chechen war criminal. Now it was considered criminal not to support the military crusade in Chechnya. Thus in January 1995, 54 percent of those polled wanted Russian troops pulled out of Chechnya (27 percent supported the troops' presence there, and 19 percent had no opinion). By contrast, in November and December 1999, between 61 and 70 percent of those polled approved of the operation in Chechnya. Even after the substantial losses in Chechnya became known—including thousands killed and wounded among the Russian army and civilians—in July 2000, 70 percent of respondents felt that there should be no negotiating in Chechnya but that order should be imposed on the republic with the help of the army.

After the military attack on Chechnya began, Putin no longer needed to continue the difficult struggle for power. All he had to do was point to the enemy, who were Chechens, naturally. War lifted him to the peak of the political Olympus.

Other circumstances guaranteed Putin's move to real power. First among these was the quite effective game played by the Kremlin. The people who constituted Yeltsin's political circle were not political geniuses. When threatened, however, they succeeded in finding a mechanism for their survival, which was not at all sophisticated but which worked, at least for the time being. The ruling team managed to restore control over power resources and, at least partially, over society's moods by working on people's darkest fears and ratcheting up the desire for stability at any price. Chechnya turned out to be a good excuse for consolidation because it served simultaneously as an internal and an external enemy.

After August 1999, the widespread desire for security in Russian society in effect led to consolidation Soviet-style. The planned, albeit crude, manipulation of public opinion by the state-run mass media aided the reimposition of central control. But it is important to acknowledge that many Russians at that particular moment acquiesced in and perhaps were relieved by the turn back to the old and familiar pattern of rule. They had been through lifetimes of change in a dozen years. Russian society, cut off from its traditions, uncertain of the future, disoriented and helpless, was stuck between floors in the elevator of history—between past and future. The weary, disillusioned post-Soviet citizen could find in the return to clear-cut decisions, authoritarian style, and the search for the enemy a bit of calm and comfort, if only temporarily.

To ensure Putin's ascension, the Kremlin now needed to clear the field of his main opponents, Luzhkov and Primakov, who had created their own political movements, Fatherland and All-Russia. (The two had put off working out their relationship and deciding who would be the leading challenger for the spot in the Kremlin.) The Kremlin killed Luzhkov and Primakov politically through a dirty campaign in the state-run media, pressure on members of the opposition, and bribery of members of their movements. The demoralized political class quickly reoriented itself, focusing on the strongest player: the Kremlin, once again. The habit of obeying central power reasserted itself, as those who had sworn fealty to Luzhkov and Primakov yesterday were bowing today to the Kremlin's new appointee. It was frustrating to watch the journalists, analysts, advisers, and plain hangers-on who only recently had crowded around Primakov and the Moscow mayor. Some of them vanished from the political scene. Others ran next door and began seeking access to Putin.

At last, the relevant Russian officials realized how important television is for politics. In the 1996 presidential campaign, the people at Russian television had just been learning how to manipulate public opinion, crafting an image of an active leader out of the ailing Yeltsin. Now television had become the primary political ax for destroying Putin's opponents. Sergei Dorenko, a well-known news anchor on state television, was assigned the task of demoralizing Luzhkov and Primakov. Behind Dorenko was Berezovsky, one of the shareholders of the state television's Channel 1. Every Saturday night in prime time, Dorenko poured another load of filth on the Kremlin's rivals. He accused Luzhkov of many and varied crimes: His wife transferred money outside the country, he was a thief, he had been party to the murder of an American businessman. Luzhkov couldn't wash it off fast enough. Once he finished with Luzhkov, Dorenko moved on to Primakov, using every means possible to paint him as a sick old man. The place for him wasn't the Kremlin but a retirement home, was the message on state television.

The Kremlin, using all its resources to destroy the opposition, deliberately forgot about the Communists, according them favored status. The battle among similar species was more vicious than the one between different species. The Kremlin's equanimity toward the Communist Party had a definite goal. The Yeltsin–Putin team needed a good showing by the Communists in the upcoming parliamentary and presidential elections, so that Gennady Zyuganov would be Putin's main rival. That guaranteed Putin's victory. The ruling team wanted to use again the strategy it had employed successfully in the 1996 elections, when the fact that Communist candidate Zyuganov was the main competition facing him helped Yeltsin stay in power. Left with the alternatives of the Communist past or an indefinite future with a sick leader, Russia had chosen the second option. So this time the Kremlin was even prepared to support Zyuganov, both materially and organizationally, to keep him around as the only opponent. The Kremlin team did not show much imagination, but at that moment they did not need it to have their way with the demoralized Russian electorate.

During an amazingly short period of time in the autumn of 1999, the spectrum of Russian political life shifted radically. Back in the summer, the political class would have supported Primakov as Yeltsin's successor. Society was ready then to accept an elderly, extremely cautious leader and to endorse the constitutional amendments that would have created a strong cabinet and an influential parliament. In the autumn, society and the political class, seeming to forget Primakov's existence, turned to the young unknown whose very appearance symbolized strict order and harsh personal rule.

In other words, it became clear that the Russian mindset was still flexible and unformed and could be controlled. Political institutions meant nothing. A few people in the Kremlin controlling all state resources determined the fate of the presidency and the enormous country along with it. Employing blatant manipulation and pressure, they changed the characters, sets, and content of the play. The preceding period of Yeltsin upsets had beaten down society sufficiently that it readily agreed to participate in the show the Kremlin was proposing.

The public observed this with calm resignation, even though the Kremlin intrigue was primitive and obvious. Why did Russia accept the humiliating spectacle unfolding before its eyes? Perhaps it was another manifestation of Russian fatalism—you can't do anything about it, you can't fight city hall. Only a small group of intellectuals and journalists protested. But who paid any attention? That the president's clique was appointing a successor and few people were surprised or shocked—on the contrary, most people found it natural—was telling. It showed either that the tradition of autocracy still lived or that Russians did not care much about the political regime, having become convinced that they would find ways to survive under any form of rule. And a lot of people had already come to like the new candidate for the throne.

At that moment at the end of 1999, the small steps Putin was taking as the new prime minister, especially his reliance on the state apparatus, could be interpreted as a return to the Soviet past—without communism, but with Communists. There was a sense of déjà vu. But it was too soon to draw final conclusions about the essence of the new regime. After all, Putin's life had included the Saint Petersburg period with the liberal Anatoly Sobchak, which could not and cannot be discounted. It remained to be seen how Putin coupled Soviet habits and a KGB background with the liberal principles acquired in Saint Petersburg.

The new premier had a positive reception from the country in the last months of 1999, and his ratings rose quickly. According to the All-Russian Center for Public Opinion Research (hereafter VTsIOM), in October, 65 percent approved of Putin's policies, compared with 52 percent in September and 33 percent in August. Their poll at the end of November found that 29 percent of respondents would vote for Putin for president, whereas 17 percent were for Zyuganov and 13 percent for Primakov. It became clear before the Duma elections in December that the Luzhkov–Primakov "second party of power" had no chance of success.

As for the Chechen war, in November 1999, 48 percent of Russians supported Putin's "antiterrorist operation" (29 percent demanded even harsher policies toward Chechnya, and only 7 percent thought excessive force unjustified). For the first time in many years—at least since Gorbachev came to power—Russian society had returned to the saving idea of military patriotism, which became the refuge of all in Russia who feared and who felt vulnerable.

Even the liberals joined the war camp. "Today in Chechnya it is not the question of Chechnya that is being decided, but an incomparably more important question—today in Chechnya the Russian army is being reborn," announced Anatoly Chubais, leader of the liberals and a recent favorite of the West, in November 1999. After the West accused Russia of human rights violations in Chechnya, Chubais flung back an accusation: "I consider the position taken by the West as a whole … on Chechnya to be immoral. I consider the position of the West dishonest." Thus a leading liberal and friend of the West suddenly turned anti-Western. Well, he wanted to survive. A politician who had been considered brave and principled turned out to be weak and conformist. He could have believed what he was saying, though; many such do.

On November 14, 1999, Yeltsin publicly embraced Putin and confirmed once again that he was "the only choice for Russia." There were almost no doubts left about the scenario Russia would follow. The successor was already appointed. But the new leader still had to be tested by election—first the parliamentary elections, then the election for president.

The old resources for the legitimation of power in Russia—through the "leading party," Marxist ideology, blatant coercion—had been exhausted. The Kremlin gang turned to elections. The role of elections in Russia was now clear: They had become a mechanism for supporting the appointed monarch. Only the unexpected could stop Putin's path to the Kremlin.

Chapter 2

THE END OF
THE YELTSIN ERA

The parliamentary elections of 1999. The difficult fate of Russian liberals.
The Communist Party as a still powerful element. Yeltsin amazes
everyone and departs. What Yeltsin leaves to his heir.

Elections for the Third State Duma, the lower house of the Russian parliament—the bicameral Federal Assembly—took place on December 19, 1999.[1] For Putin and the other candidates who would compete three months later in the presidential election, the parliamentary contests were akin to primaries. Not long before the balloting, to neutralize their main opponents—the Luzhkov–Primakov alliance—and to create a base in the new parliament, the Kremlin formed, in a matter of a few weeks, a movement it called Unity (or Medved, for the bear that was its symbol). One of the leading organizers of the pro-Kremlin movement was Boris Berezovsky, a media oligarch with an inexhaustible supply of ideas. It was Berezovsky who traveled to the regions and persuaded governors to support the Kremlin movement rather than the OVR (Fatherland and All-Russia) Party of Luzhkov and Primakov.

That Berezovsky—who had helped oversee the demoralization and degradation of power under Yeltsin—was one of the main people smoothing the way for Putin, Yeltsin's chosen successor, colored the undertaking, which was meant to guarantee the continuation of Russia's pattern of rule and ruling team. All of Yeltsin's Family was actively engaged in preparing for the victory of its heir: exerting pressure on the media, seeking the support of oligarchs and governors, collecting *compromat* (a Russian term for compromising materials) on possible rivals. This aggressive campaign in support of Putin might mean that reciprocity on the part of the next Kremlin boss was anticipated. Could the artificially created new leader escape his puppet-masters, who included Yeltsin's daughter Tatyana and her close associates? It was natural to assume that in his desire to legitimize his power, Putin would be unlikely to tolerate his creators or any mention of those who pulled the strings. It all depended on what bound them together and to what degree Putin depended on the Yeltsin Family. It also depended on how strong, determined, and willful the new leader would be.

At first, very few people believed in the attempt to create a new Kremlin party. How could such an undertaking be serious—organizing a new movement, without even the most elementary program, just a few months before the elections? But gradually the idea was given material expression. People supposed to embody muscular force were named leaders of the new Unity movement: minister of emergency situations Sergei Shoigu; world champion wrestler Alexander Karelin; and General Alexander Gurov, who, being in the Ministry of Internal Affairs, fought the Russian mafia. It was a simple-minded public relations game, waving the heroic, macho images of rescuer, wrestler, good cop. Those images were chosen to resonate with the average Russian in need of protection and security in these uncertain times. The three types would be seen as honest and straightforward guys, salt of the earth. And they would generate excitement, however bogus. Thus its creators manufactured the movement that would serve as the base for Putin and his regime.

Among the first to join Unity were the governors who were not on good terms with the law, including Kursk governor Alexander Rutskoi, Primorye governor Alexander Nazdratenko, and Kaliningrad governor Leonid Gorbenko. The Bears also got support from regions that totally depended on Kremlin subsidies. In short, the new movement attracted dependent people and people with murky reputations.

Unity was a virtual creation. Right up to the elections, it had no ideology and no structures. It was a ghost movement. I remember the early meetings of the Bears; the nondescriptness was astonishing. One could have gotten the impression that previous political waves had exhausted the country's intellectual potential and left the Bears with the refuse of the political process. These new types of politicians shared, however, one amusing characteristic: self-confidence. They did not pretend to have wise thoughts or ideas or even ambition. They wanted only to be Putin's supporters and were sure this would guarantee them victory in the upcoming elections and afterward some role within the Kremlin network.

Of course, the creators of the Kremlin party did not need many vivid personalities or experienced politicians; they needed an obedient mass. Putin became Unity's platform and compensated for the lack of other party planks. The Bears had one shining hope: to take to the political stage on the coattails of the new leader. Their party was the latest refuge for the state apparatus that had managed to adjust and survive in every regime—from Stalin, Khrushchev, Brezhnev, and Gorbachev to Yeltsin. Now it was prepared to serve a new leader without even knowing which way he would turn.

But the new "party" could become a real power only on the condition that Putin supported it openly. He vacillated until November 24, 1999, when he declared that he would support Unity "as a citizen and friend of Sergei Shoigu," one of its leaders. Things fell into place—the new structure, still fleshless and amorphous, was perceived as "the party of Putin." In late October, Unity's approval rating was below 4 percent (according to VTsIOM, which is headed by a well-known sociologist, Yuri Levada), but by late November it had already climbed to 19 percent. The party quickly took on people who sensed an opportunity to be catapulted into power.

Simultaneously, Putin made an approving gesture—albeit a more restrained one—toward the newly formed Union of Right Forces (the SPS, established in August 1999).[2] Several liberals—Yegor Gaidar, Sergei Kiriyenko, Boris Nemtsov, and Irina Khakamada—headed the Union, but the real leader and financier was Anatoly Chubais, the "privatization tsar." Chubais and Putin had a difficult and controversial relationship: The usually aggressive Chubais, accustomed to having his own way, now had to be cautious in dealing with Putin—who hardly needed such a powerful and ambitious figure around.

For Putin, supporting Unity and maintaining a condescendingly approving attitude toward the Union of Right Forces was a bold step. If those two movements lost the parliamentary elections, Putin would likely vanish from the political arena and Yeltsin would have to find a new heir. Putin decided to go for broke. It was a risk, but the whole plan of bringing a new man without political experience to power was a risk.

The Kremlin administration swung into gear behind Putin's candidacy. It organized an active campaign against OVR and Grigory Yavlinsky's Yabloko, the political blocs sponsoring alternative presidential candidates. The goal was obvious: to destroy these blocs with a centrist and democratic agenda in the parliamentary elections and thus cripple their candidates in the presidential election. Yeltsin's team wanted to guarantee Putin's victory.

The Kremlin put extreme pressure on Russia's governors to give up Luzhkov and Primakov, Putin's major opponents. The regional leaders preferred not to resist the Kremlin and quickly left the ranks of OVR. Some regional barons proved miracles of flexibility, having spent time in every pro-Kremlin movement that functioned under Yeltsin—Yegor Gaidar's Russia's Choice, Democratic Russia's Choice, and Victor Chernomyrdin's Our Home Is Russia. After their temporary halt with OVR, they switched to Unity as if on signal.

The results of the December 1999 balloting for the parliament confirmed that Russian democracy was fully or nearly fully controllable. As a result of the Kremlin's machinations, Unity received 23 percent and the SPS, which had jumped on the "Putin train" in time, also got good results—9 percent of the vote. Those movements formed a solid base for Putin in the Duma. The Communist Party received less than usual—24 percent of the vote. OVR got 13 percent, the Zhirinovsky bloc 6 percent, and Yabloko 5 percent. They formed the following factions in the Duma: The Communists had 85 seats, its allied group the Agrarian-Industrial Bloc had 43, Unity had 83, Unity's ally the People's Deputy group had 56, the SPS had 32, OVR had 49, the progovernment group Russian Regions had 47, the Liberal Democrats had 12, and Yabloko had 17.

The other 21 seats were taken by independent deputies. (In the 1995 Duma, the Communists had a total of 157 seats; their Agrarian ally had 20; the progovernment Our Home Is Russia, predecessor of Unity and OVR, had 55; the Liberal Democrats had 51; Yabloko had 45; and Democratic Choice of Russia, predecessor of the SPS, had 9. The rest of the seats were divided among smaller factions.) This unique primary showed that Putin had a good chance of winning the presidential election: Votes for pro-Kremlin Unity and the SPS were in fact votes for a new leader.

The "antiterrorist campaign" in Chechnya that had begun in September and been embraced by the majority of Russians had a profound effect on the vote, because Unity and the SPS were its two biggest backers among the competing parties. An article in the liberal magazine *Itogi* on December 23 went further: "The Duma election campaign of 1999 enriched Russian political science with one indisputable revolutionary discovery: A large-scale military operation, it turns out, can be cold-bloodedly used as an election technique."

With strong Unity, People's Deputy, Russian Regions, and SPS factions in the new Duma for the first time, a Kremlin leader had strong support in the parliament, which had given Yeltsin no breathing room. The weakening of OVR–All-Russia, which had constructed grand plans in the summer, almost automatically meant the final defeat of Primakov, Putin's main rival in the struggle for the Kremlin. The Russian political class had made its choice in the Duma elections, and it was for Putin. The Primakov–Luzhkov faction in the Duma soon joined the Kremlin camp. Russian centrists were not ready for independent life; they needed a shadow of power to survive. In the end, they would start competing with Putin's Unity for the role of the faction most loyal to the president.

After some thought, Primakov dropped out of the presidential race, knowing he had no hope of winning. Later, he would throw his support to Putin and become a frequent visitor of the new leader. And in truth, why should he have stayed in the opposition once Putin began realizing a philosophy of power that was quite close to Primakov's own? Besides, Primakov had always survived and thrived because he connected with all of Russia's rulers.[3]

The parliamentary elections also showed that it was too soon to bury the Russian Communist Party, which had lost some of its influence but remained a powerful force. In the course of the Yeltsin years of development, the Communist Party had evolved into a fixture of the Russian System that helped preserve stability. The Communists kept the protest voters from overreacting. They also compromised with the Kremlin team at key moments. In exchange, they got a few things that helped satisfy the groups that supported them. The Kremlin always took care of the interests of the agrarian lobby, the military-industrial complex, and the regions that supported the Communist Party.

Yeltsin's successor was inheriting a fully formed left-wing opposition that had demonstrated its unwillingness to undermine the presidential regime. The Communist Party had accepted the rules dictated by the ruling team, confirming that it was no longer interested in a serious struggle for the Kremlin and would settle for the role of eternal opposition. This was convenient and not dangerous. So the Communists, once elements of the Yeltsin regime, easily fit into the Putin regime. Of course, a postcommunist system in which the Communist Party is an important element is a paradox. But it was not the only paradox in the new Russia.

Another paradox was that the Communists, despite losing some of their local administrative support, increased their voter base. It was not only pensioners who were casting their ballots for Gennady Zyuganov's party—which was the major residue of the Soviet past and ironically the most influential party in postcommunist Russia—but also doctors, teachers, and military personnel disillusioned with the reforms of the last dozen years. Such people were voting not for communism but for a more socially oriented policy. And because social stresses were unlikely to decrease in the near future, the left wing of the political spectrum would not shrink either.

It was also possible that under the influence of its new base—because there was no other alternative to the Kremlin—the Communist Party might move toward real, rather than rhetorical, opposition to the Kremlin. But with the same leaders as in the Soviet past, the Communists hardly could have become a constructive force in Russia, as did former communist parties in Eastern and Central Europe.

The very existence of an eternal opposition in the form of the Communist Party, which preserved a large measure of Sovietism and antiliberalism, increased the odds against the appearance of another opposition force in Russia, including democratic alternatives. With the Communist Party as the main opposition, the authorities could pretend they were running a liberal democracy, though in reality the government was not fully liberal and hardly democratic. The Communists helped the administration maintain a liberal image. Without the Communist Party, neither Chubais nor Gaidar, much less Putin, could have pretended to fill the liberal niche.

The liberals who had come together within the framework of the Union of Right Forces, the SPS, found themselves in a difficult position after the Duma elections. The SPS had managed to unite a large part of the reformist electorate (taking a portion of Yabloko's supporters) and had hoped to become a serious ally of Putin, if not the leading one.[4] Putin, however, did not feel obligated to the liberals, and apparently did not want to depend on anyone at all. In that, he followed the Yeltsin tradition. After the Duma elections, Putin openly ignored the SPS liberals, while making a deal with the Communists in which they divided up the Duma committee posts. Putin also supported Communist Gennady Seleznev for speaker of the lower house.

With these actions, Putin showed that ideology was not an important consideration for him; he would stick with pure pragmatism. At this point, the president's aim was to get the loyalty of the parliament, where the majority of members were from leftist and centrist groups. Putin was not worried about the sentiments of the SPS members. He was sure they would not dare create resistance and would come to accept the situation. The SPS leaders did in fact swallow their pride, and in the presidential election three months later they again supported Putin.

The leaders of the SPS, primarily Chubais and former prime minister Kiriyenko, unconditionally endorsed Putin's policy in Chechnya and his leanings toward statism. Kiriyenko—attempting to justify himself and his fellow liberals while seeking a place in the new government structures—formulated the new credo of the Russian right, replete with theoretical constructions, in the April 14, 2000, *Kommersant-Daily*.

Kiriyenko defined the new liberalism as "liberalism of lifestyle." The old version, which he termed "liberalism of outlook," had become obsolete, he insisted. Russian liberalism, he said, "is following the demands of the new generation," and the new generation is "the generation of statists and great power advocates." So the liberals should be thinking not about individuals, rights, and freedoms but about a strong state. The liberals can't oppose Putin's policy, argued the ideologue of new "liberalism." "What opposition, when there is no time left?" Kiriyenko would exclaim with feigned simplicity.

A majority of the Russian liberals united in the SPS considered their number one goal to be cooperation with the president and implementation of his policy. They proved yet again that economic priorities—the market and not democracy—were important to them. Several outspoken "liberals" (for example, Petr Aven) called on Putin to become the "Russian Pinochet," suggesting that only a dictatorship could continue the country's market reforms. Behind that simple idea was another, one more important for many supporters of the market and the oligarchs linked to them: They perceived authoritarianism and totalitarianism as the best means of protecting their positions from social backlash and from their rivals.

I remember the talk in Moscow during that period. Analysts asked one another who had gone to serve Putin and who was still waiting it out. Almost all the oligarchs and the majority of liberals who were close to privatization tsar Chubais had "lain down" under Putin. That was understandable, because the property and prosperity of the former depended exclusively on the government's attitude toward them. As for the latter, none of the leading liberals had martyrdom in mind in the fight for freedom and democracy. They were saved by the fact that Putin believed in the market; that allowed for minimal loss of face when they joined up with Unity and got jobs from the new leader.[5]

The majority of Russian liberals close to power were behaving like the technocrats in the bureaucratic-authoritarian regimes of Latin America, who were prepared to service even dictatorial regimes if they accomplished economic modernization. But the point is that in Russia, with the traditionally enormous role of the state apparatus and shadowy rules of the game, Russian liberals could become merely a front for a corrupt system. And they were too smart not to notice that.

A few SPS leaders, such as Boris Nemtsov and Irina Khakamada, seemed clearly uncomfortable with the new situation. They permitted themselves to make critical, albeit moderate, statements about the Kremlin policy. The "father" of Russian reforms, Yegor Gaidar, chose to stay silent, and that meant that he was also critical of the administration but preferred not to speak out. The dissatisfaction of individual liberals and their criticism of the Kremlin allowed them to preserve their influence on some part of the opposition groups within the society and even attempt the role of "constructive opposition" (later, SPS leaders invented the term "ruling opposition" in trying to justify their attempt to perform two mutually exclusive roles simultaneously).

Some Russian observers believed that SPS leaders intentionally divided up roles—Chubais and Kiriyenko usually praised the government and the president, while Nemtsov and some others criticized them—and in this way tried to keep incompatible parts of the electorate under the SPS's control. For the authorities' part, allowing mild venting by a dissatisfied minority that did not threaten them in any way helped them keep up a civilized image.

The SPS liberals, in their desire to be part of the government at any cost, were prepared to continue in the role of stabilizer that they had taken on during the Yeltsin administration. The SPS was in the same trap that Democratic Russia—the first Russian democratic movement formed in Gorbachev's time—had fallen into when it supported Yeltsin in his power struggles in the early 1990s. Democratic Russia, too, had tried to become the president's ally, hoping to get its share. But when Yeltsin ignored it, the movement accepted the role of unrequited ally, supporting the president despite it all.

Subsequently, the liberals of the second wave, united around Gaidar's Russia's Choice and, later, Democratic Russia's Choice, no longer made demands on Yeltsin, having become part of the government without preliminary conditions. They became an important element in Yeltsin's shadow spider web, initiating moderate reforms from time to time. Who will do it, if not us? the liberals in power asked. Ultimately they, like the Communists, became a stabilizing element of the regime. So Yeltsin's regime, now being passed on to the new leader, managed to rest on supposedly eternal and irreconcilable enemies—the SPS liberals and the Communists.

But in the final analysis, the stabilizing role of the SPS liberals within the framework of elected monarchy discredited the idea of liberal democracy. Moreover, the splintering of economic liberalism and democracy inevitably led to lawless, oligarchic capitalism; there simply could be no other kind of capitalism under such conditions, where economic freedom was not accompanied by political freedom and the rule of law, and economic freedom was limited by the manipulations of the state apparatus.

As for the only democratic (noncommunist) opposition to Putin—Yabloko—it lost more than 900,000 voters somewhere between the previous elections in 1995 and the 1999 elections. The Yabloko faction in the Duma dropped by more than half, from 45 seats in the old Duma to 17. Yabloko's defeat was the result of society's disillusionment with liberal democratic values. The movement paid for its defense of those values, including the antiwar stance of its leader, Grigory Yavlinsky. Part of Yavlinsky's base supported the war in Chechnya. Moreover, a large segment of liberal-thinking people preferred the SPS to Yabloko because, they said, "You can't keep on criticizing the government, you finally have to help the government." Yavlinsky replied to this, "If we start cooperating with an administration that will use us as cover, then we will annihilate ourselves"—and he was right. But the drama for Yabloko at that historic moment was that the niche for a democratic opposition was too narrow.

The weakening of Yabloko's influence reflected Russia's need for new forms combining the human rights movement with more constructive ways of influencing the administration. The small party of the intelligentsia, always in the opposition and never going to come to power, did not suit many ambitious people who regarded a political party as a trampoline for advancement. Besides which, the regime's consolidation around the idea of order, which appealed to society and elites, would of course not help to strengthen the opposition democratic alliance. Those who feared a new "iron fist" preferred to avoid criticizing the administration. People grew more cautious—the memory of Soviet times was too recent. Yeltsin's heir from the KGB was a reminder of Soviet repression and at the same time a factor that restrained political emotions. Russia's political arena was taking on a conformist look.

After Unity's victory in the parliamentary elections, Putin's drive to power was inexorable. But with society's unstable moods and the unpredictable nature of the Chechen war, there could be no firm guarantee of Putin's victory in June 2000, when Yeltsin's term ended. The authors of Project Putin who were at the core of Yeltsin's entourage—his daughter Tatyana, his adviser Valentin Yumashev, his presidential head of staff Alexander Voloshin, and their friends the oligarchs—worried that they might not be able to keep Putin's ratings high until June, that something could happen to spoil their plans. Putin had to be brought to power immediately.

———————— ✑❧ ————————

And here Yeltsin astonished the world—on December 31, 1999, when the whole country was celebrating the New Year, Russia's first president announced that he was retiring. Reading his statement to the people, he shed a tear. "I've made a decision," he said in the taped broadcast to the nation. "I've thought long and hard. Today, on the last day of the departing century, I am retiring. . . . I want to ask you all to forgive me. Because many of our dreams did not come to pass."

Yeltsin looked solemn and sentimental, even sad. New Year's Eve and the approaching new millennium turned out to be very suitable for the first postcommunist president's farewell. Russians at their festive tables with champagne glasses in hand were prepared to forgive their leader many things, including the empty promises Yeltsin so liked to make. Russians are not rancorous. The unexpected announcement did not shock the country, or cause major upset. "About time!" captures the reaction of most Russians to the Kremlin's New Year's present.[6] Yeltsin's retirement meant that Putin would be in charge of the Kremlin and Russia and of his own presidential elections. And the Kremlin need not have worried: No one tried to ruin the scenario, and no "strangers" had any pretensions to the throne.

Preparations for Yeltsin's departure resembled a secret military operation. Only a few tested and trusted people were in on it—those who had persuaded Yeltsin to make Putin his successor, first among them Tatyana. In his memoir, *Presidential Marathon*, Yeltsin, or his ghostwriters, tried to make it look as if the president himself had made the decision and had informed his entourage at the very last moment. "I didn't know anything until almost the last moment," Tatyana declared to *Kommersant-Daily*. But Yeltsin was in no condition to plan and carry out his resignation on his own. He was not the director, the producer, or the screenwriter of this performance. He was merely the aged star dressed in the tatters of his former charisma brought in to play his final part.

According to Yeltsin's book, the first conversation he had with Putin about him resigning and Putin becoming acting president took place on December 14.[7] Putin, Yeltsin recalled, had doubts. The heir was evidently ambiguous about Yeltsin's offer. Here is how Putin reacted to Yeltsin's proposal of succession, according to Yeltsin in *Presidential Marathon*: "You know, Boris Nikolayevich, to tell the truth, I'm not sure whether I'm prepared for this, whether I want it, because it is a rather difficult life." Colonel Putin apparently hesitated. That was the correct response. No need to rush things. Putin's reaction merely convinced Yeltsin that he had found the right man, one who was in no hurry to climb onto the throne. Let us not deny Putin his sincerity—apparently he truly was not sure of himself at first and wanted more time to prepare for power. But after the conversation with Yeltsin, Putin agreed to take the Kremlin job.

Had Putin known what the president would suggest on December 14? He must have. Starting in August, he must have realized his loyalty and his performance were being tested. Members of the Family held numerous preliminary meetings at their dachas, during which they discussed the details of the transfer of power. They were preparing Putin for Hour X, and he was preparing himself for it too. As a former intelligence officer, he understood—or should have understood—what was going on. Moreover, the operation relied on his cooperation, his brains, and his intelligence officer expertise.

When Yeltsin met with Putin again, on December 29, Putin knew that he was Russia's new boss. The talks between the departing monarch and his successor were a formality, a symbolic act, like the signing of a treaty. Yeltsin's entourage and Putin had already agreed on all the basic details of the project. Obviously, the ruling "Family" could not give up power just like that. Roles were assigned. The parties' mutual obligations were ratified. It was, simultaneously, a complex transfer of personal power, the perpetuation of the ruling corporation, and the endorsement of the formed-by-Yeltsin elected monarchy. The corporation had taken its time selecting the heir, expended great effort destroying its real or imagined foes, and used every means possible to reach its goals—from smear campaigns against opponents of the Chechen war to provoking society's neurasthenia. To call things by their real names, the process was a conspiracy by the Kremlin entourage to hand over power to a specific person and to ensure his success.

The parties then turned to the stage set and the creation of a semblance of legitimacy for the event of Yeltsin's resignation. They made sure the news did not get out beforehand. The videotape of Yeltsin's message to the nation, which had been recorded in the utmost secrecy, was delivered to the Ostankino television studios in an armored car accompanied by a military escort. All national stations were to begin broadcasting the tape precisely at noon on December 31, when the Russian Far Eastern time zone entered the New Year. Thus, the population of the Far East and Siberia got the news about the change of scenery in Moscow while sitting at their tables celebrating New Year's Eve.

Meanwhile, the Kremlin was busy organizing meetings. First, Yeltsin and Putin met with Patriarch Alexii, and the Russian Orthodox Church blessed the transfer of power. The Orthodox Church always satisfied the desires of the state; there was something monarchical about that. Then came the transfer to Putin of the nuclear briefcase, a symbol of power and confirmation of Russia's great-power status. This too was taped. Then came a meeting of the retiring president and his successor with the power ministers—*siloviki*. This was the most important meeting, because the transfer of power had to have the agreement of the Defense and Interior Ministries and the security services; there could be no threat from them. Then came a farewell banquet with the power ministers, and the entire company watched Yeltsin's broadcast on television.

Around one o'clock in the afternoon, Moscow time, Yeltsin shook everyone's hand. Then journalists with cameras were allowed inside, and they taped Yeltsin's last minutes in his role of the leader. Russia soon watched Yeltsin leave the Kremlin. He looked like he was having trouble speaking and moving. The cameras showed him leaving the presidential office for the last time—he stopped for a minute, gestured around the room, and turned to Putin, as if he were leaving it as a gift: Here, now you are master of all this. Slowly, treading heavily, he went out on the steps of the Kremlin and said something more to Putin. Later, we learned that he said, "Take care of Russia." Theatrical, almost touching. But Yeltsin was an actor, and a good one, especially in his best years. Everything that has a beginning has an ending, I thought, looking at the footage of Yeltsin in a new role—in the role of a pensioner.

Putin looked tense and pale throughout the invented-by-the-Kremlin ceremony that all of Russia watched. There was no expression on his face—his gaze was remote. That is how he experienced the significance of the moment. A boy from Saint Petersburg, a regular guy from a worker's family, a recent gofer, was receiving a huge country to rule—that was enough to make his head spin. But at least outwardly, he controlled his emotions, if there were any. The Yeltsin period was over. Russia rang in a new year with a new leader.

While Yeltsin was on the way to his dacha—where he had been hiding for more than a year and which became now his official residence—Bill Clinton called. The American president was true to his warm and fuzzy and slightly teary self—he felt he had to say good-bye to the man that political fate had placed beside him on the world stage. Clinton definitely liked Ol' Boris. Yeltsin, overcome by emotion and very weary, could not talk and asked to move the call to that evening.

From the point of view of guaranteeing the succession, Yeltsin's premature retirement was a well-planned and well-executed act. Yeltsin's team, which had been so pathetic and inexperienced at the beginning, had proven that it could learn the art of intrigue. In any case, the Kremlin team did succeed with Project Successor. A man in almost total isolation, who had not dealt with the outside world for at least a year, Yeltsin would have never done this alone. So even if we were to presume that Yeltsin had chosen his heir himself, it might have seemed an independent act to him while not being so at all.

To ensure Putin's victory in the presidential election, Yeltsin had to leave early. Rumors of his retirement had circulated for a long time.[8] But not everyone believed Yeltsin would be able to subjugate his ambition and pride to reason. The unexpectedness of his exit was a crucial element in the whole play and the guarantee of the planned outcome. It is difficult to say what persuaded Yeltsin—pressure from the Family or an understanding of the political realities and the desire to find a successor who could preserve his legacy or revive the moribund reforms. Did the ailing Yeltsin think about anything besides his constant illnesses? To what degree did he understand the problems he was leaving his heir? Most likely, the need to guarantee his and his family's personal safety was uppermost in whatever calculations he made. Otherwise, why would he have chosen a man who had no experience in public politics and dealing with high-level government management, who was unknown to society at large but had shown that he could be loyal to his mentors?

Putin's behavior as chief of the FSB was the determining factor for Yeltsin and the Family's choice of him as successor. Putin had been cautious and had not exhibited excessive ambition. He was precise and disciplined. He had no connections that tarnished him. (But perhaps it was just the reverse—there was something in his past that allowed the Family to control his future.) He knew how to wait, never hurried, and seemed to be a rational, pragmatic man. But most important, he had proved that he could be trusted at a difficult time for the president. It was these qualities that determined Putin's fate and the fate of the state.

There were two more things. The first was Putin's relative youth—he was 47 years old at that time. Yeltsin liked young politicians; he felt they were the future of Russia. Second was the fact that Putin had in his life a liberal period in Saint Petersburg. Of course, those who moved Putin to the top knew that without public acceptance he could not be placed on the throne. Therefore the victory of the pro-Putin movements in the parliamentary elections became a significant factor in the final choice of successor.

Yeltsin handed Putin his present, which was Russia. There was no doubt that from then on all the state's resources would be used to guarantee Putin the presidency.

Thus ended the rule of Russia's first president, Boris Yeltsin.[9] His rule began with the faith of millions in a better future for Russia, and it ended in disillusionment and insecurity. Yeltsin himself, the symbol of renewal and strength in the late 1980s, had by the late 1990s turned into a doddering old man whom many regarded as another Brezhnev. The Russian people awaited his departure impatiently and worried that the mumbling half-ruin of a man would do something unexpected before he left, like starting a new shakeup or engaging in a new political or military conflict. Enough was enough, Russians thought, with little pity and much scorn and weariness.

People could have supported almost anyone else to be rid of Yeltsin. He was doomed, not only because society did not accept him any longer but also because this proud maverick couldn't keep going after having lost his old self-assurance. Russia wanted to close Yeltsin's chapter. Ironically, very soon some of those who had wished for Yeltsin's departure, considering him a political ruin, would change their minds on his rule and start to remember his times with nostalgia—finding in his rule more and more positive signs. You have to compare to make your final judgment of people and history.

Yeltsin, who had seemed upon his arrival in the Kremlin to be breaking many traditions as well as destroying the communist empire, merely confirmed the Soviet tradition of no leader leaving in time. His predecessors had had to be carried out of the Kremlin feet first, or forced out. He himself, recently powerful and willful, proud and ambitious, stayed on until it was painful to watch him. It will be interesting to see whether Putin manages to break that tradition, and if so, how.

Yeltsin left behind a complex political structure overgrown with powerful vested interests—regional, oligarchic, bureaucratic interests. The pattern of leadership he bequeathed reflected both the strengths and weaknesses of his character and of his conception of the presidency. The regime he created had facets of suspicion and egocentricity, and combined a desire for autocratic total power with an unwillingness to use that power like a dictator. It was a continuation of Yeltsin's personality and at the same time a continuation of the ancient Russian tradition of autocratic monarchical rule. It perpetuated at least some aspects of the Russian pattern of governance—the Russian System with its reliance on the leader-arbiter's staying above the fray, its fusion of state and society, of politics and the economy, its paternalism. No matter what form of leadership Yeltsin's heir tried to build, it would be extremely difficult to destroy Yeltsin's political thinking and the habits embodied in the structures, philosophy of power, and political complexes that survived him.

Russia will return to Yeltsin's personality again and again in an attempt to understand his legacy and decide whether it was ultimately positive or negative. Society will ponder what he was for his tormented country—reformer or stabilizer, liberal or conservative, statist or destroyer of the state? Where was he directed? If to the future, what kind of future? Or did he try to slow society's forward movement and preserve part of the Soviet and pre-Soviet past, afraid of too much change too fast?

That there is no agreement in Russia in evaluating Yeltsin suggests that the study of his role may be subject to certain shifts and that much depends on what his successor becomes and how he uses Yeltsin's legacy. Yeltsin could be regarded more kindly in the future than he was at the end of his political life. The fact that after several years of Putin's presidency even former Yeltsin critics look at the first Russian president in a more favorable way points to that.

For now, one thing is clear: Yeltsin in the early 1990s became Russia's leader first of all because he combined in his personality and his rule a connection to the past and a simultaneous rejection of that past. In an amazingly analogous way, Putin began by claiming continuity with Yeltsinism and at the same time rejecting it.

Yeltsin's political style embodied rudiments of a typical Soviet politician alongside a desire to destroy the communist instincts he possessed. He could behave like a haughty boyar out of Old Russia, disdainful of subordinates. He preferred making decisions personally and behind the scenes, resorting to intrigues characteristic of the Soviet *nomenklatura* and even of feudal times. He could not function in a system with a separation of powers, striving as he always did for a monopoly in that commodity, power. He gathered power in his fist, muscling out anyone else who might lay claim to it.

At the same time, Yeltsin showed a feeling for democracy. He understood the significance of basic civil liberties and did not attack them. He could tolerate criticism, albeit with difficulty, even when it was ruthless. For instance, he never touched journalists, even those who made it their business to attack him. He knew how to appeal directly to the people in his struggle with the state apparatus and his opponents, and he understood the power of the people. He was not vengeful and never persecuted his enemies and opponents. That was new for Russia, which was accustomed to revenge in politics, not forgiveness and tolerance. Thus Yeltsin had already begun undermining the traditional Russian System of rule.

In the early years of his administration—1991 and 1992—Yeltsin unquestionably had major goals: to see Russia integrated into Europe and to make Russia a civilized, powerful democracy. Cooperating with the West and drawing a line below the communist past were paramount for Yeltsin in the beginning, though he may not have given much thought to how to achieve them. But when he began to feel resistance, which started in early 1992, and he realized that he had no clear vision of what exactly he wanted to achieve, he turned to what he had always known—fighting his opponents and strengthening his personified regime. At that moment, he began thinking of reforms only in the context of protecting his position. If reforms did not interfere with his power, he continued them; if they complicated his life, he slowed them down or rejected them completely. Outwardly, Yeltsin was still the guarantor of the new orientation toward the West and liberalization. But beginning in 1993, he stopped being the moving force behind the reform process, which was growing moribund.

Not only the style but the politics of the first Russian president was marked by contradiction. Yeltsin made anticommunism his ideology. He managed to train the political class to operate in an atmosphere of pluralism. He gave his first government to the young, unknown liberal technocrats, exploding the Russian tradition of gerontocracy that had denied the young power except for the brief revolutionary period during the 1920s. Yet he ended up returning to an almost monarchical rule. He failed to rule in a different way. His *elected monarchy* functioned as monolithic, undivided personal rule. Such has always been the way in Russia. It is true that now it requires democratic, electoral legitimization. But personal rule distorts democracy, turning it into an imitation. Besides, this old–new hybrid political structure is doomed to be internally torn, unstable and ambivalent.

Yeltsin took power at a decisive moment in Russian history thanks to the contradictory nature of his politics: He was a rebel who came out of the bowels of the old system and still belonged to it when he began dismantling it. It is hard to imagine the dissident Andrei Sakharov as leader of the new Russia. Václav Havel or Lech Walesa is unthinkable as a leader of Russia. Their rise to power in Czechoslovakia and Poland reflected the previous regimes' greater experience with liberalization, which occurred even under communist rule. Russia had to undergo liberalization and democratization at the same time, and that is why it needed a leader who could unite the two parts of society: the one that was not ready to leave Soviet life and only wanted a renewal of socialism, and the one trying to escape the past, to get rid of its vestiges fully and forever. Yeltsin, still functioning in two eras, was the ideal politician to combine temporarily two incompatible desires and agendas for the future.

Theoretically, we could imagine another path for overcoming communism: a radical uprooting of all elements of Sovietism, including a replacement of the elites and the construction of new institutions. But such a radical transformation would have demanded a leader ready to use violence to neutralize the strata not prepared for decisive changes. In Russia, those strata formed the majority. Besides which, that kind of transformation demanded the presence of an organized democratic force with a plan of action and a leader with the political will to unite the groups interested in a critical breakthrough.

There were no such forces or leaders in Russia at the time of the break with communism, nor do they exist today. And even with an outwardly successful radical transformation from above, we could expect to see an eventual deformation of the new forms and institutions by the cultural milieu, historical characteristics, and traditions of Russian society. In short, Russia's revolutionary transition to the liberal-democratic rules of the game in the early 1990s was dubious. Russia did not follow the example of Poland and Czechoslovakia—a pact among the main political forces and a peaceful division of power between the old and the new elites. The anticommunist opposition in Russia was too weak and the *nomenklatura* too strong to achieve reforms on the basis of consensus. The irony and drama in Russia's postcommunist transformation were related to the fact that its engine and its base were still the old Soviet-born establishment. Continuity in the new Russia explained the nature of change. The more change, the more it was the same thing.

For an evolutionary, bloodless exit from communism when there was no national consensus regarding the past, present, or future, Russia needed a leader of a special type, a politician with an enormous amount of charisma who could serve as a substitute for the lack of new elites, structured agenda, and readiness to build new institutions. Such a leader could embody the complexes of the past and the desire to put an end to those complexes. But he could not be politically and ideologically monotonous, pure and definite—he would have to vacillate, have weaknesses, explode into conflicts, move in opposite directions. The cost of that leadership would inevitably be a delay or even U-turns in the liberal-democratic breakthrough.

The best thing for Russia would have been Yeltsin at the stage of overcoming communism and a new leader at the next stage, someone who could unite the nation on a democratic platform rather than an anticommunist one. After 1996, Yeltsin should have retired from public life, both because he was sick and not up to it and because he did not understand what he should do next and did not know how to change. He did not know anymore what goals to set other than his own survival. He should have left office so that Russia had a chance to keep moving toward further liberalization and more structured democracy, and so that he could keep his dignity and stay in history as an undoubtedly transformational leader.

Yeltsin, however, had already begun focusing on his own survival, on keeping power at any cost after 1992, when he fired Gaidar as head of his government. It was surprising how quickly he began fading, for a man who had been physically strong. Living on the edge, heavy drinking, stress, and other immoderate habits took their toll. He aged much more quickly than Gorbachev, even though they were born the same year.[10] But it wasn't so much a question of physical wear and tear as that he was losing his intuition, could not understand new problems and challenges, got confused, and then fell into depression or tried to respond with his old method of firing officials and appointing new ones.

Keeping Yeltsin in the Kremlin after 1996 led inevitably to the degradation and demoralization of power. The chance of rescue was nonexistent because the president had worked for years to destroy all possibility of alternative elites and leaders coming to the fore. That the majority of Russian liberals had bet on the leader and rejected the need for independent institutions discredited the very idea of liberal democracy in citizens' eyes. Russia was in a trap. On one hand, Yeltsin's reelection to a second term condemned government to stagnation. But on the other hand, there was no democratic alternative to him, and that was at least partially the fault of the liberals and democrats. The only alternative to Yeltsin in 1996 was the Communist Party's return to power under Zyuganov. Thus

Yeltsin had to remain on the political stage, even though there was no further need for an anticommunist consolidator and he had become an obstacle to a new stage of transformation. He was a lesser evil.

In the Yeltsin regime, the democratic-populist principle was constantly in conflict with the authoritarian-monarchical principle. The conflict between the incompatible combination of democracy and leadership through personified power led to democracy's becoming a facade hiding a completely different interior.

Autocratic leadership had existed in Russia for many centuries, changing only its ideological colors and method of legitimization. During the Communist stage, autocracy was legitimized by the Party and hid behind the mask of collective leadership, which did little to change its essence. After the collapse of communism, Yeltsin revived a tradition that had long distinguished Russia from the rest of Europe and that once again made monolithic power, this time without any "collectivist" cover, the nucleus of politics. In the 1990s again, the leader's power, not society, was the main subject of the Constitution. All the major institutions of Russian politics were functioning in the space created by central authority, as had happened for centuries. It was true that in Yeltsin's era, political actors in Russia acquired freedom and politics became spontaneous and unpredictable. For the first time, uncertainty of the outcome was introduced into the Russian political process. But this happened not because power underwent a crucial transformation and those in authority understood the rationale of political fragmentation and freedom but because authority was weak and confused. Moreover, the uncertainty of the political process was the result of the uncertain rules of the game.

Yeltsin's elected monarchy, functioning in a stratified society with a corrupt bureaucracy and weak power structures, could be nothing but a parody of the old totalitarianism and of the authoritarianism of the 1970s and 1980s. To survive, the elected monarchy had to share power with influential groups, to make constant deals and bargains, to face multiple constraints and obstacles. Consequently, the outwardly authoritarian leader who took so much power into his own hands was only quasi-authoritarian.

This type of regime resembled what Guillermo O'Donnell has labeled "delegative democracy"—a system of power based on the premise that "whoever was elected to the presidency is thereby entitled to govern as he or she sees fit."[11] For Russia, Yeltsin's "delegative democracy" in the 1990s was a definite step forward from the previous pattern of totalitarian and authoritarian rule. But because of its internal contradictions and traps, this rule could not be durable or effective. The question was how Russia could extricate itself from the trap of weak and demoralized omnipotence.

The monolithic nature of Yeltsin's rule seemed to aid the cause of economic reform. But the breakthrough into the effective and civilized market soon turned out to be illusory. It was indeed easier under presidential autocracy to implement market reforms and neutralize the resistance of social groups unprepared to give up state paternalism. At the same time, however, the return to personified power made impossible the development of a systemic politics that combined the activities of manifold independent institutions, each working on issues of concern to its members. Though in the short run market reform benefited from the superconcentration of power, in the long run it lost out because of the slow progress in creating a liberal-democratic society. And market capitalism in the absence of independent institutions, clear rules of the game (first of all, the supremacy of law), and independent individuals can be only a parody of the market.

We could be less critical of Yeltsin's work if we accepted that the number of challenges facing Russia in 1991 was huge and that ways of solving those problems on the road to liberal democracy were limited. But let us not forget that Yeltsin held many levers of power in his hands and that, before post-Soviet politics and society took definite shape, he had great influence over the course of events. There is no justification for his failure to push liberal transformation more energetically. He bears personal responsibility for the missed opportunities in Russian reforms.

Faced with the same obstacles, a leader who tried more consistently to escape the limits of autocracy and the traps of court politics, who understood more clearly Russia's challenges, could have helped the country make more determined strides toward a civilized system of governance, independent institutions, civil society, and a system of checks and balances. But here is a problem: How many leaders who had complete power had the ability and courage to share it with other forces and institutions voluntarily? Moving toward a liberal-democratic system means first of all the ability to share power.

We should give president Boris Yeltsin his due. Russia under his rule escaped destructive scenarios for itself and for the world, and there were plenty of them. Even if he did not handle it as well as might be envisioned, he presided over the rather peaceful decline of a nuclear superpower and the initial stage of its transformation. The price of this transformation for millions of Russians was huge and unbearable. But it might have been much heavier.

At the same time, just because Russia escaped apocalypse under Yeltsin and there were no other strong candidates for the presidency, we should not soften our assessment of his leadership. That after his departure society wanted an "iron hand" and longed for order is a judgment on his rule. He helped society to get freedoms, but he failed to understand the role of the rule of law and accountability, first of all on behalf of authority. If we look at the need to accomplish the democratic project and the opportunities, albeit limited, that he had, then Yeltsin was a weak, inadequate leader.

Yeltsin and his leadership were stitched together out of insoluble conflicts. He had enormous formal powers and at the same time was incapable of executing his decisions. He personally tended toward bossism but was left without mass support and was constantly forced to ingratiate himself and be a populist. He was a leader whose ideal was a superpresidential regime but who had to function in an era of disintegration. He was a politician who hated compromise and yet had to make many deals and concessions. He was a man who proclaimed the goal of democracy and oversaw the creation of an elected monarchy. He was a president who won two elections only to become a screen for the clans behind the throne. He was a model of a powerful, dynamic personality who ended up fighting his own uncertainty and weakness.

Yeltsin turned out to be a revolutionary who made permanent revolutionary shakeups his means of surviving. The more uncertain he felt in a new situation, the more he turned to revolutionary rhetoric and actions. Revolution for him became a means of preserving the status quo, the pattern of rule he got used to—one more paradox of the transition reality. He was the destroyer of communism, yet thanks to him the Communist Party became an important factor in the functioning of his regime. And that regime—established at the beginning of the 1990s with high hopes and many good intentions—ended up souring a significant part of the nation on democracy.

Yet Yeltsin made a return to communism in Russia an impossibility. He habituated the political class to a relatively civilized method of dealing with international issues. Since his presidency, it is harder for Russia—perhaps impossible—to return to a cold war with the West. In many ways, he guaranteed the peaceful dissolution of the USSR and the appearance of independent states on its territory. He taught the political class to exist in an atmosphere of pluralism and free expression. (Although the course of events under Putin will show that some backtracking is not ruled out.) And finally, Yeltsin made a return to a planned, centralized economy an impossibility.

There is another result of his administration that I feel is worthy of approval: Yeltsin's weak, chaotic, often helpless leadership forced a significant part of society to think for itself, to depend on its own strength, and to come out of the shadow of the state. Frustration with the leader made people learn to walk on their own. That fact may help Russia survive under any leader.

Russia will have to pay a high price to rid itself of the disabled, half-hearted form of autocracy that Yeltsin revived. But first we must see whether Putin will manage to make Yeltsin's quasi-autocracy work. If it turns out that he cannot (which is likely), society will have to pay for the mistakes of both the father of the regime and his heir who tried to keep the hybrid torn from within the regime alive. It may be that Yeltsin's success as transformer will be determined by how quickly his elected monarchy can be dismantled and by how enduring the democratic habits and the new mentality that Russia acquired under him will prove to be.

That is the legacy Boris Yeltsin left to Vladimir Putin. The very act of handing over power to Putin, as regent and heir, highlighted the principle of elected monarchy inherent in the system Yeltsin created. Yeltsin's early retirement had little to do with democracy; on the contrary, it demonstrated the imitative quality of Yeltsin's conception of democracy. His departure was preferable to the slow fading of the politician, but the artificial advance of elections, the way they were manipulated, had only one goal: to guarantee rule by a single political group.

So Putin's taking power, still in the role of acting president, confirmed the logic of Yeltsin's regime. Now Putin had a chance to show how flexible that regime was and how much it could evolve and in what direction. The new Russian leader had to survive several harsh trials, the first of which was a test of his gratitude—reciprocity with the old ruling team.

Before Yeltsin's retirement in December 1999, Putin played the role of obedient appointee ideally. He did everything to show that he had no ambitions of his own. At the moment, he really might have had none. He seemed to be trying not to cast a shadow; he wanted to be a mere functionary rather than a notable person or a leader. Perhaps he was still wary of responsibility and was afraid of his own inexperience. He may have been worried that at the last moment Yeltsin would change his mind and name a new heir.

Right down to the wire, there could be no certainty that this heir would be the last. Who knew what the sick man or his daughter might think of next? So Putin had to be obedient, not attract attention, and patiently bide his time. Perhaps this was a natural role for him, in keeping with his career in intelligence work. He had always been in supporting roles and found public life difficult. He had not yet learned how to function in it. Or we might be bad shrinks; we cannot rule out the notion that Putin did not much care whether he would be the new monarch or not.

With Yeltsin's retirement, Putin was front and center. There was no doubt that Putin would win the presidential election scheduled for March 2000. But it remained to be seen whether he would follow the logic of Yeltsin's legacy or begin changing it. Regardless of how Putin felt about the Yeltsin regime, he would have to live with it for a long time, either in peaceful coexistence or in conflict. And Russia will spend a long time clarifying its attitude toward the man who left the stage unexpectedly on the eve of the year 2000.

Chapter 3

PUTIN, THE NEW RUSSIAN LEADER

Presidential elections without a choice. What course to take? The new Kremlin spider web. Formation of the government. Taming of the governors. Whom to rely upon. The intelligentsia is concerned.

I mmediately after the New Year 2000 celebrations, Putin, as acting president, promulgated his first decree, which granted Yeltsin immunity.[1] Under the decree, Yeltsin could not be prosecuted for criminal or administrative wrongdoing for any of his actions as president. Moreover, Yeltsin's aides (his daughter Tatyana and the rest of his inner circle) were declared as having been responsible only to him—that is, they were absolved of legal responsibility. Putin's decree created a zone of immunity around the former president that could be extended at will to the members of Yeltsin's entourage.

As foreign observers noted, Putin's decree "gave foundation to all the charges laid against Yeltsin by his enemies."[2] Many Russian observers felt the same way. But we had to admit that in Russia a guarantee of immunity to the departing leader was the only way of assuring that the old ruling group would leave the stage without a fierce battle.

In the meantime, Prime Minister Putin's popularity and the administrative levers he had inherited made the outcome of the presidential election, set for March 26, 2000, inevitable. According to the Constitution, the presidential election is supposed to be held in June. But Yeltsin's early retirement made it possible to reschedule the election for an earlier date to guarantee Putin's victory while he was still popular.

There were ten other candidates besides Putin. Some of them were the usual suspects who had been competing with Yeltsin during the previous elections, among them the Communist leader Gennady Zyuganov, the leader of the democratic Yabloko Grigory Yavlinsky, and the leader of the nationalistic Liberal Democratic Party, political clown Vladimir Zhirinovsky. The rest of the presidential hopefuls entered the race without the slightest chance not only of winning but even of getting substantial support. They wanted publicity and television coverage so that they could pursue other goals afterward.

In any case, participation in the presidential campaign would never be a liability. Konstantin Titov, Ella Pamfilova, Sergei Govorukhin, Yuri Skuratov, Alexei Podberezkin, and Umar Dzhabrailov (in the order of votes received) all ran in the name of running, not in the name of winning, as if demonstrating that the goal is nothing and process is everything. Everyone knew that no one but Putin had a chance, because the entire might of the state was working on his behalf.

The second Chechen war allowed Putin to play the strong, determined leader, but there were other, no less crucial, factors that assured his success. On one hand, Putin was Yeltsin's official successor, blessed by the first Russian president, which guaranteed the support of the bureaucracy and a smooth transition. On the other hand, his image as a hard-edged, stern leader was a positive contrast to the impotent, feeble Yeltsin. This successor could be acceptable both to the portion of the public that was loyal to the regime and to the protest voters—to those who wanted an arranged, seamless succession and continuity and those who demanded change at the top and break with the past.

Most important, Putin had become the optimal way of getting rid of Yeltsin, both for the ruling class and for society as a whole, which was fed up with the erratic leader. Even his former close lieutenants and staunch supporters were thinking: Enough is enough!

The vagueness of Putin's political image made him a tabula rasa on which everyone could write what he or she wanted. It may not have been conscious on Putin's part in the beginning, but he tried to be all things to all people. Every social and political group could hope that in the long run he would support its formula for bringing order to Russia. He combined the determination and clarity always associated with the military in people's minds with a certain amorphousness. This vagueness allowed Everybody's Man to appeal to all strata of society and to avoid precise answers to the questions that were worrying Russia. For someone beginning his political career and preparing for elections for the first time, this was a sound strategy.

The ruling class unequivocally supported Putin, hoping that the new leader would preserve the current rules of the game; in backing him, it endorsed the status quo, which it benefited from extensively and wanted to continue.[3] Then there were those who hoped that Putin, as a representative of the security services, would return society to the way it had been in Soviet times, or offer a pure authoritarian regime. Some of the liberals hoped that Putin, with his market-oriented past in Saint Petersburg, would continue the long-stalled economic reforms. But the overwhelming desire among the political class and Russians in general was that Putin prove himself a leader who could bring order to Yeltsin's chaos and end the unpredictability of the Kremlin.

Before the election, Putin refused to elaborate on his credo, attempting to maintain credibility with his disparate supporters. But he could not keep silent forever. So far, he had spoken only once on the direction of Russia's development, in an article with the pretentious title "Russia on the Cusp of the Millennium" that appeared on December 30, 1999. In it, Putin leaned too much toward the past. He called for melding universal human values with Russian traditions, patriotism, collectivism, statism, and social justice.[4] Those principles had been truly popular in Russia in Soviet times, when the country was trying to mark out its own "special path." But with the fall of communism, the Russian alternative and claims of uniqueness were all void. Putin—whether he realized it or not—was trying to revive an idea that had been proven to have no future. Perhaps he was trying to impress conservative-minded Russians. But either he or his advisers made a mistake here.

Putin brought down on himself the criticism of liberals and the pro-Western contingent. He could have overlooked their displeasure, for these groups were in the minority in Russia. It was apparently far more important for him to win understanding and support among statists—those who supported a strong Russian state, a much larger group. But because he knew that liberals were powerful in the mass media and among entrepreneurs, he quickly adjusted his position, rendering it even more amorphous.

In an open letter to voters in February 2000, Putin and his staff showed that they had learned their lesson: This time, they tried to avoid any ideas that could inspire attack or even criticism. Yeltsin's successor attempted to eliminate all ideological accents and mentioned only consensual values that even competing forces—liberals, the left wing, or statists—could not reject. It all came down to an increased role for the state (without specifying where the increase would come), further market reform, and a revival of the idea of social justice.

At the same time, Putin tried out a critical stance toward the Yeltsin administration. "Our first and most important problem is the weakening of will. The loss of state will and persistence in completing started affairs. Vacillation, dithering, the habit of putting off the hardest tasks for later," he wrote, attempting to distance himself from Yeltsinism and appealing to people critical of Yeltsin's policy.[5]

Putin basically refused to campaign for the March election, stressing his duties as prime minister and acting president, which were covered extensively on television and by the other media, which followed the prime minister's every step. His team wisely chose to present him not as a charismatic leader but as just like everyone else, the "man on the street." Looking at Putin—with his plain face, ill-cut clothes, and straightforward, slightly awkward manner—every ordinary Russian could imagine himself as president. Even Putin's occasional use of street slang (for instance, his promise to "wipe out" the Chechen terrorists "in the john"), which shocked the intelligentsia, impressed the rest of the country with the new leader's folksiness.

The psychological factor was also important in Russians' attitude in the months leading up to the election. Russian society includes a large "wandering mass" of people who have supported someone new in each election, in search of a hero. In the 1996 elections, they supported General Alexander Lebed. Then they rushed to the support of Yevgeny Primakov in early 1999. Their new hero was Putin. His jump in the ratings was tied in large part to a drop in support for other politicians. Those guys had been around for ten years, some even longer, and they were becoming annoying. Putin was a new face, and people went for the freshness. They would have been attracted to any alternative to the rotting Yeltsin regime. But the irony was that they supported an alternative handpicked by Yeltsin's circle. Russian citizens, it seemed, were not ready to support someone from the opposition. They were neither frustrated enough nor angry enough to make their own independent choice not approved by the ruling team.

The last polls before the balloting for president, conducted by VTsIOM, showed Putin as the almost certain victor. At that point, 53 percent of voters intended to vote for the acting president (down from 58 percent a bit earlier). Putin's rating was beginning to slide, but not dangerously. Zyuganov, the head of the Communist Party, was stuck at 21 percent; and Yavlinsky of the liberal Yabloko was the choice of just 6 percent of the electorate.

When asked what Russia needed, 71 percent of those polled replied "a strong leader" and 59 percent "a strong state." "Democratic institutions" were not a priority—only 13 percent of respondents named them. Society was backhandedly passing judgment on the Yeltsin era, associating it with a weak leader and a weak state. But it was disturbing that Russia was once again trying to escape the crisis of Yeltsinism by searching for a new savior and not through the forming of enduring institutions.

Also disturbing was the fact that Russians did not believe Putin would come to power honestly, whether because of others' machinations or his own—and that many who thought so planned to vote for him anyway. People were frustrated by the Russian-style election, which was used to legitimize choices made through sweet deals. But at the same time, they accepted these choices. The majority of those polled—54 percent—felt that Putin's presidential campaign was dishonest, and 72 percent thought there would be chicanery when the votes were counted.

On the eve of the election, 63 percent were reported to trust Putin fully, down from 76 percent two weeks earlier (though only 25 percent were bothered by the fact that he had worked for the KGB-FSB). According to VTsIOM polls, the biggest factors in the drop in Putin's ratings were the confirmation of his ties to the oligarchs (58 percent) and the continuing war in Chechnya (57 percent). Fifty-five percent worried about his lack of a definite program. But despite all that, people did not see any other option.

The portrait sociologists created of the typical "Putinist" on the basis of these polls showed that the acting president's main backing came from young people and those more than 60 years old. He had more female than male loyalists. People with a middling education gave him the strongest backing; those who were leery of him most often had attained higher levels of education, were between the ages of 30 and 50, and lived in large cities. Support for Putin was weaker in Moscow, always more dynamic, sophisticated, and advanced than the rest of the country.

A VTsIOM survey on March 9, two weeks before the election, showed that a very large percentage of voters who supported Putin rejected the idea of extending the presidential term from four years to seven. Only 24 percent backed term extension, while 65 percent were against it (11 percent had no opinion). This showed that Russians no longer approved of lifelong rule and suggested that the longing for stability based on one leader might have been transitional.

Yeltsin's early resignation did not give Putin's opponents time to prepare for the rescheduled election or the public time to get sick of Putin. The other candidates in the presidential contest made it look something like a real race, allowing Putin to legitimize through an electoral victory his appointment by Yeltsin's circle. In this situation, Putin needed only to turn his de facto presidential powers into de jure ones. Vladimir Vladimirovich was doomed to win because he could not lose—there was no one to lose to, and he could not lose. Even if he had wanted to.

Right up until election day, the ruling group and its candidate managed to sustain an image of a strong, effective leader that was built on almost nothing. The image was created solely on the strength of Putin's continual trips around the country and other manifestations of his physical activity. The public remained totally uninformed of his real plans. When a reporter asked him what his program would be, he replied cagily, "I won't tell." This outrageous statement was the essence of the Putin election campaign—say nothing concrete, promise nothing. For those accustomed to Western political standards, the statement was a challenge of sorts, as well as an expression of disdain for public opinion—"You know you'll elect me even without a program." He was right.

On March 26, Putin won the presidency in the first round with the support of almost 53 percent of voters. His main rival, Zyuganov, got

29.2 percent; the leader of the democratic opposition, Yavlinsky, finished with 5.8 percent. Governor Aman Tuleyev got 2.95 percent; professional nationalist Vladimir Zhirinovsky, 2.7 percent; and governor Konstantin Titov, 1.47 percent. The rest of the candidates together got even less than 1 percent, and "none of the above" got 1.88 percent.

A huge factor in Putin's victory was that he was the only candidate sponsored by the ruling group, which had employed "administrative resources" to neutralize his opponents and organize support for him. The central and local authorities on all levels did everything possible to get him the win—"everything possible" being a multitude of methods, from persuading and pressuring voters to harassing other candidates to assuring a "correct" count of the vote.

Russian sociologists Lev Gudkov and Boris Dubin, explaining Putin's victory, noted Russians' desire to join and support the victor's camp, embodied now by Putin. No one seemed to care about the new leader's aims and ideology. The important thing was that he had already been sitting in the president's chair and was supported by the power structures—the army, Interior Ministry, and intelligence agencies, which were the only Russian institutions (besides the Orthodox Church) that were still fairly well regarded and thought to be relatively free from corruption.

Thus in the presidential election, Putin got the votes of 12 percent of Communists, 40 percent of Yabloko supporters, 40 percent of Zhirinovsky's Liberal Democratic Party, more than two-thirds of the Union of Right Forces (SPS) liberals, and 70 percent of the Primakov–Luzhkov Fatherland and All-Russia Party. These voters supported Putin because they believed he would win and because he and his team stood for order and demonstrated strength. And in new unruly Russia, people were longing for order and respected strength.[6]

The election for the first Russian president, in 1991, won by Yeltsin, was an election for radical change. The elections of 1996, which Yeltsin also won, were a vote to draw the communist past to an end. In the 2000 presidential election, Russia was voting for stability. There was no widespread desire for radical change. Society was tired and wanted peace and security. The desire for order was not absolute, however, because people clearly did not want to lose the liberties Gorbachev and Yeltsin had granted. The new leader had to find a new correlation between freedom and order.

The inauguration of the second president of Russia took place on May 7. The eclectic style of the new leadership was in evidence; the Kremlin tried to give the public elements of ceremony borrowed from different epochs: tsarist autocracy, Soviet times, and the anticommunist period. It was too much for good taste: Yeltsin and Putin watching the parade from the porch where the tsars had stood to greet their people; a typically Soviet style of attendance lists for guests, who were divided according to their rank and ordered to stay in their assigned hall; and the new leader taking the oath of office on Yeltsin's Constitution. The ceremony reflected the hybrid style and substance of the new ruling group, which embraced seemingly incompatible features—the KGB past of the new Kremlin boss, his liberal activity, and his nearly monarchical ascendancy to power orchestrated by anticommunists and revolutionaries!

The "postmodernism" of Putin's rise to power would continue to be displayed in his administration, which contains echoes of various eras. Tsarist-style intrigues and succession, elements of Soviet-type loyalty, new-age utilitarianism and pragmatism—all would become an impetus for mutually exclusive trends and possibilities. We will see how this man—who by training has to be unambiguous and determined, have no doubts, and seek definite solutions—will live and rule in a pluralistic, fragmented, and contradictory environment. Postcommunism in Russia was obviously not a sharp break with the past—neither pre-Soviet nor fully post-Soviet. Those who understood that and could move in the atmosphere of mixed signals and bows to seemingly incompatible principles had a chance of staying on top.

Putin looked nervous during the inauguration. The scenario called for him to take a long walk through the halls of the Kremlin to reach the room where the ceremony was to be held. As he climbed the endless Kremlin staircase, the television cameras showed his tense, pale face, his sturdy yet small figure all but lost in the vastness of the Kremlin's opulence. In his ill-fitting suit, he seemed wildly out of place in the monarchic ritual. A staff officer of the KGB, an assistant to Saint Petersburg's mayor, a nondescript member of a presidential administration—a person accustomed to being in the shadows, permanently behind the boss, running errands—found himself master of the Kremlin. This was breathtaking.

The guests were gathered in various ballrooms, depending on their place in the hierarchy as determined by the Yeltsin ruling group. Thus the main room held a very motley crowd: oligarchs, children of oligarchs, "gray cardinals," retired prime ministers, and pretty young women who did not seem to have a direct connection to the proceedings. Neither Luzhkov nor other political heavyweights could be seen in this room. But Gorbachev had been invited, on Putin's personal initiative. This at least was a good sign—Putin was bringing Gorbachev back into politics.

This was Yeltsin's last official appearance, and all eyes were on him— how did he look, could he speak, how did he walk, what did he feel in his new role? Yeltsin tried to give a memorable speech, but it was too long and lecturing. Putin, standing next to him, began giving him impatient looks. Then Putin delivered his own speech, brief and energetic, without a single hitch. Putin's very appearance underlined the difference between himself and the patriarch next to him, and the difference was for many reassuring.

The new Russian leader was in an exceptionally good position; Yeltsin might have envied him. Vladimir Putin had no opponents who threatened his power. The ruling class seemed loyal to him, even servile. The public regarded him hopefully, but their hopes were not excessive. That was also good for Putin, for if the hopes were not realized, there would be no mass disillusionment.[7]

Russia's economic situation in early 2000 was rather stable. Moreover, the country had even achieved some economic growth. In February 2000, monthly inflation was running at only 0.7 to 0.8 percent. Production had increased by 11.0 percent during the past year. The budget showed a surplus. And the price of oil was steady and relatively high at $21.50 a barrel, which was good for the economy's basic revenue stream.

The Chechen war, despite the obvious fact that it was a dead end, still had the support of the public, which wanted the Russian army to go on fighting until the separatists were crushed. All this meant that Putin had a lot of room to maneuver in setting his course.

At the same time, having seemingly unusual freedom of action, the new president was severely constrained by the system of power he had inherited from Yeltsin. Under the logic of the superpresidential regime, the president has to manage even the details. If he stops pushing the buttons, even for a short while, the system goes off into unguided flight. Besides, failures of the administration, even at the local level, damage the president's legitimacy, because in the people's eyes he is the one who controls all the levers of power and is responsible for everything.

At the same time, the system fosters the president's irresponsibility, because even if there are errors and failures, it is very hard—perhaps impossible—to remove him from office. In addition, the new leader inherited a bureaucracy and power structures (the Interior and Defense Ministries and security services) that had become overgrown with vested interests, whose aim was to preserve the former shadow rules of the game, and which waited and watched, prepared either to support Putin or to sabotage his policies. The newcomer had to learn the logic of the system he took over and decide whether he would follow it or fight it.

A no less serious problem for Putin was the merger in Russia of power and capital, politics and economics, the public and the private—a Soviet tradition Yeltsin had not only failed to break but in some areas had even reinforced. Beyond triggering the dire enough consequence of the corruption and degradation of the Russian state, the fusion of power and business had preserved and even expanded the gray zone. In that shadowy space, huge quantities of goods and services were produced and sold with no one paying a kopek in taxes. Now not only corrupt officials and some wheeler-dealers but a significant portion of the population had settled there. Millions of people worked in the gray zone. And at that time, up to 30 percent of the country's gross domestic product was produced there.

The gray zone had become the safety net for the officially unemployed, the underpaid, and those owed back pay by the government. The zone thus helped society to survive the transition. The state missed out on gigantic sums in taxes, and criminal elements profited. Yet if the state tried to destroy the zone, the loss of this workplace—where so many earned the money they needed to survive in postcommunist Russia—could undermine social stability, unless fresh legal venues for economic vitality were simultaneously created. And not only the economy but politics too had moved into the shadows, with fundamental decisions made behind closed doors and under pressure from powerful lobbies. The gray zone could not be controlled, and it contained a threat to the leader's power, if he did not want to obey its rules.

Nor did the positive economic background to Putin's administration have a solid foundation. Just as before, during the communist period, revitalization was due to high oil prices. Without structural reforms, massive investment, and the development of other sectors of the economy, the apparent economic well-being could crumble if oil prices dropped.

It was not difficult for Putin to see that the majority in the political class feared a continuation of market liberalization. His own entourage presented a problem for economic policy. Its members espoused various schools of thinking, and from the start, each competed to win him over; they did not form a cohesive professional team that could urge him to implement decisive reforms. The majority of the oligarchs from the Yeltsin era, who retained much influence, were strongly against changing the status quo and first of all breaking the fusion between power and business, for any alteration would cut into their profits and possibly topple them. In early 2000, only 15 percent of the population backed an unfettered free market, and they were a disparate bunch, incapable of providing substantive support to the regime. Fifty-two percent of Russians supported state-owned property and the priority of state regulation. The rest made up the always doubting "swamp."

Some vacillating Russians were moving toward rejection of the market. Thus in 1993, 27 percent supported private ownership of major enterprises, but by 2000 only 20 percent did. As for the state fixing firms' prices, the 45 percent who were in favor in 1993 increased to 51 percent in 2000; only 10 percent disapproved of all state interference in price setting. In 1993, 13 percent of Russians thought foreigners should be allowed to own large properties, whereas by 2000 the figure had fallen to 5 percent.[8] These were disturbing signs for any reform-minded leader.

Putin must have realized that the window of opportunity would not be open forever. If he wanted to push through any major liberalization measures, he had to hurry. Popularity and trust are highly unreliable commodities, inclined to shrink.

Further poll results suggested to Putin the political direction he should take. Thirty-nine percent of respondents did not like the new leader's ties to Yeltsin and his entourage. Clearly, Putin had to think about how to cut the old ruling team's leash. Only 12 percent criticized him for lacking a clear political line.[9] Because the figure was low and Putin's avoidance of definite policies had won him support among varied social groups, he could keep on as he was for a time. It was possible that inertia could guarantee him a quiet existence for his full term, and even reelection in 2004 if the economy held up.

But buoyed by his initial approval ratings and favorable circumstances, Putin could still make incremental yet telling changes on the economic and political fronts. In fact, he would lose an important opportunity and probably regret it if he did not undertake structural reforms for the sake of the benefits they would bring Russia. It was also possible that making radical changes without forming political backing might have toppled him, as had happened with Gorbachev and his *perestroika*. The status quo and stagnation often are more instrumental for preserving power than is revolution.

Putin embarked on his new job with a minimum of political experience and years of career habits that might work against him. The highest office in the country had fallen into his lap after a "training period" of four months as prime minister. He did not have (nor could he have acquired in his previous posts) his predecessor's political sensitivity or bureaucratic mastery. He was not a public figure with the ability to appeal to the masses in case of need. He had to learn on the job, starting with the basics of managing a national political apparatus and making presidential decisions. His work in the KGB had taught him to follow orders and to be a subordinate; now he had to wield power and exercise leadership. His only personal decision early in his administration was to begin the "antiterrorist operation" in Chechnya, which indicated a readiness to apply simple remedies to complex problems. This decision may have been the result of political immaturity, or of following certain principles, or of placating Russia's large conservative contingent—or it might have been his KGB conditioning in action.

They say, with good reason, that working in the secret services, especially in the Soviet KGB, is not a profession but a way of thinking. That way of thinking is usually characterized by hostility toward dissent of any kind, an inability to tolerate variety in the environment, the rejection of everything alien or not easily understandable, an excessive suspiciousness, and a tendency to make decisions in secret. People with such a mindset feel comfortable and secure only in their narrow circle of initiates. How characteristic that clannish way of thinking was of Putin Russians had yet to see. One could take hope in the fact that he had worked in Saint Petersburg for the liberal mayor Anatoly Sobchak and had found his way in the new atmosphere of risk, striving, and tolerance of other views.

In unfamiliar areas, Putin displayed caution and did not rush; he waited, pondered, and tried to get to the heart of the issues. His desire to understand the details, to touch everything personally, to hear out his interlocutors—these are certainly among his positive qualities. He expanded his audience, inviting people from all walks of life to the Kremlin, attentively posing questions and amiably listening to the answers. I know many people who were wary of, if not downright skeptical about, Putin until they met him, and then became his active supporters. He knew how to recruit friends. He created alternative sources of information, and he was not isolated the way Yeltsin had been.

In a situation where strategic decisions must be made quickly, however, Putin's assiduity and persistence, his desire to get at every detail, could keep him from seeing the main points. Besides, a leadership style that insists on monitoring all problems daily is exhausting, and for all his stamina and relative youth, Putin was unlikely to keep up the pace for long. Yeltsin had tried at first to be involved in every detail of management, until he realized that was impossible. Sooner or later, Putin would have to decide between strengthening institutions and redistributing some responsibilities to the cabinet and parliament, or yielding some of his responsibilities to people close to him, following Yeltsin's example.

In his first months in office, Putin did not make haste, and his hesitation made him appear bewildered. But looking back, one sees that such cautiousness was the only way to secure his position. Putin had no one at first to lean on except for the Yeltsin team that held him in its grasp. But somehow he had to begin doing things, to demonstrate his ability to control the decision-making process. He had to learn the art of governance. It was not an easy task. Unlike many others and all his predecessors, he had to become a politician after taking the job. And there were no guarantees that even if he became a politician he would go further and become a leader.

Many people characterize Putin as pragmatic and intelligent, a quick study. Early on, he demonstrated an ability to think and speak logically and precisely. He figured out how to communicate with a wide audience and even added a certain charm to his pallid personality. He learned to talk to the press and give thoughtful answers. He was extremely hardworking, and very soon he acquired huge quantities of information about various areas of governance. He had a brilliant memory, just like Yeltsin in his best years. The new leader proved to be both amazingly methodical and intellectually curious, and he turned those qualities to the task of understanding the inner workings of Russian power.

Putin said perfectly reasonable things, and soon he began to take steps in the right direction—if we consider moving Russia toward a more effective market economy the right thing to do. He recruited the liberals German Gref, Andrei Illarionov, and Alexei Kudrin, and others whom he knew from Saint Petersburg, and he brought them into the government. He asked Gref to develop a new strategy for the country's development and to prioritize economic reform tasks. The presence of these liberals, whom Putin made part of his circle, suggested that he would not permit antimarket overreactions, even if the public was growing more statist. He had grown accustomed to market thinking and could function in the framework of a market economy.

Undoubtedly, the new Russian leader had positive potential. That potential could be used for the greater good, but the exigencies of survival—or even Putin's personal complexes and prejudices—could bury it. He had only started to build his presidency.

Already a trait of Putin's stirred anxiety: He divided everyone up into friend or foe. His colleagues and comrades in arms from the Yeltsin entourage were accorded the presumption of innocence (for instance, former administration head Pavel Borodin, frequently accused of corruption).[10] Putin did not extend the same right to those who disagreed with his policies or did not show enough obedience. He soon demonstrated this with tycoon Vladimir Gusinsky and his media empire Media-Most, and then with his "godfather" Berezovsky.

Putin's attitude toward freedom of the press caused perhaps the most consternation. The new leader gradually began to regard every criticism of his policies as a challenge to the state and did not lose any opportunity to strike back at the critics. The first victim of his dislike of media independence was Andrei Babitsky, a reporter for Radio Liberty who criticized Moscow's Chechnya policy in his battlefield reports during 1999 and 2000. Babitsky bore the brunt of the Russian judicial and repressive machinery: He was charged with spying for Chechen rebels, held in an isolation cell, interrogated, and even exchanged like a terrorist for Russian soldiers and handed over to an armed Chechen group. His interrogators apparently wanted him to vanish without a trace.

The Babitsky incident can be defined as a *syndrome of totalitarianism in a pluralistic society*—a return to a typically Soviet way of treating independent journalists who had the courage to confront authority with views differing from the official line. The security services persecuted Babitsky, apparently with Putin's knowledge. Putin had to have known, because the Babitsky case became the topic of the day in the Russian media. In a group letter of protest, journalists wrote:

> Not once since the start of perestroika have the authorities permitted themselves such blatant lawlessness and cynicism toward representatives of the mass media. If the journalist Babitsky has committed an illegal act from the point of view of the authorities, then the question of his guilt or innocence must be decided in an open judicial trial. If the actions against Babitsky are a reaction to the

contents of his reports from Chechnya, this is a direct violation of the principle of freedom of the press guaranteed by the Constitution.[11]

The Kremlin did not dare keep Babitsky in prison or execute him, apparently concerned by the reaction from the international community and inside Russia. Babitsky was let free, and the charges against him were dropped in the end. This forced restraint by the security services signaled their recognition of the new political reality. Babitsky went abroad. The rest of the media community learned its lesson: Russia was not becoming a friendly place for independent journalists. And the fact that the persecution—unthinkable in Gorbachev's or Yeltsin's time—occurred at all was enough to rouse anxiety about the new Kremlin residents' attitude toward the press.

A crucial factor in any administration—and one that is much more important when the executive is strong and balancing institutions are weak—is the people with whom the leader surrounds himself and to whose advice he listens on policy and politics. In Putin's new Kremlin, the ties of the Yeltsin era continued to bind, and old courtiers held onto some or most of their power.

After the election, Putin was unable to rid his team of members of Yeltsin's entourage (for example, the head of the presidential staff, Alexander Voloshin). The new president proclaimed his "equidistance" from all the oligarchs. But the oligarchs' representatives remained part of his inner circle, exercising significant—though not open, as before—influence on important decisions. New oligarchs even began to rise to power, among them Sergei Pugachev, who had known Putin from his Saint Petersburg days. Pugachev's discreet presence in the Kremlin's corridors sent a signal that the new leader was not preparing to root out the class of oligarchs entirely; he was simply dividing them into loyal and disloyal ones.

Out of gratitude, but more, perhaps, for practical reasons, Putin continued functioning within the "paradigm of loyalty"—a system of mutual obligations within a certain circle, based sometimes on friendship and previous connections but more often on deals and fear of compromising materials. Perhaps it was this paradigm that kept him from severing old ties and that explained his unwillingness, and perhaps inability, to break with the past at this point. Once he became part of the circle of cronies hand-cuffing him, it would be difficult or even impossible for him to rid him-self of the Yeltsin entourage and other dubious hangers-on unless he cre-ated his own base and learned the very specific art of Russian governance. In early 2000, the impression was that Putin was not ready to break free.

Gradually, the president began bringing old colleagues into the Kremlin, people he knew from Saint Petersburg and whom he could trust. For the most part, however, they were people with connections to the power structures, mainly to the security services. Among them were those who had persecuted dissidents. That alone was enough to trouble democratically minded Russians and human rights activists. And their concern was justified: Given the weak democratic mechanisms and the influx of former KGB people into the higher levels of the administra-tion, some return to totalitarian behavior seemed inevitable.

For some time, even before he became president, Moscow society had been trying to determine who was "in" with Putin. It seemed that the man was surrounded by a constantly shifting kaleidoscope of new and old faces, all trying to find a spot as close to him as possible, familiar fig-ures mixing with totally unknown characters in the inevitable black suits and white shirts. Gradually, order came to the Brownian motion: Many people from the Yeltsin era gradually moved to the sidelines and took on an entreating look. In the center were new people who looked more and more confident and were becoming proficient at finding their way around the Kremlin's corridors. Things quieted down, and several circles formed around Putin.

The first circle was made up of people from the old Yeltsin political group. Preeminent was Voloshin (again, the head of the presidential staff). It was obvious that Putin kept Voloshin on not out of a sense of grati-tude but because he knew how to get things done and had gradually become quite a skillful fixer and in this capacity was still irreplaceable. Voloshin was continually hand in glove with the former members of Yeltsin's entourage and was often visited by Tatyana Dyachenko and Valentin Yumashev, leading lights of the Yeltsin Family.

The second group in Putin's entourage was the liberal technocrats, most of them from Saint Petersburg. German Gref, Leonid Reiman, Ilya Klebanov, and Alexei Kudrin were members of the government, holding key positions on its economic staff. In Moscow, they were considered people of Anatoly Chubais, long one of the preeminent Russian liberals and a permanent member of Yeltsin's team. Chubais had left the political arena in good time, but he continued lobbying behind the scenes. The relationship between Chubais and Putin was not without its dark spots and mutual suspicions. The new boss of the Kremlin would not be very likely to tolerate such a powerful and willful politician in his circle. Moreover, Putin certainly had been informed that it was Chubais who in 1999 had first objected to Putin's appointment as prime minister and, therefore, as Yeltsin's successor. Chubais knew that with an energetic president he would no longer be needed as gatekeeper and crisis manager. As for Chubais's people, they were happy to switch to Putin.

The third group in Putin's entourage was his people—those who had become friends in his Saint Petersburg phase or had been colleagues in the KGB. These *siloviki*, as they were called in Russia, were the only ones he could trust and rely on. They were, first of all, Sergei Ivanov, at the moment head of the powerful Security Council, which was coordinating the policies of the power ministries; Victor Cherkesov, a colleague from the Federal Security Service (FSB); and Nikolai Patrushev, the head of the FSB. A significant portion of the Russian public had positive feelings about the appointment to high office of people from the special services. Thus, 44 percent saw it in a positive light (21 percent as totally positive) and 35 percent in a negative light (a mere 9 percent as extremely negative).[12] The phenomenon was probably a consequence of Russians' disillusionment with the groups that arose under Yeltsin and their desire to cleanse the ruling class, because the people coming from the special services were perceived as less corrupt than others.

Along with the secret service officials were young people who had worked with Putin for Sobchak in Saint Petersburg, including Dmitry Kozak, Igor Sechin, and Dmitry Medvedev. The internal struggle between the Saint Petersburg liberals and the Saint Petersburg secret service people allowed the old Yeltsin entourage, which had brought Putin to power and had equal numbers for the corridor battles, to maintain their influence.

These groups were incompatible in their origins. But for the time being, Putin needed them all to perform their different functions. Members of Yeltsin's team continued to handle internal political conflicts. Still, they were acting as chief screenwriters. The liberals ran economic policy. Putin's secret service colleagues tried to handle, not always skillfully, the more delicate projects dealing with the consolidation of Putin's power. At the same time, they studied Kremlin intrigues. Soon we'll see that they were not very successful in learning the art of sweet deals. But they were the ones with the direct access: Putin let them in on his plans, and they could help determine where he would strike next. It was obvious that these teams of Putin's would hold differing views and strive toward different goals and that the winners would influence Putin's behavior. Maneuvering behind them, several oligarchic groups, among them Petr Aven and Mikhail Fridman's Alfa and Gazprom, exploited the battle of the political "elephants" to promote their people and create their own niches in Putin's entourage.

The time had come for Putin to show the character of his presidency. The main test, which would demonstrate not only the intentions but also the content of the new administration, was the formation of the government. Putin had two options. He could select an independent cabinet headed by a political heavyweight that would have total responsibility for economic policy and let the president take charge promoting internal stability, foreign policy, and relations with the regions. That would have been optimal for Russia because it divided the executive power and gradually moved the country toward an independent government and parliament. The second option was the creation of a totally dependent cabinet headed by an obedient prime minister and the continuation of the practice in which the president formulated all cabinet policies yet avoided all responsibility.

Putin put an end to his doubts and presented a candidate for prime minister to the Duma. The candidate was Mikhail Kasyanov, who had been first deputy prime minister in Yeltsin's government and before that Yeltsin's deputy minister of finance. Kasyanov's appointment could be interpreted as Putin's decision (probably forced) to maintain the influence of the Yeltsin political Family. It was widely known that Kasyanov was close to Yeltsin's clan.

Quite a few rumors circulated about Kasyanov. Allegedly, he had been incriminated in dubious deals involving Russian and Soviet debts. That was how he had gotten his nickname, "Misha Two Percent": It was said that he took 2 percent off the top of every debt deal he helped organize. He ignored the accusations and rumors, preferring to pretend he knew nothing about what the Moscow political world was whispering. Of course, we must give Kasyanov his due—he was also known as an experienced negotiator with Western financial institutions. And he soon showed himself to be a good administrator who knew how to survive in the shark-infested Kremlin pond.

The choice of Kasyanov signaled which model of power the new president intended to build: the obedient cabinet headed by an obedient prime minister. Putin selected the "leash" model of governance, perpetuating Yeltsin's model of the cabinet that got orders from the presidential staff and at the same time was responsible for all the president's errors— "a boy for beating," as they say in Russia.

Putin was forming a new cabinet with a strong whiff of the old. Kasyanov was immediately confirmed by the equally obedient Duma, and Putin's first government was formed.[13] It retained odious figures accused of corruption, such as Minister of Atomic Industry Yevgeny Adamov and Minister of Transportation Nikolai Aksyonenko. Putin kept the cabinet a coalition of the various groups of influence. Kasyanov represented the interests of the old Kremlin team, while Deputy Prime Minister Kudrin represented the Chubais group. Other clans, notably the group of Yuri Maslyukov, a visible Communist Party activist and representative of the Soviet defense establishment, also had a presence. The cabinet retained the old power bloc, with the exception of the head of the Foreign Intelligence Service—for the moment, the heads of the Defense Ministry, Internal Affairs Ministry, and security services were people appointed by Yeltsin. This was the result of an agreement between Putin and Yeltsin—Putin had promised not to replace them for a year.

The composition of the government showed that the new president could not yet defend his own people. Thus Gref, who had wanted a central role in the cabinet, ended up with a secondary post as director of the Ministry of Economic Development and Trade. Despite some independent moves, the new president still had to coordinate his appointments with the Yeltsin people.

A government like this, built to reflect the balance of power in the Kremlin entourage rather than to address political and economic priorities, could not be expected to be effective. The cabinet could be likened to a landmine, its members occupied not with implementing coordinated policies but with struggling to advance the interests of their groups or of their strategies.

In this context, the oversight agencies—the presidential staff and the Security Council—took on a special role: They became the key decision-making bodies—first in the field of domestic politics and second in the foreign policy area. The former was still headed by Voloshin and the latter by Putin's man and personal friend Ivanov. Given their composition and their vaguely defined powers, the two agencies were bound to have conflicts. The configuration of the center being built by Putin re-created the system of informal checks and balances that had existed under Yeltsin. The president's constant conciliating presence was necessary to keep the struggle among the group interests from becoming destructive. With a weak parliament and judicial system and the absence of local self-government, the president had to play the role of judge and arbiter.

While the members of the new ruling circle entered their orbits around the president, he kept silent, creating the impression that he did not know what to do next. "Putin is a puppet," the mass media joked. It was hard to avoid feeling that the president had allowed his team to turn him into the product of a public relations campaign: He read prepared speeches and used rehearsed gestures that hid his personality and made it difficult to distinguish the artificial Putin from the real one. It began to look as if the "man of muscle" created by his image makers was in truth baffled by mounting problems and emergencies.

In the summer of 2000, if anyone still labored under the illusion of Putin's independence, or wondered who really ran Russia, their doubts were settled once the prosecutor general was appointed. This was a key position. Much depended on the person in that post, including whether the oligarchs and the people in the Yeltsin contingent would feel comfortable. It was in the interests of Yeltsin's Family to have a manageable person as prosecutor general. When Putin tried to propose Kozak, his close ally, the Yeltsin entourage exerted unprecedented pressure on the president to change his mind. Papa himself—Yeltsin—was called in, according to a story in the *Obshchaya gazeta* of May 25–31. Yeltsin called Putin in the middle of the night and applied force until Putin rewrote the decree appointing Kozak, naming instead the acting prosecutor general, Vladimir Ustinov. The decree was sent to the upper house of the parliament for its approval with indecent haste and without the proper paperwork.

This business made Putin look pathetic. All Moscow was abuzz, saying that the new Kremlin boss had tried just this once to be independent and had not been allowed. The incident was the first major blow to the new president.

The president not only gave up his choice for prosecutor general but in the end did not support his own candidate for governor of Saint Petersburg, then–deputy prime minister Valentina Matvienko, whom Putin himself sent to run in his home city. When Putin saw that incumbent governor Vladimir Yakovlev—his personal enemy, who had wrested power from Sobchak and thus cost Putin his Saint Petersburg job—was likely to win the gubernatorial contest, he stopped backing Matvienko. That looked like weakness. Yeltsin would have jumped into the fray. Putin, coming upon an obstacle, retreated and waited. His training in the secret services or his characteristic indecisiveness was showing. At the time, it was not clear whether a new move would follow. But it soon became evident that, with few exceptions, the new leader was not looking for a fight and would rather avoid confrontation. The macho appearance that Putin had thus far tried to cultivate seemed misleading.

To somehow make up for his defeat in forming his cabinet, Putin redoubled his efforts to cement his superpresidential regime by limiting the independence of Russia's regions. He must have thought that he would meet less resistance there. The idea of creating new relations between the center and regions and curbing the power of the local barons had long been discussed in Putin's circles. Putin had waited for the right moment to launch his attack on the governors who were too sure of themselves.

In May 2000, the moment had come. Putin, who was inaugurated as president May 7, felt himself ready to show his initiative. He was definitely tired of being accused of being weak and indecisive. He thought it was time to act. He promulgated a decree (on May 13, 2000) on the formation of seven federal *okrugs*, or regions (whose borders happened to coincide with those of the military *okrugs*), among which the 89 republics and other components of the Russian Federation were divided. The creation of the *okrugs* was meant to improve the center's control over the activities of the regional leaders and newly formed regional elites. Representatives of the president were named to head the *okrugs*, of whom five out of seven were from the power structures—*siloviki*—and were close to Putin.[14]

The public reacted to Putin's initiative with confusion, but not fervent resistance. Putin then sent to the Duma for approval three new laws that weakened the role of both the regional leaders and the parliament's upper chamber, the Federation Council, the legislative body for the regional governors and heads of the regional legislative bodies.[15] Putin's goal was to overcome the broad federal tendencies in Russia's development and build a stricter system of subordination of the regions to the center—in fact returning to Moscow the powers that Yeltsin gave up to the regions in his day.

These first steps in neutralizing the regional leaders were successful. The governors and republican presidents never did organize to resist Putin's attack. Even the education of the regions in the center's deviousness attempted by Berezovsky—who by that time had left the Kremlin camp and was trying to create an opposition to Putin among the regional leaders—failed. The local bosses had decided to fight for survival separately—which is what destroyed them. Putin played his hand well, depriving the Federation Council of its role as counterbalance to the president, and depriving the governors of a sizable chunk of their power. In a way, he was taking his revenge for not being allowed to form his cabinet independently.

The political establishment gradually rebounded from the shock Putin's initiatives caused, and it became evident that its members had mixed feelings. Only recently, the president had been accused of delayed reaction, and now he was accused of overreacting. Putin had begun

changing the mechanism of power, the regime itself. And that would
affect many groups. But the observers were not sure that Putin's "revolution" would achieve its goal—the creation of the smooth and reliable
superpresidential regime. Yeltsin before Putin had tried to do the same
and failed.[16]

No one disagreed that the regions' feudal lords had long been in need
of curtailing or that local legislation had to be brought into line with the
Constitution. Of the Russian Federation's 21 republics, the constitution
of only one, Udmurtia, fully complied with the national Constitution.
Up to 30 percent of local acts adopted by the republics went against
norms established in the Constitution, according to the May 16, 2000,
Vedomosti. But the problem could have been solved in two ways: by
emphasizing bureaucratic control, or by strengthening judicial control
over the work of the regional administrations and using the financial and
economic instruments of pressure that the center had available. Putin
chose the former.

Of course there were reasons for adopting the bureaucratic solution
other than Putin's desire to increase his own power. Creating a system of
judicial and financial control over the provinces required time, whereas
building a system of control through cadres loyal to the president was
much faster. But Putin must have forgotten—or he did not yet know—
that bureaucratic control always hides elements of anarchy and uncon-
trollability.[17]

The creation of the federal *okrugs* raised the most questions. Many
observers doubted that the president's representatives could exercise
effective control over the regions if they lacked the right to use financial
transfers as carrots or sticks or to control the power structures. If, conversely, Putin gave the representatives in the *okrugs* those powers, he ran
the risk of making them into influential figures. Where was the assurance
that one of them would not turn into a new Yeltsin?

Moreover, there was also a feeling that the presidential envoys were
intentionally being appointed to take on the responsibility for what happened regionally. Putin could always pass the buck to his representative
and say, "Talk to him, he's accountable for everything." That helped the
president to retain his reputation, but it did not help make the governance more efficient.

The possibility of Putin being able to fire governors seemed to his critics like giving away too much power to the center. The Kremlin's desire to form the Federation Council by appointing political nobodies—many of whom had never been to the regions they were supposed to represent—elicited a unanimous negative reaction. It was hardly a way to make the upper chamber work effectively in fulfilling responsibilities like vetoing Duma decisions, acting as a buffer between the president and the Duma, and deciding questions of war and peace. It did not take a constitutional scholar to realize that the existence of an upper chamber of the parliament in which representatives of the executive body convene ex officio and function as a legislative branch is contrary to the principle of separation of powers. But at the same time, with the Duma so compliant, the Federation Council was the only barrier on the path to strengthening the authoritarianism of the leader. Critics disliked even more the Kremlin's decision to liquidate local self-rule, making it dependent on the moods of the governors.

The regional leaders' acceptance of the new rules could be explained by their unwillingness to engage in battle with the center and by their hope of negotiating concessions separately. Bearing in mind the ancient tradition of fighting under the carpet and the apparatchik arts of the regional bosses, an attempt to block the Kremlin's initiatives was to be expected. I remember a conversation with the powerful leader of a rich Russian donor region (a region that contributed more to the federal budget than it got). When I asked why the members of the Federation Council had surrendered voluntarily to Putin, he replied with a smile, "The best way to survive in Russia is not resistance, but sabotage." To me that meant the provincial bosses were hoping to wait it out, paying lip service to the president while continuing their former policies at home.

Putin did not stop with the bid to fortify the center's control over the regions. Now that he had felt his strength a little, he was apparently sure of himself and ready to fight his real or perceived enemies in the open. In October 2000, the Kremlin forced Berezovsky to give up control of the major Russian First television channel. Berezovsky sold his shares to the state. Then Putin struck a blow at the media empire of one of the most powerful oligarchs, Gusinsky, who had supported his opponents (Luzhkov and Primakov, and then Yavlinsky) in the elections. The new leader had had all he could stomach of the popular broadcasts on the NTV television channel, the radio station Ekho Moskvy, the journal *Itogi*, and the periodical *Segodnya*—all controlled by the ambitious and arrogant Gusinsky.

On May 11, four days after Putin's inauguration, police raided the headquarters of the Media-Most holding company that controlled NTV and Gusinsky's other media. Then the government took over Gusinsky's Most-Bank (which, however, had been in trouble for a long time). Putin's proponents concluded that the president had begun an attack on the oligarchs. But that was not the whole truth, because the police did not touch other oligarchs who had ties to the Kremlin. It was clear that the Kremlin attack was selective in nature.

If Gusinsky had supported Putin and his media outlets had not attacked the Kremlin team, and if Gusinsky had not tried to demand preferential treatment from Putin, Gusinsky would not have been touched. The Most affair showed that the Kremlin had begun taking on its critics or potential competitors. The fate of the Media-Most empire was a test of the degree of political freedom that Putin would allow, and gave a taste of the rules he would impose on the game with the influential groups.

Years after it was all over, one of the leading Russian news anchors, Vladimir Pozner, gave his interpretation of the motives behind the Kremlin's campaign against Gusinsky. "I am convinced that all NTV problems were the result of personal animosity between Gusinsky and Putin. Gusinsky tried to dictate to Putin: either you support me or I'll show *compromat* (compromising materials) on you. I don't think that the president has the right to seek his vengeance. But presidents are human beings after all." Personal animosity might have triggered conflict between Gusinsky's media and the Kremlin. But the fundamental cause was much deeper and had to do with the fact that independent media did not fit into the plan of presidential personified rule.

Another test was the fate of the Channel 3 television station, which was under the influence of Luzhkov, one of Putin's two main rivals in the presidential election, who financially supported it. The Channel 3 team also was intimidated by the Kremlin. The impression created was that the ruling group was going to stoop to traditional Russian methods—suppressing or at least scaring off enemies and even just potential political opponents.

This time, the attack was directed against the media groups that were under the influence of Putin's former rivals. The Kremlin found support for such a policy not only among the *siloviki* but among the portion of the public that saw free mass media as channels of influence for the oligarchs—which in fact was true to some extent. In November 2000, VTsIOM polls found that only 7 percent of Russians thought that the main networks were independent, 79 percent thought they were dependent on the oligarchs, and 18 percent thought they were dependent on the state. Thus the struggle against independent mass media was perceived by a large portion of the population as a struggle against the tycoons, who were especially disliked and even hated in Russia.

Putin's political handwriting was becoming clearer, as was his plan of expanding presidential power. His previous silence might have been just a tactic, wary as he was of resistance. The reform of the Federation Council and of the center–periphery relations showed that Putin intended to construct his own system of governance. Yeltsin's successor was gradually morphing into the terminator of the Yeltsin regime. Putin had sent a clear signal that he was planning to liquidate the basis of Yeltsin's power, which had been the mechanism of mutual back-rubbing and tolerance. Maybe the authoritarian at heart had been pretending to be the old guard's tame creature and hesitating guy while in fact he had known all along what he wanted. But more likely Putin had a more complicated personality that combined stubbornness and indecisiveness, sense of purpose and lack of vision, suspicion and distrust of everything and the longing to rely upon faithfulness. Russia's ride with him promised to be an unpredictable adventure.

The new leader began building his power edifice on the foundation of another principle: subordination. The president was at the very top, above everyone else, from which vantage point he sent down directives to his subordinates, who passed them down lower. Direct subordination and compliance ensured a flawless connection between management floors. The mechanism of subordination did not require an active parliament or opposition or a developed multiparty system or independent mass media. Management through subordination must have impressed Putin, as a man from the secret services and a technocratic manager. Leaning on executive power allowed him to implement decisions quickly, without wasting time on endless coordination. Besides which, this management style gave him the resources of power he needed, so that he was no longer dependent on the old clans.

In fact, the state Putin was trying to re-create was the one that had always existed in Russia, except for the brief Yeltsin interregnum. By consolidating power and trying to take it all into his own fist, he was also strengthening the Russian System—a system based on power personified. That state, however, built as it was on vertical subordination, lacking communication from the bottom up, was weak and exceptionally inefficient because its energy went into the constant generation of fear, enforcing of discipline, and supporting of the vertical chain of power. The previous version of that state had collapsed in 1991. Sooner or later, a new version of the Russian System based on the "transmission belt" would collapse under its own weight, especially if it lacked a strong mechanism of repression.

The new ruling team, especially the Saint Petersburg newcomers, could not understand that an efficient state has a more complex structure that includes numerous horizontal supports and a network of counterbalances. By the way, such a state is also more conducive to its leader's survival, because he does not have to worry about preserving his inaccessibility or finding an heir who will not throw him in prison when he loses power. But for the time being, Putin was not thinking about such things. He started down the more familiar path, perhaps urged on by insecurity, by a desire to protect himself, or by the inertia of Yeltsin's legacy. Perhaps he saw no trustworthy partners out there with whom he could build institutions. He might have been fascinated by the idea of turning Russia into a huge corporation based on vertical ties, with himself in the role of chief executive officer. But Russian society was already a more complicated entity that couldn't obey rules mechanically imposed from above and didn't want to be compartmentalized by junior managers. Sooner or later, the president had to realize that.

At this point in time—1999 and 2000—Putin, like Yeltsin, was evidently not concerned with questions of how to combine the market and democracy, political and economic freedoms. Just like his predecessor, he began creating a system relying on his instincts and what felt comfortable to him. But Yeltsin was wise and experienced. He knew Russia, and his intuition told him that Russia had changed. Therefore, after some attempts to discipline the country, he had preferred to rule by allowing all the forces in Russian society to develop and not hindering anyone who was not a direct threat to his power.

Yeltsin, like Chinese leaders, let a thousand flowers bloom. Putin wanted to sow the entire field in one vegetable. His instincts, honed in the power structures, provided simple guidance: control everything, trust no one, be strong because power is the only thing people understand. Those were the political bricks with which regimes in Russia had always been built. With the public's astonishing approval ratings—more than 60 percent of respondents backed him—they seemed to be telling Putin, "We want what you want. We want to obey, keep going." But it was still unclear to what degree people who had grown accustomed to Yeltsin's freedom would be willing to line up again. Then, too, the regime of subordination went against Putin's goal of building an efficient market economy, which demands freedoms and initiative. Government is always a balancing act, and balancing authoritarianism and the market is an even trickier one.

At the same time, the new leader defied the attempts to put him into a definite ideological cluster. He proved that he was ready for complicated policy design. Leaning toward traditionalism in the process of shaping his rule, he put a new mark on Russian foreign policy. Even before the presidential election, he invited Lord George Robertson, secretary general of NATO, to Moscow, reviving Russia's relations with the alliance. He did this despite the resistance of the Russian military. He invited U.K. prime minister Tony Blair to Saint Petersburg and persuaded him that he wants to pursue warmer relations between Russia and the West.

Putin's intention was to rebuild bridges to the West after their deterioration during the later years of the Yeltsin administration, and especially after the spring of 1999 saw both NATO enlargement and the NATO bombing of Kosovo, which chilled relations between Russia and the West. It was also clear that Putin was worried by the negative reaction in the West to the war in Chechnya. He demonstrated that his goal was to join the international club, that he wanted civilized relations with the West. He understood the importance of the West in solving Russia's economic problems.

One could assume that as a member of the intelligence community and with his KGB experience, deep in his heart Putin might harbor distrust of the West. It is possible that, like many of his colleagues, he would secretly accuse the West of trying to weaken Russia and exploiting Russian weakness for its own profit, and of having a double standard in its policy toward Russia. In any case, at the beginning of his presidency, Putin still used in his rhetoric the idea of a multipolarity promoted by his predecessor Primakov, albeit more cautiously—which meant that he still cherished the illusion of Russia's "special path," or that he was unsure about the new Russia's identity and development agenda, or that he was not ready for more decisive breakthrough—for the time being. But realistically, one had to wonder which countries or groupings a weakened Russia could attract as one of the poles. In the beginning, Putin may have hesitated in setting an agenda, but with his new policy toward NATO and Europe, he was clearly turning toward the West.

Putin faced an even more complicated task, that of choosing his base of support, or the groups he would rely upon. The selection in Russia was limited: large private businesses, in the persons of the so-called oligarchs; the state apparatus, with its numerous ministries, government committees, and other institutions that constitute the backbone of the system of governance; the regional elites; the power structures, meaning the Defense and Interior Ministries and the intelligence services; medium-sized and small businesses; and society.

Selecting that base was not easy. With his statist orientation, Putin could not entirely trust big business, which had demonstrated its vested interests and inability to curb its greed. Still, the new leader could not or did not want to distance himself fully from some oligarchic groups, at least for the time being. But he hardly considered sharing power with them.

As for the state apparatus, it shared Putin's desire for centralization. Moreover, the apparatus could easily forge a union with the power structures; such a union, after all, was long the basis for the Russian regime. But relying solely on that union was even more dangerous for Putin than an alliance with the oligarchs and big business. He knew that such support could lead to an excessive emphasis on the grinding of administrative gears, slowing down the development of the free market and increasing isolationism in foreign policy. The apparatus and *siloviki* in Russia still could support the repressive dictatorial regime. Putin was at least outwardly in favor of preserving the civilized rules of the global game, and as we have seen, there were signs that he leaned toward establishing normal relations with the West. If he kept on this course, he had to cut his links with the apparatus and *siloviki*.

Society had not developed sufficiently to provide a base of social groups that could lend liberal support for an administration. Small and medium-sized businesses in Russia, which of all groups had the strongest interest in equal rules and fair competition and in ousting the oligarchs, were as yet too weak to be a pillar of the new rule. The intelligentsia was tired and frustrated, having been disappointed by the previous reform effort. As for civil society at large, it was still unstructured and amorphous after a mere decade of postcommunist evolution, and thus not a powerful pressure source.

It came down to a choice between the main political forces in Russia: the oligarchy and the state apparatus. Naturally, the two forces were entwined. During Yeltsin's presidency, the state apparatus helped enrich the oligarchy, earning a bit for its cooperation. However, the apparatus, traditionally powerful in Russia, had won much less from the transformation than had the oligarchs, so revenge and domination were very much on its members' minds.

The apparatus and the oligarchy had clashed several times in the postcommunist era. The first involved the skirmish between the faction of Alexander Korzhakov, Yeltsin's former chief of security, and the oligarchs (Berezovsky, Gusinsky, and others) during the 1996 elections. The two groups fought not only for control over Yeltsin but for different paths of development for Russia. The bureaucrats and military men in Yeltsin's entourage tried to persuade the president to cancel the elections and hold on to power by force, which would have made him hostage to them. The oligarchs, conversely, were in favor of going ahead with the elections, which would keep more freedoms and thus allow them to survive. In this case, the interests of the oligarchs and democracy coincided. In the spring of 1996, the oligarchs and the liberal technocrats who joined them—in the person of Chubais and his group—won.

The next clash between the oligarchy and the apparatus came in 1997, in the "bank war." In the course of the fighting, which centered on the privatization of Russian communications giant Svyazinvest, roles were reversed, and the liberal technocrats—Chubais and his people—became statist bureaucrats attempting to rein in the appetites of the oligarchs of the Berezovsky-Gusinsky group.[18] During Primakov's time as prime minister, the third open clash of interests occurred, with the state apparatus and Primakov on one side and the oligarchs, led by Berezovsky, on the other.

With Putin's accession, there were signs of a new conflict. They were blurred because some influential oligarchs remained in Putin's camp and this time the attack was on two representatives of big business, Gusinsky and Berezovsky, who were trying to play an independent role in politics. But the bureaucratic and power-structure supports of the regime were demanding that Putin also push the other oligarchs out of the Kremlin orbit. In forming his base, Putin seems to have chosen the variant that corresponded best to his psychology—not betting everything on one card, avoiding direct confrontation especially with powerful foes, and gradually weakening everyone by slowly narrowing their space for maneuvering. The president stressed the bureaucratic-power component but left untouched those oligarchs who had sworn fealty to him. He obviously wanted to create a system of power in which each influential group found its own place but no one group could claim to have a special role or influence in the Kremlin and so leave its allotted niche.

The problem was that none of the fundamental forces in the president's entourage—state apparatus, oligarchy, or power structures—was interested in consistent reform. It was not clear whether the president would manage to stay above the fray and avoid being captured by some political force. The much more experienced Yeltsin had not managed to remain an arbiter.

In the new context, the situation of the liberal technocrats, especially those from the Union of Right Forces (SPS), provoked mixed feelings. Under Putin, the majority of liberal technocrats moved to progovernment positions. It is unlikely they felt comfortable there, when the regime's basic supports were apparatchiks and power structures. The liberal technocrats had hoped to influence the Kremlin under the Putin administration. Under Yeltsin, albeit for a brief period, Yegor Gaidar did determine the vector of economic development. In this connection, the story of "Putin's Gaidar"—German Gref, head of the Center for Strategic Development— is edifying.

In 2000, Gref proposed a new concept of liberal reform to the president. But Putin could not give Gref carte blanche to realize his ideas, just as Yeltsin before him could not give Gaidar free rein. One sees that neither the oligarchic nor the bureaucratic-power structure version of rule allows the liberal technocrats independence. They were relegated to an auxiliary role when the oligarchs were in power, and that looked likely to be the case under bureaucratic domination as well. Liberals still could not become soloists in Russia. It was true they were able to slowly advance some reform measures, like the 13 percent flat income tax that they had succeeded in implementing under Putin. But being in the minority, they were forced into numerous battles that often ended in compromises that eviscerated reforms.

While the oligarchs and the bureaucrats fought over primacy, the Kremlin began constructing a new political stage. There were signs that a search was on for ways to break up the Communist Party and create a left-center movement that would be loyal to the Kremlin. At the same time, preparations were under way for a new law on parties, intended to create a tame multiparty system. As for the pro-Putin Unity Party— which had announced its aim of transforming itself from a movement into a more structured party with individual membership after the presidential election—it was beginning to look more like the former ruling Communist Party of the Soviet Union. The process of turning Yeltsin's political chaos into a "democracy" controlled by the center had begun.

One of the leaders of the SPS liberals, Boris Nemtsov, called this democracy "castrated." The old colleagues Putin had brought in from the security services, once they became acclimatized, starting acting more harshly than the old Yeltsin cadres. They did not hesitate to intimidate independent media in the regions, and they openly used the courts and prosecutor's office to crack down on politicians and groups that expressed their dissatisfaction with the new regime.

Thus in late May and June 2000, weeks after his inauguration as president, Putin overturned his early reputation as a slow-moving politician. He must have decided that it was time to create his own system. He wanted independence. But like most offspring, he still was unable to sever all ties to the old regime.

The outward calm and tranquility of the political scene were giving way to still-spontaneous spots of dissatisfaction. The first to become agitated were the independent mass media and the human rights activists. For them, the Putin regime was taking on more and more obvious authoritarian traits. A collective editorial by the editors and journalists of the liberal newspaper *Obshchaya gazeta* on May 25 was the first to call what Putin was building a "dictatorship." "The impression is being created," wrote the journalists of *Obshchaya*, "that the consolidation of ever more power in the hands of the president is not a means for implementing some policy (the president has not announced any clear political priorities unrelated to this consolidation of power) but an aim in itself."[19] The democratic segment of the membership of the SPS, in the persons of the old human rights activist Sergei Kovalyov and Yabloko members, spoke out against Putin's reshaping of power, accusing him of trying to reinforce robber capitalism and give it a dictatorial impulse.

Putin could not present a counterargument—after all, having initiated his top-down system of governance, he retained special-interest clans that had arisen under Yeltsin, represented by all the oligarchs still sitting in strong positions in the Kremlin. Now, with his effort to concentrate major power resources in his hands, he gave the democrats reason to suspect him of acting more harshly in the interests of the narrow groups of influence—old and new—that occupied the Kremlin. Even if he was power hungry solely on his own account, the question arose: What next?

For the time being, the Russian president proved only one thing: that he was not a democrat. But neither was he a dictator.

There was no mass resistance to Putin's initiatives, nor could such resistance appear. There were several reasons for that: media controlled by the central authorities; the lack of a strong opposition; society's passivity and fatalism; the hope that Putin would pursue honest politics; and a reluctance to criticize him. The president continued to be above criticism in Russia. Russians behaved as if they could not afford to lose hope in their new leader. Therefore, the Kremlin could disregard the scattered hotbeds of dissatisfaction among intellectuals and a few stubborn liberals.

Society followed the leader, but its loyalty and support were conditional—as always in Russia.

Chapter 4

THE MOMENT
OF TRUTH

Putin repeals the taboo on persecution of the oligarchs.
The victor in the boring wilderness. A harsh August and a feeling of suffocation.
Reinforcing the superpresidential regime. Military reform.

It is the summer of 2000. Putin's first attack on the largest independent Russian media empire, Media-Most, failed. The Kremlin so far
had succeeded in taking over its bank, but the rest of the media holding belonging to the oligarch Vladimir Gusinsky survived. Gusinsky
mobilized public opinion in Russia and the West in support of his company. But the president's men retreated only to regroup. A new assault on
the media conglomerate was inevitable, everyone realized. The print and,
especially, the electronic media independent of the state constituted a
serious obstacle for Putin on the path to building his pragmatic authoritarianism. The president understood the role of the mass media in the
political struggle. During the run-up to the parliamentary and presidential elections in late 1999 and early 2000, television had been the decisive
force in transforming Mr. Nobody into Mr. President, and Vladimir
Vladimirovich did not want this powerful political resource in the hands
of his opponents—or even his mildest critics.

Putin's personal animosity toward the ambitious Gusinsky, whom he
knew rather well, may have contributed to the president's attitude toward
the oligarch's media outlets, particularly the highly popular network
NTV. The media tycoon was arrogant enough to believe that he could
influence Putin and even dictate rules of the game to him. This the pres-

ident could not abide. Putin was also outraged by the lack of respect shown him in NTV's broadcasting. The popular NTV program *The Puppets* made the Kremlin boss a caricature, pitiful and even vicious at times. Journalists from NTV, accustomed to saying whatever they wanted under Yeltsin without fear of the Kremlin's wrath, did the same under Yeltsin's successor. They had not noticed that times had changed and that Putin had no intention of tolerating the free-for-all. Yeltsin would not watch television programs that criticized him. Apparently Putin tuned in.

In June, the thunder roared—Gusinsky was arrested. The move would have been almost unthinkable in the Yeltsin era; then the oligarchs had been untouchable. That was Yeltsin's understanding of democracy. He could be displeased by one or another representative of big business. But to arrest him? I believe the first Russian president saw arrests and persecution as basically communist means of governance, and therefore he loathed them. Later, after the oligarchs helped him retain power in 1996, it became impossible for him to take such action. Yeltsin knew how to show gratitude. Besides, he never destroyed anyone, not even his worst enemies.

The last political arrests in Russia went back to 1993, when Yeltsin had put in prison his rivals, vice president Alexander Rutskoi and speaker of the parliament Ruslan Khasbulatov. They had mounted opposition to him that flared into armed insurrection among thousands of followers after Yeltsin dissolved the parliament and ended with the president ordering the army to fire on the parliament building. But Yeltsin was the one who let Rutskoi and Khasbulatov out of jail and refused to prosecute them further. He tried to forget them. Most likely, Yeltsin was merciful to his opponents because he did not consider them a threat to him.

As for his mild reaction toward the tycoons, it is quite possible that Yeltsin regarded the oligarchy as the natural base for his regime. And perhaps he realized that the oligarchy made not only the market but also nongovernmental—that is, free—media possible in Russia. Yeltsin had respect for the freedom of mass information. From time to time, he grew irritated or angry when journalists or politicians treated him poorly or made him the target of crude, even brutal criticism. Sometimes, he called editors in chief on the carpet in the Kremlin and tried to give them orders. But he never persecuted anyone for criticism or personal attacks. The first Russian president remembered that his rise was made possible by the freedom of the press and freedom of expression. He behaved as if all critics and opponents for him were nothing more than annoying gnats, and his reaction was simple—shut the window so you wouldn't see or hear them. Apparently, he also felt that free speech in Russia was important evidence that the country had abandoned communism—his life's goal.

Putin, as soon became apparent, was quite different. He perceived a threat differently. He considered critics and the unruly to be enemies of the state, and therefore his enemies, because he identified the state with the president—that is, himself. He could have said after Louis XIV, "L'Etat, c'est moi"—"I am the state." And they were enemies, as he saw it, to be plucked or squeezed out of the political scene, not given the freedom to speak their minds. At least in his view of politics and power, Putin was more like a Soviet leader than a postcommunist one, and he could act more like one where his critics were concerned. Besides, he wanted the consolidation of the state, which called for more reliance on subordination and discipline. The story of the independent media showed that Putin retained some traits of the Soviet elites that Yeltsin seemed to have been lacking, among them distrust and suspicion. As for vindictiveness—this feature has a more universal character.

Note that the charges against Media-Most were not political but economic: nonpayment of debts to the state. Media-Most did have overdue debt with Gazprom, the state-owned natural gas utility, which reflected its dubious relations with the state. Gusinsky's independent media empire, which included one of the most popular Russian television networks, NTV, could not have been created without close ties to the state. The Kremlin had awarded Gusinsky broadcasting rights for channel 4 as payment for the extremely active participation of all his empire—radio and television stations, newspapers, and magazines—in Yeltsin's 1996 reelection campaign (which the NTV journalists later regretted). Gradually, Gusinsky created professional news on television—a new phenomenon in Russia. But he did it with the help of millions of dollars in loans that again could not have been received without the close cooperation of the authorities. The state monopoly Gazprom guaranteed loans for him from state banks and Western creditors. And there were doubts whether Gusinsky intended to repay the money—most likely not.

The prehistory of the other oligarchic empires in Russia was similarly murky. All the oligarchs had debts with the state, and most were mixed up in fishy deals and machinations. But the authorities continued to regard them benignly, allowing them the occasional serious misdeed. The other broadcasting companies had even greater debt—foremost among them state-owned ORT and RTR—which they had no intention of repaying. The blow fell on Gusinsky because he had violated the system of loyalty and tried to become a political force in his own right.

It is highly likely that Putin personally approved the arrest of the media oligarch. In any case, it couldn't have happened without his knowledge. As he apparently saw it, the arrest was a major step in bringing order to Russia and showed all potential critics that this president would not joke around when it came to maintaining political stability as he saw it. Thus he did away with one of the fundamental taboos of the Yeltsin regime: the prohibition against persecuting both an independent media and the oligarchs.

The Kremlin did not expect Gusinsky's arrest to create the negative reaction it did among Russian democrats and especially in the West. The Media-Most journalists destroyed every attempt by the Kremlin to justify Gusinsky's arrest. Others—politicians and oligarchs—came to Gusinsky's defense for the good reason that they saw a threat to themselves in what had happened to him. The West got involved again. The Western press made the Kremlin's crackdown on Gusinsky's media its lead story, and Western leaders prominently raised the issue with Moscow officials, which was the most unpleasant aspect for Putin. In the end, Gusinsky was released from prison and the charges against him were dropped—as it turned out, only temporarily.

The Gusinsky affair signaled that the authorities would now be using the prosecutor general's office for political ends. The prosecutor's office was being turned into a guard dog of the new regime. The president's warning was clear: No one had immunity anymore, and his critics could find themselves in an extremely unhappy situation. The prosecutor's office and the courts stood behind Putin, prepared to demonstrate that opposing the regime was futile. After Yeltsin's permissiveness, this was indeed a new tendency in Russian politics.

The signal sent by the Kremlin was received by the press and the political world. Gradually, the reaction inside Russia to the continued attack on Gusinsky's media and most of all on NTV began to diminish. People, still remembering not-so-distant Soviet times, decided not to provoke the president. "God knows what is on his mind and how far he might go if he is threatened—better not to test his patience," they were thinking. It was true that in the West, where Putin was being closely watched, observers voiced concern. But Putin must have felt that Western governments would deal with him under any circumstances. He was probably correct.

Putin sent another message as well. If one of the richest and most powerful men in Russia could be arrested and kept in prison just like that, without a fair trial, what could ordinary people expect? The Russian human rights community was seriously concerned. But this small group had little influence now. They were regarded as incurable romantics and idealists. That most of their funding came from the West was a reason for many other Russians to regard them, as they had in Soviet times, as an instrument of Western, primarily American, influence, which only increased their isolation in Russia.

It was soon revealed why Gusinsky had been released—an unseemly story. Gusinsky was forced to sign an agreement with representatives of the state (created by Gazprom's own organization dealing with the media, Gazprom-Media) that in essence traded his property for his freedom. He agreed to sell Media-Most, so disliked by the new regime, on the condition that all charges against him were dropped and he was released from prison. The agreement took the form of a special protocol and was signed by Mikhail Lesen, the minister of the press, television, and mass communications. The state behaved like an out-and-out racketeer. It put Gusinsky in prison, but as soon as he agreed to give up his trouble-making property, he was released without a trial. Under the cover of legal institutions, a cynical deal was concluded.

All this had nothing to do with the "dictatorship of the law"—the principle coined by the president and said to be the foundation of his system of governance, which supposedly demanded strict obedience to the law. Analogous blackmailing using law-and-order agencies was tried out on several other oligarchs and mostly succeeded. Thus Vladimir Potanin, one of the initiators of the "loans for shares" auctions (in the course of which the oligarchs who had helped reelect Yeltsin got property at half price), was forced to pay several million dollars in taxes to avoid an investigation. He was the first in line who experienced the new scare tactics of the law enforcement agencies. Soon he would be followed by others. All the Russian oligarchs had received property because of their access to the Yeltsin entourage. Now the new regime wanted to restore control over them and their activity by blackmailing big business.

Gusinsky was no fool. As soon as he was released, he went public about the terms of his agreement with the Kremlin. He also announced that he had signed the agreement "at gunpoint" and therefore did not intend to comply with it. The state did not get his property. We can imagine the reaction at the Kremlin to Gusinsky's "treachery"—yet all he was doing was playing by the rules the new ruling team set. Putin's team and Media-Most entered into a new unequal battle. The state, including the prosecutor's office and judges and the law enforcement agencies, openly declared a war against a private broadcasting company. The NTV network was the major object of the state attack.[1]

Meanwhile, the moods within society began to change. A large portion of the Russian political world and quite a few journalists supported the government against Gusinsky this time around. There were several reasons. Many found Gusinsky annoying personally and resented NTV's role during the Yeltsin administration, especially its great impact on Yeltsin's reelection in 1996. Others stressed the financial aspect of the conflict between Media-Most and the government, insisting that debts need to be paid and refusing to see the political component of the conflict.

Still others were afraid of drawing down the wrath of the authorities and tried to show their loyalty in every way. There were people in journalism and in politics who understood that the NTV case was about destroying the freedom of the media under cover of talk about repayment of debt but who did not have the courage to admit it. Some people were irritated by the resistance the NTV team put up. One episode in Russian political reality became a gauge of the current level in Russia of public understanding of political issues, and of human decency.

———— ❧ ————

The summer of 2000 was a triumph for Putin. He succeeded in everything—taming the governors, fighting the oligarchs, liquidating the independence of the Federation Council, pocketing the Duma, weakening all the other political institutions, and cowing the press. It is true that he didn't succeed against Gusinsky—not yet. But after his political victories in Moscow and in the regions, he had no influential political opponents, no political rivals left. Even the traditional critics of the authorities like Grigory Yavlinsky, leader of Yabloko, stopped baiting the Kremlin, seeing that society was quite happy with Putin and that people were irritated with any criticism of his actions. Yavlinsky announced a personal moratorium on criticism of Putin until the new president's policies on other issues were clearer.

Nothing threatened the president on the political stage. He was the only force around, the only real source of power and influence. All the other forces, groups, and institutions reacted to what he did rather than acting in their own right. Putin became the sole embodiment of politics and power in Russia. The rest were too insignificant and even pitiful.

The causality is important here. Putin increased his power so much not because he was striving to become omnipotent—Yeltsin probably was by nature far more authoritarian—but mainly because Russian society at that moment was longing for simplicity and security. People were too tired to think, much less to choose from among the choices that political pluralism and democracy suggested. The list of available politicians was too short, and those who were available did not inspire much hope or trust. And besides, the people were fed up with them.

Those who only yesterday had mocked Putin as a politician who would never crawl out of Yeltsin's pocket were now expressing concern about where the president's excessive powers might lead. It was beginning to look as if Vladimir Putin, having gained confidence and while his approval ratings were high, wanted in one fell swoop to destroy all groups of influence that did not depend on him and to fortify the supports of his personal authority. If things continued this way, Putin would literally have no opponents in four years, and his reelection would be guaranteed. And no other influential people would be left in the political arena.

Someone in Putin's entourage—I believe it was Alexander Voloshin—noted, "Everything we do succeeds. How boring. . . ."

Indeed, in comparison with the Yeltsin years, the Putin era was growing boring. The political conflicts of every variety that had constantly exploded on the Russian stage had disappeared. Almost all the independent political actors were gone, leaving only those who sucked up to the president—Kremlin courtiers rather than political actors. The style and rhetoric of power had changed—now there were positive, affirming words and intonations harking back to the era before Gorbachev. If politics is a combination of independent institutions and organizations, channels of influence, and mechanisms for regulating conflict, this was, if not the end of politics, the extinction of many of its aspects. Not only had the struggle for power disappeared, but the struggle to maintain power had become unnecessary. "He's come for a long stay, perhaps forever," said even recent democrats and liberals, fretting about finding a niche that would help them survive in the new climate.

Putin, in the meantime, switched to international affairs. After all, activity in the global arena would boost his legitimacy, his recognition factor, and his acceptance as a player in the world political club. The summer 2000 meeting in Okinawa of the Group of Eight industrial nations (G-8) turned into a coming-out party for him. He spoke well. The members of the world club liked his calm, modest, businesslike demeanor. It wasn't hard to please them—after Yeltsin, any Russian president who could stand without help would be considered a success. Putin had a successful debate with U.S. president Bill Clinton on the Americans' possible abrogation of the 1972 Anti–Ballistic Missile Treaty, feeling the approval of France and the understanding of Germany behind him. The meeting demonstrated Putin's quick reactions and down-to-earth, technocratic approach.

Just before the meeting Putin had gone to North Korea, where he had heard from its leader, Kim Jong Il, a suggestion of his willingness to trade away the Korean missile program for Western money. Putin skillfully introduced the idea at the G-8 meeting. But Kim made a U-turn and withdrew his idea, embarrassing Putin. The new Russian leader had to learn that he must be cautious and avoid becoming a card in somebody else's game. But the embarrassment with North Korea did not change the generally positive impression that world leaders gained of Russia's president. German chancellor Gerhard Schröder suggested that in the future no G-8 meetings should be held without Putin. In other words, Putin joined the highest international league and carried it off with dignity.

Polls in Russia continued to show unprecedented popularity for the new leader. In July 2000, according to VTsIOM, 73 percent of Russians approved of Putin (17 percent disapproved of him, and 10 percent had no opinion). At the same time, 60 percent endorsed concentrating all power in one man's hands as a means of solving Russia's problems (27 percent supported the independence of the branches of government, and 13 percent had no opinion). Russians supported their new president, hoping that he would deal with Yeltsin's chaotic legacy, though they were still not confident that anyone could bring order to the country. At the same time, people agreed that they did not know the leader and his agenda. Fifty-nine percent admitted that they knew little about Putin, only 23 percent felt they had learned a lot about him, and a mere 10 percent felt that they knew what kind of a leader he was.[2]

Russian politics do not stay boring for long. The person who spoiled Putin's triumphal march was another media oligarch—Boris Berezovsky, the master of Kremlin intrigue for much of the Yeltsin era, and one of the smartest political animals in Russia. Berezovsky had been a moving force behind Project Putin. He had helped mold Putin, prepared him for the highest office. But after Gusinsky's arrest, he sensed that his creation was turning on him and other oligarchs whom he could not control. Berezovsky was among the first to realize that the president was beginning to act on a plan to free himself from the more odious part of the Yeltsin entourage. Knowing he would be at the head of those kicked out of the Kremlin, Berezovsky switched to the opposition before being shown the door.

The other oligarchs also felt the change in Putin, but they just laid low. Yet the gray cardinal and leading Kremlin spin-doctor could not tolerate being tossed aside without a word of thanks. Beyond mere feelings, Berezovsky came to the conclusion that if Putin was not stopped from gathering all power to himself soon, he would leave no room for any independent political actors, even those to whom he was obligated. He was sensing danger emanating from the new leader that he had failed to notice before. The rebellion of the country's main intriguer was a desperate attempt to stop the steamroller that could mean oblivion or political death for some, particularly himself. Besides, Berezovsky also had a business empire to save.[3]

Berezovsky was the first to openly protest Putin's reform of the Federation Council. Soon afterward, he began daily attacks on the president using his media resources, first of all his newspapers. The political silence had ended. Someone had begun criticizing the leader who had managed to hypnotize everyone, proponents and opponents alike. Berezovsky pointedly resigned from the parliament in July to protest Putin's policies. That might have seemed a foolish gesture, for parliamentary deputies had immunity from prosecution. But Berezovsky was not a petty player.

As Putin's major critic, Berezovsky could now claim to be a defender of democracy.[4] If Putin suddenly began investigating Berezovsky's machinations, the latter could point to his halo marking him as a persecuted victim of the regime. That would assure him support or even political asylum in the West in case of need. He would need it sooner than he might have expected.

Though the most restive tycoon said all the right things about the threat to the gains of democracy, no one in Russia thought he was sincere. Everyone remembered his role in the evolution of the Yeltsin regime and assumed he was only trying to save himself and his empire now. The fact that Putin's main critic turned out to be this oligarch who had more shady baggage than almost anyone strengthened the president's standing with Russians. Ordinary citizens reasoned simply that if Berezovsky was unhappy, Putin was doing the right thing. What irony: When there was a real threat to democratic freedoms in Russia, their most energetic defender was a manipulative tycoon with a suspicious reputation.

Berezovsky went further and attempted to create a "constructive opposition" to Putin. He was beginning to look at his battle with his former friend Vladimir as a personal vendetta. He might have wanted to prove that once again—as with the reelection of Yeltsin in 1996 and the organizing of Putin's own ascendancy in 1999—he could do the impossible. However, his well-publicized campaign to create an opposition failed. At the press conference he called to announce his intentions, Berezovsky was joined by people who seemed randomly selected: a second-rate actor, a columnist, a playwright, and a writer who lived abroad. It was pathetic. This time, the great intriguer was out of luck— the prosecutor general's office began investigating his deals, and he was forced to emigrate.[5]

Berezovsky's defeat showed how much the mood of Russian elites had changed. A short time before, everyone would have answered the call of that demon of Russian politics. Now Boris Abramovich was politely heard out but got no response. No one wanted to become his ally. Oligarchs could be supported and joined only when they were acting on orders from the regime. It seemed there was no independent role for either the oligarchy or the opposition in Putin's Russia.

The Kremlin godfather's vendetta against the president was the beginning of an unpleasant chain of events for the Kremlin just when it had seemed on the verge of invincibility and all its plans were successfully fulfilled. A powerful explosion went off in the underpass below Pushkin Square, in the center of Moscow, on August 8, 2000. The fiery blast knocked people off their feet, killing dozens. Many agonized for days from burns before dying. The blast was attributed to Chechen separatists. And once again, the Moscow police started endless antiterrorist "special operations," which naturally yielded no results. "We must get used to the fact that something can happen at any time in any place," the Russian newspapers wrote. That was the mood of ordinary Russian people, who had longed for stability and a quiet life with Putin's ascendancy to power and found themselves facing new insecurities.

The explosion on Moscow's main street was only the beginning of Russia's disasters. On August 12, the atomic submarine K-141-*Kursk*, the pride of the Russian fleet, sank in the Barents Sea during naval exercises. It became the fraternal grave for 118 crew members. It was only learned from a dead crew member's note, after his body was brought up, that after the submarine sank, some of the crew lived and hoped for aid that never came. For hours after the accident, they banged out an SOS on the walls, and this banging was actually heard by the Russian divers who finally discovered the submarine. Then the signals stopped. Russian attempts to save the crew, started too late—on the sixth day after the accident—and executed extremely unprofessionally, were a failure. The Russian rescuers had none of the equipment needed to open the submarine hatches. The country that launched satellites and had nuclear missiles that could destroy the world could not open the hatch of its own submarine.

Russians, who had grown accustomed to the constant losses in Chechnya, were stunned by the *Kursk* tragedy. Perhaps we all thought about the horror of a slow death by suffocation, the tapping in code, and the slow realization that the rescue would not come. Someone put it very well, describing the emotion that gripped the recently callous nation: "Today we are all in the *Kursk*, and we know that no one will save us." Every day when there was news about the submarine, people stopped what they were doing to listen closely to the radio or watch the television, trying to find a glimmer of a reason to hope that the country that still considered itself great would be able to save its seamen.

It was a rare moment of unity at a national moment of catharsis. Even during the putsch of August 1991 in Moscow, people had not been really united—the democrats and Muscovites had supported Yeltsin, but the rest of the country had calmly watched the events as onlookers at their nation's crisis. Now grief brought Russians together. The tragedy awakened not only feelings of compassion but also an understanding of the impotence of the authorities and the vulnerability of ordinary people in the country where the state never cared about the life of an individual.

Putin can consider that tragic week his first serious failure. While the remaining crew members were knocking in code on the submarine wall, the president was vacationing in the Black Sea resort of Sochi. On occasions like this, Western leaders behave very differently. At almost the same time, President Clinton interrupted his vacation to meet with firefighters battling wildfires in the western United States. Chancellor Schröder interrupted his vacation to attend memorial services for the Germans who had died in the Concorde crash outside Paris. Putin continued his holiday. The country looked at television and saw the confused faces of bureaucrats. Then came clips of Putin receiving guests in Sochi, calm, tanned, and confident in a white T-shirt. He quickly hid a satisfied smile, but the cameras had captured it. Putin was surrounded by happy guests and his beaming lieutenants; they had been talking about something pleasant after a good meal.

The television footage was a disaster for the president. He definitely did not know how to behave; he was not experienced, or cynical, enough to play convincingly and pretend. Perhaps he did not feel the gravity of situation, or he did not care. He might have thought that he should remain cool and confident of himself, not emotionally involved, detached. Much later, it became known that exactly that was the advice of Putin's people.

In the meantime, the military's top brass quit. The minister of defense, Igor Sergeyev, vanished from the scene. The remaining officials blatantly put out mountains of lies attempting to absolve themselves of responsibility for delays in organizing a rescue operation and for rejecting foreign help. As usual, they had been waiting for an order from the very top. But the order was not coming. The Kremlin continued to deliberate on whether a superpower could seek foreign help. The Soviet tradition was to let your people die quietly and keep their death a state secret. The problem nowadays was that to keep secrets in Russia was impossible.

Alan Hoskins, the leader of a group of British submarine officers, revealed that the British armed services had offered to aid the Russian ship immediately after the accident. But Moscow kept silent, then asked for help when it was too late, and finally for unknown reasons turned to the Norwegians. "Apparently, Russia had some political reasons for hesitating to save the crew of the *Kursk*," Hoskins was quoted as saying in the August 31 *Obshchaya gazeta*.

The Norwegians discovered that the Russians had hidden the truth about the conditions and details of the operation, creating suspicion that they did not want the Norwegians to be more successful than they. At some point, Vice Admiral Einar Skorgen, who was coordinating the operation for the Norwegian side, threatened to pull his divers out if the Russians continued to sabotage (he used the exact word) and interfere with their efforts. "There was a total informational chaos. We were besieged by so much false or distorted information that it endangered the safety of our divers," he was quoted as saying in despair, in the August 29 issue of the journal *Itogi*. But on the ninth day after the accident, the

Norwegians did open the hatch of the *Kursk* and get inside, revealing that all men on board were dead.

While the Russian authorities lied, the press—both Russian and Western—screamed headlines about the tragedy. "Putin's silence in the first long days of the crisis shows that he was in a state of confusion, probably bewilderment," an August 28 article in the *Times* of London said. Definitely, the Russian president lost his self-confidence—the *Kursk* case appeared to be more dramatic, for him as well, than he had probably thought at the beginning.

"Putin's reputation sank to the bottom with the submarine *Kursk*," wrote a Russian journalist. Putin kept silent for almost a week after the loss of the submarine. He must not have expected a country accustomed to the loss of lives and permanent disasters to feel such pain over the fate of this submarine. And he did not know how to react to that pain. Only recently so confident, sure of himself, he now did not know what to do, which words to use, how to address his nation.

But as soon as Putin got over his confusion, he started looking around for people to blame. Meeting with relatives of the seamen, he announced that the guilty parties in the tragedy were Big Capital and the press, the latter paid off by the former: "The newspapers and others defend the interests of those who support them (the oligarchs). They are vilely exploiting this tragedy to settle a score with the authorities. ... Why? Because we are pushing them against the wall. For robbing the country, the army, and the navy."[6] It was obvious that the president was furious about the way his behavior during the disaster had been presented in the press, which he was sure was in the hands of the oligarchs. He acted as if he was concerned only by the attacks in the media, not the fate of the seamen. He refused to see the failures of his people; he had no sense that the military and the government apparatus had behaved cynically with lives at stake. He was focused on one thing: absolving the authorities.

The search for a scapegoat did not end there. Nikolai Patrushev, director of the FSB and a close ally of Putin, announced that there had been two Dagestanis aboard the *Kursk*, hinting at a trail leading to the terrorists from the Northern Caucasus. Then the authorities revealed that one possible version was that the *Kursk* had collided with an American or British submarine. But no one could explain what happened to the second submarine after the collision—after all, it would have been damaged as well.

Putin was caught unawares first by the catastrophe itself and then by the reaction of the Russian press and public. He *was* clearly puzzled. All his statements and actions demonstrated his failure to realize that Russia had become another country, one that was accustomed to openness, and that he had to learn to tell the truth. Moreover, the mass anguish over the *Kursk* had another source: The sub had been the pride of the Russian fleet, the best ship that Russia had with the best crew. If they were doomed and nobody could rescue them, what could the rest of the country expect? That was what ordinary Russians thought. That is why they were so shocked and traumatized.

The president was not to blame for the submarine accident, of course. He was not to blame for the cowardice and hypocrisy of his subordinates—most of whom had been appointed by his predecessor. He was only guilty of being unable to get past the Soviet manner of reacting to tragedy.

Putin also showed himself lacking in a sense of the moment and an understanding of emotions, without which a leader cannot rule successfully—especially in Russia. He did not have the ability to feel compassion for the trapped seamen or the grieving Russian people, or the political intuition to catch the barely perceptible shifts in the public mood. Yeltsin had that intuition; he would have known how to react. Putin behaved as a cold, rational man. It was true that he wasn't heartless—he was unable to control his tears at the funeral of his patron and friend, Saint Petersburg mayor Anatoly Sobchak. Those tears, a manifestation of his humanity, won him the sympathy of millions. But this time, he failed to feel the public mood, or he might have been afraid that being human would be seen as being weak. Also exposed were the inexperience and unprofessionalism of his team, which advised him not to react to the August events and not to take responsibility for them.

That moment in August 2000 could have been a turning point for Putin and for Russia, bringing together regime and people at a time of crisis. Only time will tell what August taught Putin. Would that cold shower wake him up and make him more sensitive to the problems of his country? Or would that tragic experience make him even harsher, more indifferent and cynical?

Putin promised to raise the submarine. In November 2000, more bodies were brought up. One bore a note that confirmed that the men were alive after the blast and that their deaths were arduous. The country suffered yet another shock.[7]

The submarine was raised in the summer of 2001, one year after it sank. The recovery was expensive and extremely dangerous—the craft carried an atomic reactor and torpedoes that could explode at any moment. Experts saw no need to raise it. But Putin had promised his country that the submarine would be raised at whatever cost, so raised it must be. He owed it to the families of the crew. The cause of the accident was confirmed—it had been the explosion of a defective torpedo. The fleet commanders had known about that type of torpedo problem for a long time but ordered the *Kursk* into maneuvers anyway. The post-communist Russian power structures still could not break out beyond their traditional irresponsibility, carelessness, incompetence, and indifference to people's lives.

Putin finally fired the high command of the fleet but, again, in a typically Soviet way—without telling the public the real reason for the dismissals. The step did not alter the dire situation of the decaying Russian fleet. Without reconstruction and modernization, there was no guarantee that a new disaster would not occur. But before beginning to revamp its navy, Russia had to decide whether it needed to maintain such a huge fleet, symbolic of Russia's superpower status and vast imperialist ambitions, when the country couldn't guarantee safety to its seamen.

August brought bitter commentary from journalists and intellectuals. "In a sense the *Kursk* means the end of the era of Russian industrialization. Russia is tremendously worn out—morally and materially. It has used up the Soviet resources and has not created anything new," declared an article in the August 28 *Vedomosti*. Boris Vasiliev, a writer who had been a Soviet tank test driver and had seen a lot of accidents, wrote in the August 31 edition of *Obshchaya gazeta*: "What was outrageous in this story [of the *Kursk*] were the lies and amoral behavior of the president. Putin does not know how to be a leader. He is Brezhnev II. But unlike Brezhnev, he is angry inside. That's the only difference."

The mood of the military was also grim. "I'm afraid that the ship turned out to be more expensive than human lives. And what are we to make of the fact that the head of the commission on the rescue did not go to the site of the tragedy until the sixth day after the catastrophe? I would not want to be saved that way," declared General Yevgeny Podkolzin, a former paratrooper commander, in the August issue of *Kommersant-Vlast'*. What he said openly was what the rank and file and the officers of the armed services were thinking to themselves.

After the *Kursk* disaster, doubts increased about the government's ability to improve the situation in the country. Only 29 percent of Russians polled in September expressed optimism, while 34 percent felt that life in Russia would not get better, according to a VTsIOM poll. This was a verdict on the new rule.

In August 2000, the relationship between Putin and society seemed about to become much less euphoric. In July, Putin had a 73 percent approval rating (only 17 percent disapproved of his performance, and 10 percent had no opinion). In August, after the submarine accident, about 62 percent of respondents approved of Putin (28 percent disapproved, and 10 percent still had no opinion). The president had lost a sizable amount of support and gained a sizable number of critics. Forty-three percent of Russians felt that Putin had behaved "with dignity, and responsibly" during the *Kursk* incident, while 42 percent thought not. It would seem that Putin had nothing to really worry about, but the shift sent a signal that society at large was not in love with its leader—at least at that moment.

That same August, when emotions were still running high because of the submarine disaster, a fire broke out at another symbol of Soviet grandeur, the Ostankino television towers, which served all the national television channels. The dark television screens seemed to say that Russia was entering an age of catastrophes. Technical and human resources were wearing out, and something had to be done urgently.

The Ostankino fire demonstrated to the full the drawbacks of Putin's "transmission belt" of governance. For three long hours, firefighters could not start putting out the blaze because no one—not the mayor of Moscow, not the chief of the presidential staff, not the energy minister or the prime minister—wanted to take the responsibility for turning off the electricity. Only President Putin could. Similarly, the military leaders during rescue operations for the *Kursk* did nothing at all while they waited for a command from above. The concentration of power at the top bred a disinclination to take action and a desire to hide from responsibility in all levels of the administration.

Political jokes are a good indicator of the psychological state of Russian society. Here are two sad jokes from late 2000:

The first joke: Ostankino had to burn down. The FSB had lost its recording of *Swan Lake*. (Tchaikovsky's music for the ballet *Swan Lake* has very specific overtones for Russian audiences—during the August 1991 putsch against democracy, all the radio and television stations in Russia broadcast it.)

The second joke: Washington officially announced that no American towers were anywhere near Ostankino. (This joke was a reaction to official declarations by the Russian military that the *Kursk* had sunk as a result of a collision with a Western submarine.)

The appearance of such jokes suggested that Russia was returning, at least in part, to the way it had been in communist times—there had been very few political jokes in the Yeltsin revolutionary era. The return of political jokes among intellectuals especially was a reflection of both their dissatisfaction with the situation and with the authorities and their fear of expressing this dissatisfaction openly. The political joke as a form of reaction to politics and power in Russia has always been an expression of a double mentality: on the one side, resentment of politics; and on the other, an attempt not to cross the boundaries, a form of survival.

Some observers hoped that after the *Kursk* the country would stand up, dry its tears, and make the Kremlin pay—which would have sent Putin's ratings plummeting. They didn't plummet. In the end, Putin was forgiven for his clumsy handling of the crisis by many, except the victims' relatives. Observers, including Russian ones, were surprised by the people's willingness to go easy on the authorities. "Well, these things happen," many citizens sighed, fatalistically. "You can't bring back the dead." The press wrote that the authorities had been given a license to make new mistakes. Apparently, we underestimated the exhaustion factor in Russian society, which leads more to a passive acceptance of whatever life brings than to a demand for anything better. The surge of dissatisfaction

with the government quickly subsided and was replaced by other feelings, foremost among them a sadness too bleak for despair and fatalism.
"We just have to bear up," Russians said.

But certain conclusions were drawn. The groups of influence that
were watching closely saw that the president was not as strong as he
wanted to appear, did not know how to handle crises, and could become
weak and disoriented. After the *Kursk* drama, a joke circulated in
Moscow that the old system of power under Yeltsin was predicated on an
absent president and the new system on a strong president. And everything went wrong when the strong president was absent.

The boss in the Kremlin must have realized that he had problems,
because in September he began desperately working on his image. He
met with people, traveled tirelessly around the country, as if trying to force
Russia to forget his moments of weakness, and made gestures aimed at
ordinary folk. On a trip to the Volga city Samara, he visited a dirt-poor
provincial household (with a television camera crew) and ate with evident
pleasure marinated mushrooms straight from the jar. Russians could enjoy
their president's simplicity and trustfulness, just dropping in on a strange
woman and partaking of potluck. Only those familiar with the security
around the president knew the work the secret service had to do before
Putin could "drop by" a random house and snack there.

But the image makers did their job. In September and October 2000,
Putin restored his ratings and once again looked confident, at least outwardly. The main decision he had reached after August soon became
clear: He must crush the media critics who had damaged him so badly
over the *Kursk*. That meant doing whatever it took to crack down on the
media conglomerates—Gusinsky's first of all.

By the end of 2000, Russia had returned to some of its old rhythms
of life, as if the ten-year Yeltsin hiatus had never happened. Under Yeltsin,
presidential portraits had not been in vogue. Now the Ministry of
Defense ordered all military bases to buy portraits of Vladimir Putin
immediately. Soon the state apparatus made a portrait of the second
Russian president not only a key element of the office furniture but a
symbol of personal loyalty and statist sentiments. Artists found work that
looked like it might become full time. At first they didn't know how to
depict the new president, because there were no instructions on that sub-

ject from above. Then the canvas size for official use was determined—2 by 3 meters—with portraits for offices somewhat smaller.

Putinomania gradually became an element of Russian life. New textbooks were introduced in the schools of Saint Petersburg, Putin's hometown, that described the childhood of little Volodya Putin. That meant something to people who had learned to read with books about the childhood of little Volodya Ulyanov (Lenin). Other Russian cities would soon follow suit with their own initiatives. In some places, the restaurant "Putin" was opened; in others, the chair and table used by the president on some occasion became a valuable item in the local museum. Putin may not have known about these initiatives, for they were probably thought up by loyal subordinates. But quite a few people heard the bugle call and got to work restoring the past.

On the political stage, players in the new production directed by the Kremlin tried to figure out which part or parts they had. When it became clear that the parliament's upper chamber, the Federation Council, would no longer be a serious institution, discussions began on what the State Council—created by Putin in September 2000 as a consolation prize for the regional bosses, or the senators, as they were calling themselves— would be doing. The bosses hoped that the State Council would be given the main functions of the upper house and even be made constitutional.

While the senators made their ambitious plans, Putin promulgated his decree on the State Council, which clarified what he wanted it to be: a consultative organ that would convene at the president's request and discuss what the president's team prepared. The governors' hopes that the president would give the State Council the right to appoint the prosecutor general and higher court judges and generally raise the body's status were dashed. And once the State Council was made the president's toy, the same fate was prepared for other political institutions.

At the first session of the State Council in November 2000, Putin proposed that its members approve the new Russian anthem. It was obvious that the Kremlin had wanted something to occupy the fledgling organ. Discussion of the anthem might have seemed like a mockery to these leaders, once omnipotent in their regions. But the governors held their peace. Instead of discussing the strategy for Russia, they began to edit verses.

They had a powerful motivation, because everybody knew that the Kremlin would get rid of all regional bosses who had not demonstrated fealty to Putin. Many of the governors were facing reelection, so the reckoning was drawing near. But even those who had tried to please the boss were not sure of the Kremlin's support.

The elections for regional head were to be held in 2000 or 2001 in almost half the republics and territorial entities. In some regions, the Kremlin had urged governors to resign "voluntarily," using the prosecutor's office and *compromat* (compromising materials) gathered on them. There was always something to be found on the governors. There was talk that Putin's electoral rival Yuri Luzhkov was thinking about retirement from his post of Moscow mayor for "health reasons," in exchange for immunity from prosecution.

After media oligarch Gusinsky, the Kremlin's second victim was Kursk governor Alexander Rutskoi, who had been vice president under Yeltsin and was a retired military pilot. Rutskoi had a controversial political biography—he had led the parliamentary mutiny against Yeltsin in 1993 and even been imprisoned. Then he reappeared as governor of Kursk, the region the ill-fated submarine was named after. No one doubted that Rutskoi, who placed family members in cushy jobs, was corrupt. But the Kremlin did not know how to get rid of him. So Putin's people chose the simplest path: The Kremlin put up its own candidate (from the security services) for the governorship and used the courts to remove Rutskoi from the race the day before the election.

Even though the democratic segment of society did not feel great warmth for Rutskoi, the manner in which he was taken out of the game—intrigue, and the executive branch telling the courts what to do—upset people. "In essence, it's the right thing, but in form, it's a mockery of democracy," observers said. And after all that, the Kremlin did not finish the job. Rutskoi was removed from the ballot, but the Kremlin's candidate did not win in Kursk; the victor was a Communist, an anti-Semite, and most likely a thief too.

Soon the practice of getting rid of people in other regions who did not suit the Kremlin, using pressure from law enforcement and threats of jail, became a popular Kremlin policy. Outwardly, the cleanup of regional government could resemble a return to legality because many of the governors Putin's people went after were corrupt or guilty of other serious misconduct. But the Kremlin's "cleanup policy" in the regions had nothing to do with the rule of law. Moscow was using the courts and prosecutors in the name of political expediency to support Kremlin loyalists and weaken independent politicians and the Kremlin's foes. The Kremlin even had a list of leaders to be discredited, details of timing and method, and names of those in the courts responsible for passing sentence on them. In some cases, the courts did clear away corrupt politicians. But in other cases they moved, under pressure from Moscow, against the political opponents of the center. The court system was turning into an appendage of the executive branch, as it had been in the Soviet era.

The Kremlin, however, did not want a total purge of the regions; it was prepared to continue the practice, instituted by Yeltsin, of making deals in them. According to Russian law, both the president and the regional governors were allowed only two terms. With Putin's approval and under pressure from the presidential staff, the Duma passed an amendment that gave 26 governors and republic presidents the right to a third term. The number included such regional heavyweights as Mintimer Shaimiyev, the president of the republic of Tatarstan. Putin must have concluded that, having given the regional bosses a scare, he could control them. Running his (that is, the Kremlin's) candidate in a region meant getting into a fight in which the wrong people might win. And besides, fighting meant tension, which Putin did not like. Thus, for the sake of peace of mind, the Kremlin agreed to de facto limitless rule for regional family clans. Later, the Constitutional Court endorsed the ruling that gave regional bosses the right to be reelected for a third and even fourth time, which guaranteed the preservation of semifeudal regimes in Russian provinces.

Tatarstan is an outstanding example of how local regimes have ruled and how they cooperated with Moscow. During the 1990s, the experienced Soviet apparatchik Shaimiyev managed to neutralize nationalist groups in Tatarstan, to become president there, and to establish relatively stable rule in the republic. His rule was based on the dictatorship of his family, which controlled the republic's basic resources—oil and gas, among others. Opposition was cruelly suppressed. Corruption and paternalism flourished. But Khan Shaimiyev gave the center what it needed, primarily outward calm and support during elections.

At the beginning, Putin demanded that the regional feudal lords, especially Shaimiyev and Murtaza Rakhimov (the president of another Russian republic, Bashkortostan, who had built the same type of rule as Shaimiyev), curtail their appetites and bring their constitutions into line with the federal one. The regional lords grumbled and resisted at first, and even directed gentle threats at the center, but in the end they caved in. Yeltsin's successor brought a greater semblance of order to the regions, but it was still the local barons, rather than Moscow, who held sway there. Putin was apparently afraid to seriously impinge on the interests of the feudal clans that ruled most regions—especially because he planned to run again in 2004 and needed the support of the national republics and controllable regions that voted the way the local boss told them to. The new president, like Yeltsin before him, needed influential leaders who knew how to count votes in their domain.

As he began building his superpresidential regime, Putin came to understand that without preserving Yeltsin's policy of deal making in the regions, he would not survive. The price to be paid was the Kremlin's toleration of regional authoritarianism and corruption. There were no organized alternatives to the regional clans—during the Yeltsin years, after a brief period of political struggle, power in most of the regions had been seized by clans dominated by Soviet *nomenklatura* with criminal ties. Putin gradually seemed to become wary of stirring up any conflict with the ruling groups in the regions.[8]

As for the regional elections of 2000, the regions were still battlefields for the Communists and the Kremlin's "party of power." Other political movements had no chance of winning there. That was one result of Yeltsin's ten years: The power struggle locally in Russia was between the old and the new *nomenklatura*. A closer look revealed that most of the new *nomenklatura* came out of the Soviet version. The ruling class had not grown younger. The differences between the Communist governors and the governors loyal to the Kremlin were minimal. Two regions chose military men as governors—General Vladimir Shamanov, who fought in the second Chechen war, was elected in Ulyanovsk, Lenin's birthplace, on the Volga River; and Admiral Vladimir Yegorov was elected in the

Baltic port of Kaliningrad. But it would be premature to see a trend of the military coming to power. Soon it would become obvious that the governors with a military background, like General Alexander Lebed in Krasnoyarsk, his brother Colonel Alexei Lebed in Chakhasia, and Shamanov in Ulyanovsk, were far from efficient managers—they were pathetic and incompetent.

In Chukotka—in Russia's distant and underpopulated North—the new governor was Roman Abramovich, a Yeltsin oligarch who won by a large majority of votes, obtained by bribing the populace with gifts. With his billions of dollars, this young man could easily develop the resource-rich Chukotka into the Russian Klondike. It wasn't clear what Abramovich wanted with Chukotka. When asked, he said, "I feel sorry for the Chukchas." Abramovich did not seem like a man with strong philanthropic tendencies. But, ironically, he might be an improvement over the previous governor, Alexander Nazarov, a shallow and corrupt Soviet apparatchik who brought the region to complete degradation with a starving population. At least Abramovich was doing something for Chukotka—for instance, he sent all the children of the place on a seaside vacation in the South, at his own expense. Actually, he could well afford to spend several million dollars of what he had managed to borrow from the state. But the residents of Chukotka, tired of the corruption and anarchy of the previous administration, were grateful to Abramovich.

That a Kremlin insider would look for a place on the outskirts of Russia spoke volumes: Yesterday's initiators of Project Putin did not feel comfortable in the Kremlin and were looking for other "warm spots." Being a governor did not confer total immunity before the courts, but at least it lent legitimacy to one's power and was a safe harbor for waiting out political storms.

In October 2002, another oligarchic family headed by Vladimir Potanin would win regional elections in Krasnoyarski Krai, and its representative, Alexander Kchloponin, would become one more governor-tycoon. It was just the beginning. Soon other oligarchs would follow suit in trying to win local elections. A new page in Russian political history was opening as powerful financial-industrial groups were beginning to legitimize their power in the provinces through elections for the local executive branch. This time, no longer hidden in the shadows, open and legal fusion between power and capital on the regional level had a real chance to challenge the presidency and Moscow's authoritarian moods.

The Kremlin attack on the remaining independent institutions continued, and only a few were left. The next institution on the victims list was the Central Bank, headed by Victor Gerashchenko—Hercules, as he was called in Moscow. Russian liberals and Western financial people disliked Gerashchenko, considering his policy damaging for liberalization. The Kremlin loathed the powerful head of the Central Bank for being too independent and ruling his kingdom without asking for advice from the president's team. Besides, there was a real problem with the bank's transparency—nobody outside knew exactly what was happening inside. The managers of the Central Bank enjoyed salaries as high as those of Western corporate executives, which was outrageous in the eyes of Russians.

A draft was prepared of a presidential decree that stripped the Central Bank of its independence and put it under the control of the government. The Duma, loyal to Putin, would support any decision of the president's. It was true that something definitely had to be done about the Central Bank kingdom. But subordinating the bank to the government would enable the cabinet to print money at will, which would spell an end to reform.

At that moment, the Kremlin did not pursue its initiative to tame the Central Bank—it would have created too much trouble, not only among Russian liberals but in the foreign business community, which for the Kremlin was more important. Putin was intent on attracting foreign investors to Russia, and he did not need scandals. But still the idea of stripping the main Russian bank of its independence continued to be on the agenda of Putin's entourage.

Running a bit ahead, Gerashchenko was dismissed in the spring of 2002 and replaced by another man from Saint Petersburg, Sergei Ignatiev, who had a liberal background, was a good professional, and was close to the Gaidar team. There were doubts, however, whether the new head of the Central Bank would defend his institution's independent status and pursue the reform that the Central Bank's previous head had so vigorously opposed, or whether he would succumb to the pressure from the president's men. Quite a few observers in Russia shrugged skeptically as they watched the changes at the bank—they feared that with its own man there, the Kremlin would be able to use the bank for its needs, which had been hard to do under Gerashchenko. In any case, Ignatiev was an honest man, but a nominal figure rather than a political heavyweight. An irony of Russian politics is that independent people are not often reformers and liberals very often do not have independent positions.

Next on the agenda was Russia's messy multiparty system, which interfered with Putin's idea of politics and gave rise to too many irritating little parties that were difficult to control and that might someday cause problems for the "party of power." On orders from the president's team, the Central Electoral Commission prepared a new law on parties. The draft required that a party have at least 10,000 members, with organizations in 45 regions of no fewer than 100 members each, to qualify for registration. Every two years, the party would have to reregister. And if, in the course of five years, the party did not participate in an election, it would not be allowed to reregister.

The authors of the bill hoped to reduce the number of parties from 188 to fewer than 20. In essence, the law was directed against the democratic parties, which were small—first of all against Yabloko, headed by Grigory Yavlinsky. Under the new law, the Communist Party and the "party of power" had the best chances for survival, which was just the way the Kremlin's people wanted it: their "party of power" competing mainly against the permanently toned-down left-wing opposition, which scared voters into voting for the Kremlin party.[9] The law on parties was approved by the Duma, like all the other laws Putin had proposed.[10]

The Kremlin also began rooting out the other organizations it considered unnecessary or harmful. The work was being done with the help of legislation written to suit the needs of Putin's team. No one could say anymore that lawlessness abounded in Russia. "Controllable democracy" was being introduced by means of the law.

The only way an effective multiparty system could be formed was with parties depending on the result of the election participating in the creation of the government and sharing responsibility for its activity. But since the government in Russia has been formed by the president, with the parliament taking no part in its selection and parties having no influence on the executive branch, there are no impulses in society for the creation of strong parties. Besides which, the Russian authorities tried to create parties from above and foist them on the public, which could support the Kremlin-blessed movements. And it supported these poor stilted excuses for parties because there were no viable alternatives.

Soon, however, the presidential team started to realize either the flimsiness of this system or its unattractiveness to the West. And the opinion of the West was important to Putin. There were signs that the Kremlin began pondering how to make the system more civilized—or, at least, to make it *appear* more civilized. Somewhere in the team, the idea of moving to a party government ripened. But that government, as conceptualized by the Kremlin technologists, had to be formed on the basis of the Kremlin-sponsored "party of power." It looked like a return to the tradition of Soviet party government, which was based on the Communist Party's monopoly and was therefore moribund.

Finally, the president's team found time to discuss other issues. Putin began thinking about military reform, prompted by an awareness of all the signs of the degradation of the Russian army. A severe breakdown in civilian control over the military had taken place during the Yeltsin period. During the summer of 2000, the system of subordination was openly violated in the army. The unheard-of happened: The chief of the General Staff, Anatoly Kvashnin, bypassed his boss, minister of defense Marshal Igor Sergeyev, and sent the president his plan for army reform. Kvashnin behaved as if the defense minister did not exist. It was a scandal, a violation of the chain of command; suddenly, what had been under the surface became public knowledge.

The highest army command was divided into two irreconcilable camps, which could not contain their conflict any longer. Putin, as commander in chief, should have fired both the minister of defense and the chief of the General Staff. He said nothing, however, pretending nothing was amiss. He had behaved the same way in 1999, when General Vladimir Shamanov blackmailed the authorities, threatening to quit if operations in Chechnya were halted. Putin's silence then proved that he did not like open conflict and did not like making choices: Faced with alternatives, he postponed making a decision. He might not have felt strong enough to rein in the military. Thus the president faced a serious problem: not only restoring unity in the military command but also strengthening his control over the armed services, which had started doing as they pleased under Yeltsin.[11]

The problem with the chain of command was not the only problem. Russia could no longer keep 3 million people in the armed services; that was an unbearable burden for the country. The army had been placed on starvation rations. It was being sapped from within by corruption and unprofessionalism. An index of the disintegration was being kept by Chechnya, which showed the army's inability to function in hotspots. By 2000, only two or three out of a dozen divisions in Russia were battle ready. The army, which had been created for imperialist goals and superpower imagery, was now yet another confirmation of the profound crisis in the system. Not only the size but also the organization of the army were completely out of sync with the economic resources of the new Russia.[12]

Putin found the strength to announce the need for military reform. The plan he proposed in the fall of 2000 reduced the army and navy by 365,000 military personnel and 120,000 civilian workers. The reductions were to take place before 2003. By 2005, the army would be reduced by almost 600,000 people, including civilian personnel. The core of the reform in the plan was the creation of powerful battle-ready troops to be based in the basic strategic locations—Southwest and Central Asia. In a speech that fall to the leadership of the armed forces, the president adopted a harsh tone for the first time. He attacked the "parquet" generals who sat around in headquarters. He spoke critically of the weakness of the officer ranks. He started doing something that no Russian leader had ever had the courage to undertake. But would he have the courage to go the whole way until he reformed the final bastion of the empire state?

The military budget for 2001 was boosted 40 percent, thanks to increased oil revenues. But there were doubts that even a larger budget would allow radical military reform, which required heavy spending. General Andrei Nikolayev, chairman of the Duma Defense Committee, said in November, "This is a budget of stabilization. There are no clear priorities. It will improve the situation, but it cannot cardinally solve a single problem." It was true that even the expanded budget was not enough to solve the problem of retiring officers, who by law were entitled to an apartment and a retirement bonus. Experienced observers concluded that the 2001 budget would not change the situation in the army.[13] The lion's share of the budget would go for patching holes and paying off debts. No deep military reform would occur without big money.

The Russian military leadership so far had failed to meet the challenges of a new security context. On one hand, it was clear that security on Russia's southern borders with Central Asia and China had to be beefed up. On the other hand, the Russian military still considered NATO a threat and demanded fortification of the Western outposts and the retention of its nuclear potential. A weakened Russia could no longer respond to all those challenges—it had to decide on a new set of security priorities instead of continuing to build the army on the Soviet model and merely reducing its numbers.

What was the point of preserving nuclear parity with the United States? Russian observers asked.[14] According to some specialists, Russia needed no more than 500 nuclear warheads to guarantee its security. China, France, and the United Kingdom were nuclear powers with a smaller numbers of warheads. And their nuclear status cost them much less than Russia, exhausted by crises, was paying.

Moreover, about 10,000 tactical nuclear weapons were gathering dust in Russian warehouses in case of a limited nuclear war with NATO. Against whom the Russian generals intended to use them now was not clear—not even to the generals. Nevertheless, millions of dollars were spent maintaining the battle-readiness of this military rarity.

The president, undoubtedly, appreciated the difficulty of reforming the army. In late 2001, Putin approved the idea of a professional army, promising to make Russia's professional by 2010. "Neither the government nor society supports the existing draft system," Putin announced.[15] His team decided to make 2002 a breakthrough year in executing reforms and bring one airborne division to a full staffing contract. But it was unclear whether Russia had enough funds to try the experiment, which would cost about 2.5 billion rubles, or $70 million, per division. At the time, the military had 132,000 contract soldiers, down from 260,000 several years before. Putin had to admit that so far Russia had failed to make contract service attractive.[16]

The military leadership was not ready for even a partial transition to a professional army. The plans being prepared by the Ministry of Defense under Putin's comrade in arms Sergei Ivanov planned to add between 40 and 50 percent contract soldiers to the Russian armed forces in 2005–2006 and to reduce the length of service for draftees to six to eight months. But those plans remained on the drafting board. At the same time, the General Staff raised the issue of reducing the categories of draft-exempt citizens. The transition to a professional army was held back by more than lack of funds. There was another factor at work—the unpreparedness of the generals for a new model for the army, which, incidentally, required a substantial reduction in generals and a renewal of their ranks.

Besides, the creation of a new model for a modern army demanded that the political class and society answer once and for all the question: Would Russia become part of Western civilization, or continue dangling between Europe and Asia, pretending to have a "special path" of development and trying to defend itself from the West?

Chapter 5

POWER IN ONE FIST

—————————— ⚬⚬ ——————————

Chechnya as a trap. The government under the gun. The Soviet anthem.
Putin enters the world. Why does the president want power?

In comparison with Yeltsin's stormy rule as president, so often roiled by failures, disasters, zero-sum games, and the threat of the old man's own collapse, the first year of Putin's ascendancy, with the exception of August, was relatively smooth. The president himself might consider it successful. Only Chechnya could really spoil Putin's mood.

The sole undertaking associated with Putin's name and begun on his initiative—Russia's "antiterrorist operation" in the secessionist republic of Chechnya, already devastated by one war (1994–1996)—was a failure. No one had any doubts about that, not even in the Kremlin. From August 1999 to September 2000, according to official sources, 2,600 Russian soldiers died in Chechnya. The death toll among civilians in Chechnya was growing—no one knew whether it was in the thousands or the tens of thousands. The authorities didn't want to know. Despite the ferocity of the federal operation, the leaders of the Chechen separatist movement—Aslan Maskhadov, Shamil Basayev, Arbi Barayev, Ruslan Gelayev, and the Jordanian citizen Khattab, known for his cruelty in the first Chechen war—were all still alive (Barayev and Khattab were reported to be killed much later in 2002). Moscow's goal in the war in Chechnya—the rooting out of terrorism and terrorists—had not been attained.[1]

Moreover, after some weakening, the resistance of the Chechen fighters grew stronger toward the end of 2000. New fighters, primarily young

134

Chechen men, were constantly joining the forces in the field. Even Chechens who had been neutral toward the federal army and were tired of the Chechen field commanders and the continuing violence—the Chechens who had pinned their hopes for a peaceful life on the federal forces—were gradually moving toward support of the separatists as Russia's mass bombing of the civilian population killed their families and friends.

In the summer of 2000, Moscow was showing signs of confusion over Chechnya, and Russians—both the military and civilians—were feeling the strain after nearly a year of fighting. Even the proponents of a military solution to the Chechen problem were forced to admit that the government was at a dead end in Chechnya. The antiwar sentiments widespread among Russians during the first Chechen war were not a problem for the regime with this second conflict; a significant percentage of Russians was still favorably disposed toward Putin. But war fatigue was setting in.

In late August, 50 percent of those polled commented in exasperation that there was no end in sight to the war, while 41 percent pointed to the heavy losses in the federal army and 26 percent to the losses among civilians in Chechnya. Half still felt that military action must be continued and that there was no other way out (only 39 percent wanted negotiations with the Chechens, and 11 percent had no opinion).[2] These data show that a large segment of Russian society was still prepared to put up with the war in the summer of 2000. But the sense of pointlessness, exhaustion, and war weariness was growing.

The Russian army had occupied almost the entire territory of Chechnya, and the problem of what was to be done now was becoming much more pressing. A partisan war had broken out in the troubled republic. The Kremlin did not know how to fight guerrillas. It wasn't clear who was a fighter and who a peaceful resident. During the day, the Chechens led ordinary lives; but at night, they took up arms and shot at federal soldiers and laid landmines along the roads. Children became combatants in this "landmine war," often because the separatists paid for each mine laid and each Russian armored vehicle destroyed, and the children and their families needed the money.

Russia had returned to 1996, when questions about civil resistance first arose. Federal forces did not find answers then. Yeltsin severed the

Chechen knot before the presidential election of 1996, accepting peace with the separatists and Chechnya's de facto independence. That peace meant defeat for Russia.

This time around, the problems in settling the war were compounded. Distrust between the federal authorities and the Chechens had only increased since the first conflict, which reduced the chances for peaceful negotiations. Nor could Moscow leave Chechnya. Russia's self-image had been tarnished, and few Russians were prepared to accept a new military failure. The fear was that the army would rebel before being forced to leave Chechnya ignominiously. Besides, Chechnya was not ready to build an independent state. If Russian troops left Chechnya, the field commanders—the same warlords who enriched themselves trading in hostages, drug trafficking, and selling arms—would take charge again as they had done after the first war. And the leaders then would not be the moderates like Chechen president Aslan Maskhadov but more intransigent people like Basayev and Khattab. The bandit raids into Russian territory, kidnappings, and Chechnya's disintegration into chaos would continue. But Russia could not win in Chechnya either. So at this point in history, Russia and the breakaway Chechen republic were caught in a situation with no exit.

In the meantime, normal life in Chechnya was almost impossible amid the charred and bombed buildings, abandoned military hardware at the side of the road, and people burdened with their few possessions slogging through the mud. Children were hungry and dirty, adults gaunt. Everyone was physically ailing and in need of psychological support. Journalist Anna Politkovskaya reported from the former Chechen capital Grozny after it had been bombed: "Grozny is a living hell. It is another world, some dreadful Hades you reach through the Looking Glass. There is no living civilization among the ruins—apart from the people themselves."[3]

Refugee camps in the neighboring republic of Ingushetia sheltered tens of thousands of families that had no hope of ever going home, for their homes were gone. These people had lived through two wars in six years and might never get back to normal life. In the meantime, Russia was barely handling its own problems and had no money, no compassion, no patience for rebellious Chechens. The Russian budget for 2001 included no aid to Chechnya. The only things Moscow could offer

Chechnya were isolation and oblivion, but only under the control of its troops, whom the Chechens regarded as occupiers.

The Chechens (and they were not alone) began to believe that the Russian authorities, at least the military authorities, simply did not want to end the war. "Many episodes evinced the army's unwillingness to complete a total destruction of the Chechen fighting units," said Ruslan Khasbulatov, a Chechen and a former speaker of the Russian parliament. "Apparently, somewhere in military headquarters, someone decided that continuing the war was useful." As Khasbulatov explained it, the war gave the generals constant promotion up the career ladder, financing for the military and special services, personal wealth, and growth of the power structure's political role in society.[4]

Khasbulatov seemed to be right—some of the top brass were definitely interested in continuing this war, which brought them material well-being and raised their political significance.[5] The death of enlisted men and junior officers did not worry the military and political leadership. People began to ask why, with the full power of the army deployed against them, the separatist warlords were still at large and moving freely around Chechnya—and also to ask where the rebels were getting their most advanced arms. Many called this very strange war a "contract" war, suspecting that there were secret deals between the Russian military and the separatists.

Despite all the obvious questions, Russian society still accepted, albeit already with growing resentment, that Chechnya was turning into a round-the-clock slaughterhouse. After all, this was taking place on the periphery, far from Russia's center, and people—worn out by their own problems, weary, and busy—got used to the constant bloodshed. Official Moscow stopped publishing information on the dead and wounded and tried to move Chechnya to the back burner. The army attempted to avoid responsibility for Chechnya, shifting the burden onto the internal troops, the militia. The militia said that it could not fight in Chechnya, and in fact it was not prepared for military action. In the meantime, a new generation of Chechens grew up, one that had known nothing but war, was trained to do nothing, and thought of nothing but revenge against the Russians. Those youngsters were more and more leaning toward radical Islam—Wahhabism and jihad, the "sacred war" with Russia, was becoming their life goal.

And even with the harsh controls the military placed on information coming out of Chechnya, the world was still finding out what was going on there. The face of the war was dreadful. Hundreds of Russian soldiers and Chechens alike were dying, often young boys who had not yet started living. The number of Russian cities and towns to which the dead were returned in zinc coffins from Chechnya was growing. Thousands of Chechen women were wearing black as a sign of mourning for their dead relatives. The press was also printing occasional stories about the Russian military's abuses against civilians in Chechnya, about arrests of people whose guilt was not proved but who were kept in special camps, about so-called cleansings—actions in the course of which soldiers looted Chechen property and often executed young men suspected of ties with the separatists. The Russian army acquired the virus of cruelty, and that virus could become contagious. The Russian occupation of Chechnya was triggering the blind and cruel vengeance of the separatists.

Putin clearly did not know what to do with Chechnya. He tried to distance himself from the war so that everyone would forget that it was this "antiterrorist operation" that had brought him to power. He sought opportunities to share responsibility for what was going on in Chechnya with loyal Chechens. There were very few to be found. The new Chechen leaders he appointed, like the new head of the Chechen administration, Akhmad Kadyrov, had participated in military action against the federal army or were suspected of corruption; they were not trustworthy. But there was no choice. Putin refused to negotiate with Chechen president Maskhadov. The latter had lost his former influence. But in comparison with the other separatist leaders, he had two important qualities: The Chechens had elected him their president, and his legitimacy had been conferred by Yeltsin, who as Russian president had negotiated with him.

The newspaper *Moskovskie novosti* ran an interview with Maskhadov on November 21, 2000. The editors took a risk offering their pages to him; the Kremlin might do more than chastise them for the decision. Maskhadov told the interviewer, "As a military man I can say: An army cannot stand, it must either attack, or defend itself, or retreat. When an army as large as that stops, it falls apart." And he was right—the Russian army, having lost its goal in Chechnya, without a clear and visible enemy, had started to fall apart. Maskhadov suggested that Yeltsin play intermediary in peace negotiations. But the time was not yet ripe for negotiations—the team in the Kremlin continued to talk of victory. And even if Putin understood by then that there could be no victory in Chechnya, entering into talks with Maskhadov meant returning to square one, and that was tantamount to an admission of defeat. Putin could not do that under any circumstances—at least not yet, even with the steady increase in losses and because of the steady increase in losses.

There had been a breakthrough in Russian attitudes toward Chechnya since the beginning of the year. In October 2000, for the first time during the second war, there were more opponents of the war than proponents. Only 25 percent felt that Putin was handling the Chechen problem successfully, and 36 percent didn't think Russia was having any success in Chechnya (18 percent felt that Moscow didn't know how to bring order to Chechnya).[6]

If Russian troops suffered major losses, only 34 percent of Russians said they wanted military action to continue, and 54 percent demanded negotiations. A growing number felt that war was beneficial for both the Chechen fighters and the Russian authorities. Fifty percent of those polled said so, and a significant 10 percent went so far as to say that Russia's leaders were involved in a conspiracy with the rebel leaders. This was serious. If the dissatisfaction with Chechnya was added to the other problems in Russia, the social problems and frustrations above all, Putin would have a hard time of it. That was enough to make the Kremlin worry.

Against the backdrop of the sad situation in Chechnya, the president and the still-new team in the Kremlin could take consolation in the painless passage of the budget—the first peaceful procedure in the history of relations between executive and legislature in postcommunist Russia. Under Yeltsin, discussion of the budget was always tortuous. The Duma tried to prove its independence then, because it had few other opportunities to flex its muscles. The Kremlin was forced to make concessions and even bribe entire parliamentary factions to guarantee passage of the budget bill. As a result, the budget was usually bloated and unrealistic. The government never even thought about following it. But this time around, the wheeling and dealing were minimal. The Duma approved almost every government proposal on the budget; the deputies and interest groups behind them did not dare argue or try to cut deals with the new president.

Mikhail Kasyanov's cabinet proposed to the parliament a truly revolutionary budget for 2001. The new budget apportioned 60 percent of tax revenues to the center and 40 percent to the regions. The money going to the donor regions (as was stated above, these are regions that contribute more to the federal budget than they get from it) was slashed by almost a third. Naturally, these regions were unhappy, but their feelings counted for little in Moscow. In addition, a serious problem for the localities could arise in the new year. Because the government had squeezed everything that it could out of its budget, there was no longer any guarantee that local authorities would have enough money for the social sphere, education, and health care, which were local responsibilities. Federal officials must have hoped that they would have a better chance of solving all of Russia's problems if they distributed funds from the center, as had been done in the Soviet Union.

No one appeared worried because the budget had a "hole" of about 8 percent of its total, which indicated that the government had hopes of additional revenue. But it was not clear where those funds were expected to come from. The government hoped to borrow about $5.3 billion from the International Monetary Fund and the World Bank to partially fill the "hole." But there were no guarantees that that loan would be granted. The Paris Club of creditor countries had been informed that Moscow had allocated only $5.3 billion to service its debt to the club in 2001, rather than the $14.5 billion it actually owed. Kasyanov was unilaterally restructuring the debt to the Paris Club without conferring with the members that had loaned Russia the money.[7] The cabinet could not have done it without Putin's blessing.

The budget was approved just before year's end. For the first time, Grigory Yavlinsky's Yabloko movement, which had always voted against government budget proposals, voted to approve this one. Putin could feel triumphant that the government and the Duma had begun working in harmony, as if part of the same organism. In the future, the executive branch would have no problems getting the budget through the lower chamber of the parliament; from now on, the branches of power in Putin's Russia had no source of disagreement. The unwavering obedience of the Duma was useful when it was indeed used by the government to pass reforms—but even in that case, the country needed an independent parliament to provide an evaluation of the legislation. There was no guarantee that the semiauthoritarian executive power in Russia would always propose reform solutions.

Gradually, things seemed to quiet down on the political scene, at least in Moscow, and the Kremlin dream was to finish the last year of the century peacefully. In late November, however, a new scandal broke out in Moscow. Andrei Illarionov, the president's economic adviser, suddenly launched an attack on the Kasyanov government, in his numerous interviews and public presentations accusing the cabinet of failing to take advantage of a unique economic opportunity for advancing reform.

And in fact, the economic results for the year 2000 were the best in Russia in the past quarter-century.[8] But instead of using the economic stabilization as a foundation for structural transformation, the government remained astonishingly complacent. "The intoxicating air of the unexpected well-being that has befallen Russia has played a nasty trick," Illarionov concluded. "The legislative and executive branches began dividing up additional revenues that are not related to the effectiveness of the economy."

Illarionov's comments were only the beginning; by signaling to the Russian political and intellectual community that the government was not a sacred cow, they encouraged criticism to fly on all sides. Some analysts warned that Russia was facing a possible shock in the economy. Some spoke of the inevitability of a repeat of the 1998 financial crisis.[9]

The lack of a clear economic policy and the cabinet's uncertainty had actually been evident earlier. It was apparent that neither the prime minister nor his team intended to undertake any decisive actions to reform the economy. Kasyanov avoided all responsibility; keeping his job seemed to be his lone goal. During 2000, only one really important law was approved: the flat income tax of 13 percent. But the indecisiveness of the government was due not only to Kasyanov's weakness. The Russian government was the president's cabinet, and only the president could set the tone of its activity.

The sudden attack on the government by presidential adviser Illarionov could be interpreted as evidence that Putin had suddenly realized that he had lost a year and was now scurrying to find culprits for his cabinet's inactivity. In the polemic that ensued, no one asked the questions, Where had the president been all that time, and what had he been thinking?

In the meantime, Illarionov created a new sensation. In late December, he blasted Anatoly Chubais—now head of RAO UES, Russia's electrical utility—charging him with a criminal restructuring of UES similar to the notorious, widely criticized "shares-for-loans" privatization scheme in 1996. As a result, Chubais's reform was temporarily halted. Later, after much hesitation, in the fall of 2002 Putin decided to go ahead with the UES reform and then stopped and hesitated again.

The situation—with criticism of the cabinet as a whole and criticism of Chubais's reform in particular—highlighted Putin's management style. The president allowed passions to flare up in his entourage. He gave each participant in the fight a chance to speak, and he did not defend any of them, watching the emotions and arguments from above. Outwardly, such a style may seem effective because it creates the opportunity for discussion and a clash of views. However, there was something about it that suggested that this president allowed passions to burn only because he did not know which side to choose. In other words, the openness and the apparent pluralism of views hid indecisiveness.

Moreover, it was noticeable that Putin often allowed these dogfights and squabbles to take place in his absence, which made it possible for him to distance himself from unwelcome problems once they had been aired. In the course of the debates, he promised his support to all the opponents, and everyone was sure that he had the president's backing. That was further proof of his indecision and wavering, his failure to establish a position, make a final choice, and pursue it.

Thus, at the end of 2000 it seemed that the Kremlin had not yet decided whether it should take on further economic reforms, and if so, which ones. Rows in the liberal camp between Illarionov and Chubais were disquieting. If the liberals on the president's team couldn't come to terms, how could any agreement between competing interest groups in his entourage be expected? And because the president's team was split more widely, consensus as to future development within society was hardly plausible.

The conflicts in the president's entourage also suggested that the administration, having quickly taken control of the main levers of power, was slowing down because it did not know what to do next. The struggle for portfolios and spheres of influence resumed.

Meanwhile, some substantial economic issues had to be resolved. In December 2000, German Gref, one of Putin's closest allies, admitted that in 2003 Russia would not be able to pay its foreign debts and declared that a restructuring of the Paris Club debt was urgently needed. Russia's debt to the club stood at $48 billion, and in 2003 the payments would be $17.5 billion, which could amount to as much as half the budget. That problem had been looming for a long time. What was not obvious was why the government only realized it at the end of the year. At the end of 2002, Russian authorities were already more optimistic about Russia's ability to pay its Paris Club debt. But again, everything depended on world oil prices, because oil revenues continued to be the major source of the Russian budget.

Perhaps the relative affluence of 2000 had a lulling effect on the Kremlin, making officials think that they could go on for a long time without doing anything except using up the gold and hard currency reserves. When they finally comprehended the coming challenges, they became bewildered and descended to blaming one another or shifted to a gloomy prognosis.

The behavior of the government was understandable—it was waiting for instructions from the president. That is how Russian power is programmed: Follow the one above you. Yeltsin had allowed some degree of independence and put up with the various influence groups, with a pluralism of views, and in the end even with chaos. But Putin made it clear from the start that he would not accept any movement outside the lines and that he demanded strict subordination from his lieutenants. But he was never quick enough to draw the lines, and sometimes he simply didn't know where they should be drawn because he had not decided on his positions. That justified the state apparatus in doing nothing.

Instead of speaking on the controversial economic prospects and establishing his own standpoint, Putin turned to simpler things, apparently hoping that they would not provoke emotional conflicts within society. He asked the Duma to extend its session until the deputies approved a package of new state symbols. The president evidently had decided that the country could get by without a clear strategy for economic development but absolutely must have a new seal and anthem to enter the new millennium. For the seal of the new Russia, Putin proposed the tsarist double-headed eagle, which would symbolize the succession from the tsarist empire. The Soviet anthem, originally approved by Stalin, would signify the ties to the communist period.

Yet another symbol, the tricolor flag revived by Yeltsin, was to represent the noncommunist period. The tricolor had been introduced in tsarist Russia, and the White Guards flew it when they fought the Bolsheviks in the Civil War in 1918–1920. During World War II, the tricolor was taken up by the army of General Andrei Vlasov, who was allied with Nazi Germany against the Soviet Union. Nor did President Putin forget the red flag that had symbolized the USSR—it was proposed as the flag of the Russian army. With this combination of symbols representing all the stages of Russian history, Putin proposed to show the ties of time and to give tangible form to Russia's glorious heritage. Russia would enter the twenty-first century under the banner of absurdity in its symbols.

The melding of symbols of schism and mutual hatred with a symbol of the Soviet empire was viewed by many as a mockery of history or the product of a lack of understanding of that history. Some even considered it a provocation, this attempt to unite the nation on the basis of irritants.

The president's thinking on the issue was more straightforward. My hunch is that the package was Putin's own idea, not something put together by his councilors, and that it reflected his own views. For Putin, a strong state could not exist without symbols approved by everyone. It was very important that the populace rise each morning to an anthem that inspired energy and optimism and that state buildings fly the flag of Russia proudly. It goes without saying that Putin was sincere in wanting a consolidation of society, and he apparently dreamed of becoming the leader of Russia's unification. He must have truly believed that a return to the symbols of tsarism and communism would put an end to the arduous debates that were tearing the country apart: What is the new Russia?

What should Russia take from its past and what should it reject? He wanted to bring into the new mainstream the people nostalgic for Soviet times—and there were still many of them.

Putin himself must have had at least a touch of that nostalgia, for it was clear that, personally, he liked the Soviet anthem. He did not take into account that there were people in Russia for whom a return to the past was unthinkable because it held not joy but tremendous suffering and tragedy. With his insensitivity and his obtuseness, the president gave new life to old divisive passions and reopened old wounds. He precipitated another clash between the people who wanted to obliterate the memory of the Soviet era, the deaths of millions in the Gulag, and those who continued to be proud of that period.

Russia fell into debate once again. The endless, repetitive, emotional arguments between friends and even strangers over the symbols showed how difficult it is to unite a country that has been through the fire for years and is still undergoing radical change, how intransigent were the interests of different groups—liberals, nationalists, left-oriented people— and how these groups refused to listen to one another.

The main irritant for the liberal segments of society was the Soviet anthem, whose heroic music by Alexander Alexandrov was perceived as the symbol of communism and the Soviet empire. Putin had not expected the notion of reinstating a Soviet song to cause such a storm. When the protests began, he started justifying himself with a certain ill-at-ease tone. "Let's not forget that in this case we are talking about the majority of the people," he said, referring to the results of polls on the symbols. The argument reminded many of Soviet times, when the leaders justified their actions by reference to the majority.[10] Putin humbly, albeit with hidden irony, added, covering himself, "I do allow that the people and I could be mistaken."

The long-silent Yeltsin spoke out. The former president gave a special interview in which he declared, "I am categorically against reinstating the USSR anthem as the state one."[11] But Putin, quite consciously, was appealing to that portion of society that yearned for some revival of Russia's might and glory in the Soviet style. Those were people for whom Putin felt an affinity. At least at the moment, they were his true base, not pro-Western intellectuals and human rights activists, and not anticommunists like Yeltsin. He would not disappoint his staunch loyalists and show weakness to his liberal opponents by backing down on the symbols.

In a December 8 vote in the State Duma, 381 of 450 deputies approved the change to the Soviet anthem. The white, blue, and red flag got 342 votes, and the imperial double-headed eagle 341. It was to be expected. The Duma continued to be faithful to the new president, and it approved everything he proposed; the liberal factions were firmly against Putin's symbols, but they were prevented from speaking on the issue in the parliament. The law making the symbols official included a provision requiring people to stand during the anthem. The joke went, "If you don't stand up on time, you'll do time."

A few days later, the Federation Council also approved Putin's symbols for Russia. The senators had the anthem—familiar for so long, now to become familiar again—played. Everyone obediently jumped up when the Stalin-approved music began, except for Nikolai Fedorov, president of Chuvashia, who remained in his seat. This was a harbinger of what was to come: At every official function, some would stand and others would remain seated or pretend to be tying their shoelaces. At least for the foreseeable future, it would be a constant reminder of the schism in Russian society and of the fact that the new president had encouraged it.

Journalists continued to mock the symbols the president had proposed. "He is the president of our mothers and fathers," they joked, because his choice of state symbols seemed to demonstrate that the past was more important to him than the future. Russia's leader was giving yesterday's answers to today's questions. That Russia was entering the new millennium to the strains of the Soviet anthem created a dark premonition in some people's minds.

Putin's choice of the Soviet anthem, particularly over Yeltsin's protests, also demonstrated that the president was moving away from the influence of Yeltsin and his political circle. His open disagreement with his predecessor on this subject was almost a challenge to the old ruling corporation. But it would be premature to conclude that Putin was now free of all obligations to those who had put him where he was.

Almost simultaneously, also in December 2000, another event transpired that showed Putin still felt himself under at least some obligation to the Yeltsin entourage. Despite the large amount of material turned over to it by Swiss prosecutors, the Russian prosecutor's office decided to drop the case of embezzlement by Yeltsin's presidential office, which allegedly involved the president's family. After several years of stories on the front page of Russian newspapers, "Kremlingate" was declared closed due to "insufficient evidence."

The Russian prosecutors explained that the piles of bank documents from Switzerland could not be used as evidence in a Russian court. They were copies, and not very clear ones, whereas Russian justice works only with originals. Of course, the prosecutors could have gone to Switzerland, compared the copies with the originals, made clear duplicate copies, and had them notarized if they themselves were not notaries. Instead, the prosecutors decided to shut down the Kremlingate investigation. One more scandal was hushed up, and the Yeltsin family and the high-ranking officials who fed at the same trough could sleep peacefully again. Kremlingate could never have been closed without direct orders from the Kremlin's current occupants. Clearly, the old Yeltsin circle still had influence, and Putin still felt an obligation to it.

In the meantime, the new president developed a taste for world travel. He seemed to regard his international trips as an important element in the reestablishment of Russia's prestige. Moreover, the experience—the receptions at the highest levels, spending time with global elites—seemed to give him a real sense of power. Other leaders must have similar reactions, because so many of them take up foreign policy once in office. And perhaps Putin felt that international problems were simpler to solve than domestic ones.

The Russian president flew across oceans, visiting several countries per trip. He flew from hot climes to cold and vice versa. His physical stamina was astounding. But he was young and his sports background helped; he was in excellent shape and had a lot of endurance (unlike Yeltsin). Vladimir Vladimirovich learned the secret language of diplomacy and felt comfortable and on an equal footing with the other leaders at world summits. He spoke logically and impressed people with his memory. A quick learner, he was turning into a worthy partner.

A partial list of Putin's travels in 2000 would include Belarus, Brunei, Canada, China, Cuba, France, Germany, India, Japan, Libya, Mongolia, North Korea, Turkey, and Ukraine. The president managed to use up his budget for international travel, and he had to seek additional funding.

That same year, a Russian foreign policy concept paper was finally developed by the Foreign Affairs Ministry. The document said quite a few reasonable things, among them that the country must drop its idée fixe of a global presence and think about promoting its economic interests. It stressed the need for improving relations with neighbors in the Commonwealth of Independent States and Europe. But at the same time, the draft incorporated thoughts that seemed to come from Cold War documents—for instance, that Russia was surrounded by hostile forces that had to be fought.

The concept paper created the impression that it was the product of a struggle between two groups, one concerned with the new image of Russia and one seeking a return to the days of confrontation with the West. The same duality could be discerned in Putin. On one hand, he announced, "We must rid ourselves of imperial ambitions." On the other hand, a painful reaction on the part of the Kremlin to the independent policies of Azerbaijan, Georgia, and Ukraine indicated that imperial moods, though weakened and less apparent, were still alive and that superpower claims were still being asserted by the Russian ruling team.

The character and frequency of Putin's contacts with Europeans evinced Moscow's desire to make relations with Western Europe the most important element of its foreign policy. Moscow clearly needed to activate contacts with European states, especially after Yeltsin, for whom no other countries besides the United States existed. Russia was genuinely interested in promoting economic ties with Europe. It had its reasons; trade between Russia and the European Union in 2000–2001 already constituted 48 percent of Russia's total trade, whereas trade with the United States made up only 5.5 to 6 percent. But one had the feeling that Putin's European orientation was to some extent a reaction to the growing coolness in United States–Russia relations.

The warmth of the personal relationship developing between Putin and several European leaders, particularly Tony Blair of the United Kingdom and Gerhard Schröder of Germany, was not, however, enough to smooth away the problems arising in Moscow's relations with the Council of Europe and its Parliamentary Assembly. Russia lost the right to vote in the Council of Europe because of its handling of the "antiterrorist operation" in Chechnya (this right was returned to Russia in 2001 after a delegation from the council visited Chechnya and concluded that Russian policy there was becoming more civilized). Nor was Moscow on good terms with the Organization for Cooperation and Security in Europe (OCSE), which Russia hoped to turn into a linchpin of European security in response to the strengthening of NATO. As a result, the Russian Foreign Ministry, unable to find a compromise with the Western countries on human rights issues, did not sign the OCSE declaration at the end of the year.

In addition to the European angle, Putin tried to restore Russia's ties with its allies from the Soviet period. That was the object of his trips to Cuba, Mongolia, and North Korea. In restoring torn ties with its former satellite countries, Moscow was not only after at least the partial restoration of Russia's world role. Economic motives were crucial: Moscow wanted to begin negotiations on the payment of old debts. Where it was impossible to get money back, Putin talked of being paid in raw materials and of an economic cooperation beneficial to Russia. The Russian president was introducing commercialization of foreign policy—a promising change on the international scene, where Russia had always been more interested in demonstrating its might, even when it meant losing economic benefits.

Moscow's attention to former allies from the Soviet period made Russian liberals wary and nationalists happy. The latter declared an end of Russia's pro-Western policies and a turn toward Asia.[12] But Putin clearly was not planning a break with the West. He applied the same method to foreign policy that he used at home—looking to each potential partner in turn, not tying himself permanently to anyone. It appeared that he wanted, with his diplomatic flurry, to remind the world about Russia after a lengthy period of foreign policy lethargy. In developing his international agenda, Russia's president definitely had some domestic priorities in mind, first of all an economic agenda. But at the same time, Putin's desire to move simultaneously in all directions created the impression that he still could not answer the question, Where does Russia belong? Or perhaps he postponed his answer for the time being.

Putin's activity on all international fronts only emphasized the cooler relations between Russia and the United States. In fact, they had begun to freeze during the Clinton–Yeltsin period. The sad irony is that it happened despite the fact that Bill Clinton was the first and so far the only U.S. leader who made Russia his foreign policy mission, who called for a "strategic alliance with Russian reform." Strobe Talbott, the deputy secretary of state during Clinton's presidency, gave an illuminating assessment of the United States–Russia relationship in the 1990s in his memoir *The Russia Hand*, revealing the hidden and dramatic clash of interests, hopes, and myths as a new era of this relationship took shape.[13]

By mid-1999, United States–Russia relations had come under considerable strain. Outwardly, the war in Kosovo and NATO enlargement had caused a major breach. The roots of bilateral discontent went much deeper, however. Both sides underestimated difficulties and constraints of Russia's transformation and of building normal ties when one state was at an unprecedented peak and the other in the process of a humiliating fall, especially when the two had been fierce rivals for so long and had been the symbols of alternative civilizations. Unrealistic hopes and an asymmetry of capabilities were serious sources of growing frustration in Russian–American relations. However, the United States had asymmetrical relations with other states that did not produce the same mutual dismay.

A strong belief among the Russian political class that a great-power role was the crucial consolidating factor in Russia, and the only way for Russia to survive as an entity, was the major cause of the growing rift between the United States and Russia. This belief was behind the stubbornness of Russian elites in pursuing the country's global ambitions, and their unhappiness with U.S. dominance and unwillingness to accept these plans. The Russian political class was not ready to redefine Russia's role in the world. Moscow still wanted to preserve the bilateral world order, with only one argument to support its pretensions: its nuclear arsenal.

In the field of security, the Clinton administration pursued a policy that Thomas Graham and Arnold Horelick described as "trading symbolism for substance."[14] It offered Moscow some concessions, such as incorporating it into the Group of Seven structure in exchange for withdrawing its troops from Eastern Europe and the Baltic Sea region. It also warded off a destructive Russian response to NATO enlargement. This policy not only helped the United States pursue its agenda but also softened Russia's transition to a more realistic international role. But in the end, the policy did not prevent the Russia–United States relationship from sliding into crisis. Symbolism and imitation partnership, which Russian elites considered to be hollow, only deepened Moscow's distrust of Washington.

In fact, the Clinton administration helped Russia manage superpower decline by assisting in resolving the security issues resulting from the collapse of the Soviet Union. But paradoxically, "superpower decline management" hardly could get support or even appreciation from Russian elites, who considered great-power status the only prerequisite of Russian statehood. Besides, the U.S. side did not always have the patience and time, and it lacked an understanding of Russian complexes, as was demonstrated by NATO enlargement, which brought such an emotional rejection in Russia.

Theoretically, Moscow and Washington could have worked it out under one condition: Russia's rejection of all claims to a superpower role and agreement to become a "normal" country that was part of Western civilization—that is, to become a new France. The bargain would also include Russia's voluntary acceptance of U.S. world hegemony. But all that seemed unlikely to happen at that time.

Because liberal democratic ideology had not become entrenched in Russia, in the 1990s great-power rhetoric remained—in the eyes of many representatives of the Russian political class—a powerful unifying factor, and no Russian leader could have held onto power without understanding that. Yeltsin, despite his deep-down pro-Western orientation, often thought that it was safe for him to play great-power advocate, which explains his zigzags in foreign policy. Keeping up the foreign policy and even the rhetoric of a superpower was doomed to be a major destabilizing factor in relations with the United States. Thus, the cooling down of the relationship between Moscow and Washington was inevitable.

The new people Putin brought into the Kremlin were sick of their country's weakness. They had been brought up believing in Russia's exceptionality and greatness. They wanted to be respected, and they wanted their country to be respected and taken into account again—and perhaps, if not feared as before, at least regarded with some wariness. The only foreign entity to which they wanted to prove something was the United States, because only in an equal relationship with it could Russia feel like a great power. However, the method of self-determination chosen by Russia's new ruling group in early 2000 was much like the old Soviet method—an exhibition of willful independence, even cockiness, a search for its own spheres of influence, an accent on what separates rather than what brings closer, and an attempt at blackmail in the threat of rapprochement with China.

The new team in the Kremlin took a series of steps to signal its coldness toward Washington. Putin indicated that he was not interested in developing a relationship with a U.S. lame-duck president but would wait to deal with Clinton's successor. When Putin and Clinton met in Moscow in June 2000, the Russian leader did not even pretend to demonstrate interest in strengthening a personal rapport with Clinton or in discussing serious issues. "It was no mystery what Putin's game was: He was waiting for Clinton's successor to be elected in five months before deciding how to cope with the United States and all its power, its demands and its reproaches. Putin had, in his own studied, cordial and oblique way, put U.S.–Russian relations on hold," wrote Talbott.[15]

One of the first signs of tougher Kremlin policy was the trial of the American businessman Edmond Pope, who was charged with espionage and attempting to buy blueprints of the Shkval, the Russian secret torpedo. More followed. At the tensest moment before the election in the United States, on November 3, Russian minister of foreign affairs Igor Ivanov informed the U.S. State Department that Russia would no longer abide by the Gore–Chernomyrdin agreement limiting Russian shipments of arms to Iran. This was a highly unpleasant gift to the Democrats at a point when presidential candidate Al Gore was defending himself against charges of secret deals with the Russians and tacit acquiescence in Russian corruption.[16] An extreme example of the new approach toward Washington was the attempt by the Russian military to lay the blame for the loss of the submarine *Kursk* on the United States.

Yet another example of the change in relations was the flight of Russian jets over the U.S. aircraft carrier *Kitty Hawk* in November 2000.

Such flyovers had not been carried out by Americans or Russians since the end of the Cold War. Putin's team in the Kremlin apparently wanted the Russian military to send the United States a message: "Beware, we are still strong and can create trouble for you!" The pilots were decorated for flying over the American ship.

The displays of arrogant self-confidence and public reminders that the love and hugs were over were a game aimed at the Russian man on the street and anti-Western elites, who faulted Yeltsin for being too friendly with American leaders. The anti-Americanism of Russian political elites had been in evidence before. But while it was veiled in Yeltsin's day, now it was mandatory for entrée into the political class. Like his predecessor, the new president of Russia enjoyed entering the circle of the "Group of Eight" and shaking hands with the U.S. leader. But at the same time, the Russian press—even the liberal papers—did not miss an opportunity to take digs at the Americans with the silent approval of some of the Kremlin's inhabitants.

Russian observer Andrei Piontkovsky hit the mark when he wrote in the December 7, 2000, *Obshchaya gazeta* about "the manic depression" syndrome of Russian elites expressing itself in relations with Washington. This syndrome could be seen on the one hand in the servility of some representatives of the Russian ruling class toward Washington. They flocked to the U.S. capital to meet with officials, speaking pleasantly, smiling radiantly, and giving them slaps on the back in the American manner. But back in Moscow, they turned on the United States. They had to keep up their image as statists, great-power advocates, for it was the fashion now. This hypocrisy concealed seemingly incompatible feelings: humiliation and impudence, a desire for revenge, and a longing to be accepted as equals.

The surge of anti-Americanism can hardly be said to have been instigated by the Russian president, who behaved in an extremely reticent and cautious way. But he never did anything to stop the mood either. It looked as if Putin was still forming his understanding of Russia's identity and Russian goals in the foreign policy field, and assessing the West and the United States and their intentions toward Russia. He apparently had worked out his own general orientation during his years in Saint Petersburg, when he had had many successful business contacts with the West. But after his unexpected ascendancy to the Kremlin, he had to

make sure his orientation would not endanger his power, and he preferred to wait and see. Meanwhile, the political class took Putin's caution
as his approval of a more active anti-American stance. In Russia, it is
always safer to play on anti-Western feelings than on love of the West.

But Washington was not interested in Russia. In the autumn of 2000,
the United States was having trouble electing a president. The electoral
endgame gave rise to jokes in the Russian establishment that boiled down
to one thing: One has to know how to control the election outcome.
Even Putin made a remark, with a sarcastic smile, about U.S. democracy
not being able to give the American people their new leader quickly. The
torturous process of U.S. elections strengthened the conviction of the
Russian ruling class that the Russian mechanism of appointing the president and using administrative resources to get him elected was much
more convenient and dependable.

When it became clear that the United States had elected Republican
George W. Bush, Russian elites first sighed in relief. They had decided that
Republicans in the White House would be better for Russia than
Democrats. The conclusion was based on three premises. First, Moscow was
disillusioned with Clinton, who despite his good intentions toward Russia
did little to help Russian reform, in the opinion of Russian politicians. The
Russian ruling class had expected a new Marshall Plan—similar to the one
the United States implemented in Europe after World War II—in gratitude
to Russia for ending communism and the USSR. Those hopes were not
satisfied. Or to be exact, they were not fulfilled completely.[17]

Second, during Clinton's presidency, Russia's international weight and
influence continued to diminish, intensifying the asymmetry between the
United States and Russia. Russian elites—unwilling to accept that imbal-
ance, or to reconsider superpower ambitions and approach the world in a
more realistic way—regarded Washington with increasing suspicion and
irritation, accusing it of hegemonic plans and trying to weaken Russia.
Any attempt by the United States to pursue its interests was perceived as
directed against Russia, the continuation of a zero-sum game.

Third on their list of reasons to prefer Republicans in power in the

United States, Moscow observers recalled that under the Democrats John F. Kennedy and Jimmy Carter, relations between the United States and the Soviet Union were, in their view, rotten. In contrast, they praised the Republicans Richard Nixon, Ronald Reagan, and George H. W. Bush, who succeeded in establishing quite amicable relations with Soviet and Russian leaders. Obviously, human memory is selective; the Russian proponents of the Republicans had forgotten Nixon's toughness toward the Soviet Union and Reagan's early presidency with his hostility to the "evil empire."

What Russian elites disliked most about the Democrats was their desire to promote democracy and their concern for rights and freedoms. The new ruling team in the Kremlin did not want to be lectured, especially on democracy. In Moscow's perception, the Republicans traditionally were less given to interfering in the internal affairs of other countries and were ready to play balance-of-power games in which Russia still counted.

Moscow saw George W. Bush's election as the start of a new era in relations between Russia and the United States. Many in Russia viewed Bush as practically the American Putin. Bush and Putin were certain to like one another, analogy lovers reasoned. Both were starting out from square one, in politics and in their relationship.

Russian observers thought that both countries would play at geopolitics and enter into a dialogue on nuclear issues that Russian elites liked so much and that gave them a feeling of importance. Consequently, Russia would once again be regarded as a partner of the United States and thereby regain its superpower status. Kremlin strategists did not wish to see that Russia was no longer a priority for either Democrats or Republicans and that Washington was tired of Moscow and its constant mood swings and desire to be cuddled and cajoled. While under Clinton there had been a willingness to accommodate and soothe Moscow politicians, the new, harsher, and more pragmatic residents of the White House were not at all sentimental when it came to the Kremlin. Thus Moscow had to prepare for a more restrained, even cold, attitude on the part of the White House, which could always point to the difference in the two countries' capabilities.

Something else came between the two new presidents: U.S. plans for a national missile defense (NMD), which meant abrogation of the

Anti–Ballistic Missile Treaty that Russians viewed as a "cornerstone of nuclear stability." Almost the entire political class in Russia, including the liberals, felt that the U.S. plan for NMD would destroy the system of international security built over the years, in which Russia was an important element, and that is why it was totally unacceptable for Russia.

This stance of total rejection of NMD and refusal to seek a compromise with Washington threatened to embarrass Moscow if the United States went ahead with the unfurling of its nuclear umbrella. Russian foreign policy circles hoped to mobilize Europe and China against the U.S. plan. Clinton's refusal to push forward missile defense during his tenure was perceived in Moscow as the result of Russian pressure on the White House. And that perception was the basis for the Kremlin team's belief that the U.S. plan for NMD could be stopped by taking a hard line with the United States. That was the prevailing mood in Moscow.

Putin deserves credit for making a distinction between a bow in the direction of Russian complexes, which he performed, and not on one occasion only, and a sober understanding of the new international situation and Russia's role in it, which he demonstrated with his cautious policy at the end of 2000. He probably understood that the United States was no longer the main threat to Russia's security. But it was still hard for him to rise above the ambitions and neuroses of the elites, and at that point he had to follow their lead, though with increasing restraint.

Overall, 2000 was not an easy year, either for Russia or for its president. It saw the sinking of the *Kursk*. The war in Chechnya went on all year, taking lives every week. Nevertheless, despite those tragedies, public optimism was surprisingly high. For many Russians, 2000 was the least difficult of recent years. Typically, it was the least difficult for people in the provinces, the elderly, and the poor—those who lived simple lives. These people had begun getting their salaries and pension payments regularly under Putin, and that was enough to lead them to consider the year a success.

For the intelligentsia, people who lived in large cities, and the politicized segment of society, 2000 was much harder than 1999. Some of these people were more disappointed by what the new president did on the political scene, for they had expected more than their regular wages from him; they had expected vision and a strong sense of responsibility. Others had no hope from the beginning, having been suspicious of Putin; now, watching the president's ambiguousness, they felt that their suspicions were justified.

Of Russians polled on the year 2000, 39 percent had higher hopes than the year before (when the figure was 29 percent); 30 percent felt disappointment (the same as in 1999); and 16 percent felt fear (slightly down from the 18 percent in 1999). Another 13 percent felt confused (compared with 17 percent in 1999), and 20 percent felt angry (compared with 23 percent in 1999). The year 2000 had been calmer for Russia and could be characterized with the words of sociologist Yuri Levada: "A bit less fear and a bit more hope."[18]

But 2000 could not be considered a problem-free year for Putin, first as prime minister and acting president, then as the elected president. By the year's end, it was obvious that the Russian public considered the war in Chechnya a failure—49 percent called the president's actions there unsuccessful, as opposed to 24 percent at the beginning of the year. But there were no antiwar demonstrations or other actions in Russia. Society seemed to remain aloof from the war, waiting it out. People pretended that the events in Chechnya and the continual losses had nothing to do with them.

Gradually, Russians began judging Putin's presidency more severely. At the close of 2000, 45 percent felt that he was handling his responsibilities well, and 48 percent felt that he was not successful. The president's activity in the economic sphere was considered unsuccessful by 65 percent, whereas on the task of defending democracy, 53 percent considered him unsuccessful. In only one sphere did the majority (63 versus 28 percent) believe that the president was successful: international affairs. The respondents did not have a clear understanding of what his foreign policy actions meant; it was more that they were hypnotized by his constant international trips.

Although the majority did not consider the president's actions successful, his administration as a whole garnered the approval of 68 percent of respondents, and 40 percent were prepared to vote for him as president again. However, those data could not have made the president feel very optimistic. He still had support, but the majority expected nothing positive from his presidency. People were supporting him primarily because there was no alternative to him in the Russian political arena.

President Putin had managed to consolidate all the basic levers of power in his hands. He had managed to neutralize all the groups of influence that had been powerful under Yeltsin. He had struck a blow against the oligarchs and forced them to give up political ambitions. But to be perfectly objective, the oligarchy as a class had been weakened in Russia by the financial crisis of 1998, and it never recovered as a political force from that blow. The power of the regional elites had been undermined as well; the Kremlin demonstrated that it could easily get rid of regional leaders it did not like. And finally, political opposition had disappeared almost entirely. The State Duma was fully dependent on the Kremlin. What we saw was an almost tranquil idyll. The distribution of power had changed radically. Politicians were no longer divided into democrats and communists. Now the demarcation line was who was pro-Putin and who was against. There were very few of the latter, or they were lying very low.

How did the new Kremlin boss manage in such a short time and without a visible struggle to destroy the numerous "political flowers" that had bloomed under Yeltsin and spoiled his life? The answer was rather simple: Society still retained a fear of authority. Yeltsin was not feared, especially at the end of his term. Moreover, he was not considered rancorous or vengeful. He was treated like an old, sick bear who could be teased a bit and not taken seriously.

The second Russian president, however, elicited other feelings. He was not very well known, and people did not know where he drew the line or whether he had *any* lines on the use of power—including coercion. So even a slight criticism from the authorities, a glance or nod from the president, was enough to send people scurrying in toadying fashion.

It turned out that the central authorities in Russia, first among them the president, still had enormous power. Putin was the leader with administrative and coercive resources, with support within the political class. There was no alternative to him at the time. He was power personified. Those in opposition had no guarantee of surviving and existing or even raising their voices—their only option was vegetating on the margins of political life. One may object that Yeltsin also had administrative resources.

But the first Russian president could never get utter support and obedience. He had to constantly fight with the Duma, the Federation Council, the opposition; he had to bear attacks in the press and the mockery of opponents. In the end, he was despised and ignored.

Why did the nondescript, shallow-looking Putin manage to bend to his will the political scene in Russia, where the powerful and charismatic Yeltsin had failed? Besides fear of power and the traditional servility of the political class and society, there was exhaustion. Yeltsin ruled in a period of social upheaval, and when the upward surge ended, society continued living in disorder. This was a time of political whirlpools and struggle, fragmentation and pluralism, freedoms and spontaneity. Yeltsin whipped up that frenzy himself and extended the revolutionary cycle artificially, not knowing how to stabilize the situation. For Yeltsin, extending the revolution was a means of personal survival.

By the time Putin came along, it became clear just how tired and disenchanted society had become. Putin was possible because the masses wanted nothing but peace and order. Rocking the boat would no longer have the support of the people. Putin easily dealt with the chaos that had developed under Yeltsin, primarily because the majority of Russians wanted it dealt with. The main proponents of order were the "swamp" that bet on Putin and understood order to mean subordination to the leader. Putin was helped by the pendulum of development that had swung from the phase of disorder and liberalization to the phase of calming down and strengthening of conservative values. Putin behaved like the concentrated expression of the pendulum's movement.

Once he had consolidated all power in his hands, the president stopped at that. His obvious victories in 2000, besides building up his superpresidential regime or "verticality of authority," as it was called in Russia, were only two—the Duma's approval of the START-2 missile reduction treaty, and the new income tax code. This was practically the sum total of Putin's achievements for the year, despite extremely propitious circumstances, the likes of which Yeltsin had never enjoyed.

At first, Putin's frenzied activity—his constant peregrinations around the country and meetings with the most varied people, his continual appearances on television—created the impression of mobile, dynamic, even aggressive leadership. Gradually, though, many people began to perceive all that activity as mere bustle intended to create a simulacrum of governing. It looked at that moment as if the president followed the principle: "The movement is everything, the goal is nothing."

Putin had done almost nothing toward a breakthrough in liberal reform. Moreover, the end of 2000 revealed a loss of impulse in his presidency, a weakening of the energy of leadership. The question was repeated with increasing volume: Why did Putin want power—for the sake of the process or for reforms? Quite a few observers came to the conclusion that power had been a goal in itself for the young Russian leader.

Besides which, other things were gradually revealed. It turned out that not one of the Kremlin boss's actions had been brought to its logical conclusion. The oligarchs had been given a scare. But those who agreed to be faithful to the regime were granted almost total freedom to act and get rich. Only the most recalcitrant had been attacked. So Putin's anti-oligarch revolution stopped midway. The fusion of power and business was retained.

The governors were lined up in a row, like soldiers, and pacified. However, the Kremlin could not achieve its goals in the regions and obtain total obedience. Very quickly, the Kremlin had to begin doing what Yeltsin had always done: offer the governors deals and compromises.

Despite all the pressure from the Kremlin on the independent media, they continued to exist. As 2000 ended, NTV was still criticizing Putin. All attempts to imprison Gusinsky, the owner of Media-Most, and to wrest control over the media from him had led to nothing.

In other words, Vladimir Vladimirovich had managed to achieve impressive results in taming Russian politics. But it turned out that he was far from having politics on a leash. Russian society, outwardly giving the impression of being tamed, continued on its own way. The Putin team was using fear. As the president put it, he had only "shown the cudgel." For the nervous and easily frightened, that was enough. But there were others in society—those who decided to wait, to observe the regime, or not to give up. There were not many, but they existed. Losing his former aggressiveness and now encountering silent and still-invisible resistance, Putin the humble newcomer began hesitating more frequently.

Yeltsin had had his own dance—one step forward, two steps back. Putin continued dancing, taking a step forward, then stopping, sometimes even retreating; it was a halting, jerky dance. That did not mean he lacked the decisiveness to entirely break the dissatisfied elements in society and complete his construction of a "manageable democracy." Perhaps he was just biding his time and gathering his strength. But it is no less possible that he did not know what to do next. Perhaps the year 2000 was only a warm-up before the jump. But a jump in which direction?

The sources of Putin's power became clear. The first was high oil prices, which created economic stability and made possible the payment of wages and pensions. Journalists joked that though Putin was formally Yeltsin's heir, he was actually much closer to another leader—Leonid Brezhnev. It was in the period of Tsar Leonid that the USSR survived on high oil prices. As soon as prices fell, the Soviet economy collapsed like a house of cards.

The second source of Putin's power was his amazingly high approval ratings, which stayed high despite the emerging disillusionment with him among some social groups. But oil prices and ratings were too unstable to serve as bases for a presidency. At the end of 2000, oil prices were slowly coming down. As for Putin's ratings, he had become hostage to them. That was reflected in his policies; the president had to reject or postpone necessary but clearly unpopular actions, such as housing and utility reform, because they threatened to wreck his high ratings.

It looked as if the Kremlin started its day with an analysis of the president's ratings. If support was faltering in some social group, the Kremlin began working on it—"turning its face to it." The president suddenly began making speeches that would resonate with that audience. If he needed to flirt with the left, he began attacking oligarchs. If the liberals were unhappy, he turned to them, talking about market reforms. It was hard to avoid the feeling that the energies of the president and his team were being wasted on following the fluctuations in his ratings. As a result, there was no time or energy to set a general course.

Moreover, the president had become a hostage to his team, which had manipulated his rise. The team helped him win the elections. But keeping the election experts on at the Kremlin turned the president's administration into an endless election campaign.

After a year in power, Putin still had not answered the question about who he was. The question, posed by the journalists at the global summit of capitalist elites in Davos in the winter of 2000—"Who is Mr. Putin?"—had not lost its bite. Putin was still an amorphous political leader who constantly changed his contours, trying to appeal to all forces simultaneously. Artists who painted portraits of him complained that they couldn't "capture" him—he slipped away, he seemed inscrutable, and they could not find the defining features that former leaders had had. Paradoxically, on one hand, Russian society already knew a lot about its president and his goals. On the other, he was still a work in progress, and he often seemed to behave like a professional intelligence officer covering his tracks and hiding his true intentions. As a result, the president's image remained a blur.

Thus the most varied political forces continued to hope that Putin would end up on their side. The liberals hoped he would join them, and the left and statists felt he was much closer to them. "Who Mr. Putin is and how he pictures the future of Russia is still unknown," a reporter wrote in the December 26, 2000, *Kommersant-Vlast'*. "Just as much is known now as a year ago. And whether it is conscious or unconscious, Putin is not letting people find out."[19] That is to say, even as president, Putin behaved like an agent in enemy territory, letting no one learn his true intentions—if in fact he had any. Because of his unformed image and his political bartering with the main political forces—something for some, other things for others—he managed to preserve his power positions and social stability. At least for now.

Chapter 6

RUSSIA
TRANQUILIZED

Back to the kitchen. Society seeks calm. Russian Gaullism.
Who loves Russia more? Pogrom at NTV. Wax dummies.

The first year of Putin's presidency ended in the spring of 2001. Instead of the animation and chaos characteristic of Yeltsin's tenure, we saw a wintry political and intellectual landscape. Now there was not even a single influential political force independent of the Kremlin, or a single public group with a strong independent voice. Almost everyone left on the scene was playing—voluntarily or reluctantly—by rules set by the authorities. People who still tried to say what they thought, especially if it was to attack the Kremlin, had no guarantee of political survival, not because they were threatened but because nobody listened to them any longer; what they said or how they acted did not matter anymore—they did not have any impact on the political process.

Political actors had become nondescript and difficult to remember. The political and intellectual personalities who just recently had raised the tone and vitality of society—liberals, oligarchs, prominent journalists, former dissidents whose public appearances were impatiently anticipated—had vanished from the open scene or spoke only in hushed voices; they were faded versions of themselves. The last of the Mohicans, famous Soviet dissident writer Alexander Solzhenitsyn, was living in seclusion outside Moscow. When he made a rare appearance in the capital, he was regarded as if he were a museum exhibit. Politics and public discourse had grown shallow and petty, reduced to the level of kitchen chitchat. No one in sight could or dared think big.

Under Yeltsin, even in the final stage of his administration and despite his personal decline, life was on at full blast, albeit not always with an influence on politics and the regime. But now even the purely external fairgrounds bustle was gone. Russians seemed less interested in both politics and the future. Weariness and indifference dominated. The outward calm often hid emptiness or lack of ambition. People's aim was simply to survive and limp along, with no claim to anything more.

In other societies, this relaxation comes as a result of satiety and material security. In Russia, the descent from activity to indifference, the giving up on hopes and slide into living day to day, was the product of disillusionment and weariness. Russians now regarded further reforms as not necessarily a good thing, because they were afraid that any reform could only make things worse.

The shift from the struggle and striving of the Yeltsin period to apathy did not occur instantaneously with the beginning of the new presidency. Putin would never have been elected in an era of vibrancy and desire to renew life. He would never have appeared as a public figure when Russian politics called for charismatic personalities, vivid leaders with electrifying powers—when the search for a goal was on. Putin in the Kremlin now was the reflection of the exhaustion of revolutionary ardor and, for many, the loss of courage and perhaps a feeling of being at a dead end. Russia seemed to want nothing but peace and quiet, and Putin seemed to be the man who could produce it. The new president became the embodiment of muddling along. Or rather, he was forced to assume that role, which he definitely did not like, for he seemed to have had much higher aspirations for himself and Russia.

The language of power and of the elites changed. Just a few years earlier, everyone had spoken of reform, progress, renewal, modernization, and democracy. It had been impossible to talk in any other way. Those words, symbolic of a new life, had become popular in Gorbachev's day. In Yeltsin's, they were the entrée into the ranks of the elites, and the passwords to power. Now completely different words filled the air—stability, statehood, order, sovereignty, greatness, power, patriotism. The change in symbolic words and rhetoric in general signified the new content of politics.

Politicians who were remnants of the past still cluttered the stage, but for the most part they were political ghosts. Some were afraid of being reprimanded by the Kremlin. Others tried to appear independent, but did not know what issues to take a stand on, what position to choose, or how to protect their independence, their freedom of expression and action. They had not decided on what issues they could disagree or were allowed to disagree with the Kremlin.

The irony was that the ruling team did not have the strength to force its wishes on Russians. The president, contrary to expectations, soon appeared to be not an ironhanded man who was ready to force people to accept his policy. Society and the political class, ready to obey the authorities, met them halfway. Politicians lined up voluntarily, without even being told. Witness the people from Unity, the propresidential party, united by one impulse: a readiness to do whatever the Kremlin said. They surrounded Putin, looking into his eyes as if begging, "Tell us what to do and we'll do it, Master." Bold, decisive, thinking people were leaving the stage. The ones who remained and who continued to disobey, like human rights activist Sergei Kovalyov, were perceived as eccentric and quixotic; no one paid attention to them. They fell by the wayside of the new life, where subordination and servility were seen as confirmation of pragmatism and rationality. Anything else was idealism and stupidity.

What was going on was a consolidation of the last echelon of the Soviet *nomenklatura*. Time and political struggles had swept away the early echelons, and power now belonged to the backbenchers of the Soviet ruling class. These were men in their forties. During the Gorbachev thaw and the Yeltsin chaos, they had neither the enterprise nor the aggression to rise to the top. Perhaps they did not have the talent either. They were young and inexperienced. This echelon had the strength only to be in proximity to power, playing secondary and tertiary roles. They bided their time, served, and worked as errand boys until their hour had come. Some of Putin's people had no ambition and ended up at the top by accident. Even for Vladimir Vladimirovich and most of his colleagues at the very highest levels, being catapulted to power came as a surprise, I think.

Most of the team came from Saint Petersburg, continuing the venerable Soviet and Russian tradition in which the leader brings people with him from his hometown. There were jokes about it in Moscow. For example: The Saint Petersburg train arrives in Moscow. Every disembarking passenger is approached by official-looking people and asked, "Would you like to work in the Kremlin?" It was true that virtually all Putin's remotely close former colleagues and even some mere acquaintances from Saint Petersburg had moved to Moscow and been given important posts. This showed that the new president trusted only his own people. An infusion of fresh blood into the Kremlin was vitally necessary to help the new president get out from under the influence of the circle that had ruled in the latter Yeltsin era. But Russia needed an influx of professionals—not shallow, locally experienced bureaucrats.

The change of personnel and personality types was palpable. In Yeltsin's day, you could come across anyone in the Kremlin, from democrats and Westernizers to nationalists and supporters of autocracy. It was a motley crew, the product of the sudden elevation of completely unexpected people. Putin's team may have vaulted to the top as well, but its members were all alike, and quite different from Yeltsin's group. They were individuals with unremarkable faces, buttoned up and not at all interested in joking. Most were statists who felt nostalgia for Russia's vanished grandeur. They must have hated the anarchy and degradation of the Yeltsin era. They could not have approved of the winners of that era—those pushy oligarchs and court favorites. The bureaucrat apparatchiks had come to power with Putin, making Yeltsin's favorites seem lively and even extraordinary. Periods of stabilization always call for average types—people who are unlikely to harbor individualism and the desire to stand out.

Putin's people belonged to a single generation and were bound by a common psychology and similar behavior patterns. Many had connections to the power structures—*siloviki*—or at least shared a worldview with the army and security services. They allowed people of another mentality— the liberals German Gref and Alexei Kudrin, for example—into their midst to achieve specific goals, but they did not give them freedom of movement. They did not, could not, trust the liberals—they were people of another blood.

Most of the new people at the top had their own principles and brand of honesty. They were pragmatic, grounded, cautious, patient, and did not set themselves unrealistic goals. But there was something in their pragmatism that undermined it. The majority of Putin's subordinates still lived in the great-power paradigm—they were unlikely to picture Russia as a state that thought about its people, not about power and greatness. It was not yet clear whether the new team could escape that paradigm and treat the state as a means of serving the people. If that were to happen, we could safely conclude that Russia had overcome its past. At that time, Putin's team worked within the model they knew.

But the larger point is that not all the newcomers were capable. They brought provincialism and a lack of sophistication, for Saint Petersburg had long since become a fairly bleak city—politically and intellectually. To some degree, this provincialism was beneficial, because it brought the Kremlin closer to the greater part of Russia. But it also made it difficult for the new team to understand current complex strategic problems, to practice the art of governance in a huge and enormously controversial society that called for daring vision, experience, and knowledge.

The most important fact of life about the new ruling team was not even its conservatism or lack of expertise but something that was not really new: Ten years of Yeltsin's reforms had not produced alternative, non-Soviet elites in Russia. Yet again, the people in power had been brought up by the old system and had the old ties. Yes, they had breathed the new air and had developed new habits. But it was not clear to what degree they were oriented toward the future and whether they could give Russia a new strategy. In all successful transformations, society can move forward only after the appearance of new elites.

The revolutionary stage is inevitably followed by a period of stabilization, many pundits said by way of consolation. One had only to look at the former communist countries of Eastern Europe after their social and political upheavals. Stabilization in Russia, however, differed from stabilization in Poland and Hungary, for instance. There, the choice had been made of a new form and manner of life, and society had agreed in principle with that choice. In Russia, stabilization meant that people were tired of pursuing a new agenda, of seeking a new future, and had agreed to a halt in the search. At least for now.

During the turbulent Yeltsin years, the motto was "We must change to survive." Now many Russians, seeking calm, subscribed to another principle: "Change is dangerous and risky." Because only a minority benefited from Yeltsin's reforms, the great majority did not want any more experiments. And it seemed that the winning minority was not very interested in changes either, afraid of a new redistribution of power and property. Many opted to settle with what they had.

Stabilization came at a time when the problems of renewal and restructuring of society had not been completely solved. In its ten years of transformation, Russia had not fully transformed its system. Russian society still was a hybrid that combined contradictory elements: bureaucratic pressure and chaotic striving, market relations and the government's desire to control everything, habituation to personal independence and a readiness to limit one's personal freedoms, servility toward the authorities and distrust and suspicion of them. Russians simultaneously wanted to be free and were afraid of freedom, not knowing how to handle it.

The outward manifestations of democracy in Russia did not interfere with the spinning of the bureaucratic spider web that was stifling the country once again. To survive, to get things done, society had to retreat once again into the sphere of shadow relations, where ties, money, power, and manipulation, rather than the fair, transparent rule of law, decided everything. Even people who considered themselves liberals felt quite comfortable in the gray zone.

Could that hybrid society based on opposing principles be sustained? If so, for how long? If not, was Russia prepared to continue reform in an atmosphere of weariness and disappointment? A breather was needed. But that meant losing time, and history does not tolerate breaks. And could Russia allow itself time off when the infrastructure built in Soviet times was falling apart—with airplanes crashing more frequently, buildings collapsing, roads falling into disrepair, and the education and health systems crumbling? Russia seemed stuck without answers. Pundits were going around and around trying to decide whether Putin was still pondering, whether he was waiting, vacillating, or perhaps preparing for a new breakthrough. There was no visible evidence of consideration and searching in the Kremlin, but the former intelligence agent knew how to be inscrutable and take unexpected turns. Meanwhile, precious time was running out.

An important index for assessing the changes taking place in the country and people's minds with Putin's ascendancy was the attitude of Russia toward the West. During the Yeltsin period, a lot of Russians wanted to be like people in the West and strove to be part of Europe. At the end of the 1990s, however, many Russians became disillusioned with the West and distrustful of its intentions toward their country. Most of their hopes for serious capital investment in the Russian economy had not been fulfilled. Institutional forms borrowed from the West did not work in Russia; to be accurate, they worked, but in the interests of the minority. Democratization had turned into chaos. Privatization had ended up enriching the few.

More and more Russians were coming to the conclusion that the Western pattern of civilization did not fit the Russian framework of development. According to the early 2001 VTsIOM polls, 58 percent of Russians had become convinced that Russia and Western culture were incompatible. This reflected not hostility toward the West but rather a lack of hope that Russia would ever catch up with Western society.

At the same time, Russians continued to borrow the Western lifestyle—and elites the most actively of any social group. The more successfully the ruling class followed Western standards in their lives, the more it turned to supporting superpower status for Russia, as if looking for a cover for its foreign ways. It was amusing to listen to people who drove the most expensive foreign cars, owned villas on the Côte d'Azur, sent their children to school in Switzerland and England, and kept their money in Western banks weigh in with typically Soviet opinions on the decline of the West and the need to "rebuff" it.

Suddenly, both in the ruling class and in the rest of society, the desire to return to traditional Russian values and seek tranquility and healing in them was manifesting itself. More and more frustrated Russians began to think that Russia was doomed to follow its "special path" of development.[1] And the characteristics of this special path are a strong, centralized government, power concentrated in the hands of the leader, and a superpower ideology.

The beginning of Putin's presidency saw an increase in the number of people in Russia who believed that their country was different from the other states and that Russians were different from other people. Although

54 percent of respondents in 1994 said that Russians had become different from people in Western countries during the years of Soviet rule, 68 percent felt that way in 2000. Seventy percent believed that Russia "was distinguished by a unique way of life and spiritual culture," and 71 percent said that Russia "is a great country that can be understood only through belief in its great predestination."[2] Such beliefs were an antidote to Russia's vulnerability and the continuing disenchantment of its people. They also help to explain Russians' attempts to compensate for domestic problems with an appearance of strength in the international arena.

These data speak of disillusionment with the notions of easy integration with the West that had come with warmer relations in the late 1980s and early 1990s. By the late 1990s, hopelessness had spread, and many Russians doubted that their country could ever become "normal." One antidote to Russia's seeming helplessness is the belief that it has been marked out for a special destiny—Russians are not like other people and should not try to be, because they are meant for something greater and the goal itself demands suffering, pain, and coping with difficulties. Russia's special path has never brought a normal life, but belief in it confers a justification of hopelessness and an illusion of strength.

Poll results must always be treated with extreme caution. If Russians were asked even at that moment of disconsolate fatalism, for instance, "Would you like to continue on the special path, if that meant continuing poverty, excessive power for the bureaucracy, corruption, and embezzlement in Russia?" the great majority would undoubtedly support normality, that is, joining Western civilization. If Russians were asked, "What is the greatest threat for society—the West, Islamic terrorism, China, or domestic problems?" the majority most likely would say the greatest challenges for Russia lie in Russia.

At the same time, it is fair to conclude that during the first years of Putin's presidency, Russia's political class and some social groups were losing their hope that Russia would ever catch up with the West and be incorporated into the Western community. Putin's own ascendancy to power was a reflection and outcome of this shift. People looking at a president with a KGB background assumed he had to be a nationalist and a strong proponent of great-power status for Russia, as were the majority of the Russian *siloviki*. With characteristic servility, they were prepared to be "more Catholic than the pope," although Putin himself was still vague about his real inclinations. Soon, however, it would become evident that the longing for uniqueness in Russia was not—thank God—a stable and dominant trend and that President Vladimir Putin would prove that appearances were deceptive.

An essential element of the new retro mentality was the attitude toward the leader. He was forgiven all weakness and failures, out of a sense of self-preservation, because no one saw any benefit in criticizing the authorities, for criticism would not lead to anything positive soon. Faith in the leader was more emotional than rational, because the public still did not know Putin's plans and program. Trust in the leader and a return to a traditional rule were for many the ultimate guarantee of relative calm. Seventy-nine percent of citizens had decided by 2001 that "Russians can't manage without a strong hand."

The desire to have someone at the helm who inspired hope led people to lay blame for failure not on the president but on everyone else—the cabinet, the oligarchs, the Duma, the governors, the West. And that was yet another paradox, for the other institutions in Russia were an extension of the presidency. All this ensured that Putin's approval ratings remained high while those for Russia's other institutions (cabinet, parliament, courts) fell beginning in 2001. Putin was protected, spared, and preserved as a symbol of faith. People were prepared to forgive him many things out of fear of him failing.

In other words, conservatism became entrenched in Putin's Russia. Russian conservatives placed the individual's subordination to the state and the regime, which was identical to the president, at the top of their pyramid. The psychological subtext of Russian conservatism was fear, accumulated over the "time of troubles" of the previous fifteen years, beginning with Gorbachev's *perestroika*. It was fear of the unknown and unexpected—fear of the mob, of the permanent disasters, of the collapse of Russia, of entry into a new world for which a very large part of society was not prepared.

A new joke posited that a conservative was a badly frightened liberal. And in fact, quite a few active conservatives had recently hailed the demise of the Soviet empire and communism and had supported liberal reforms and taken part in them. Today they were afraid of what the reforms had wrought. They now wanted the status quo, which could be bolstered by an increase in the role of the secret services and power agencies. They hailed the presidency of a man who seemingly valued power above almost anything else and who could guarantee them security. Putin was the creation of the fears of society, especially of its elites, because he wouldn't have come to power without them, and at the same time he presented himself as the answer to these fears.

Looking for analogies in history, some Russian conservatives compared themselves with French Gaullists and Putin, naturally, with General Charles de Gaulle. There were some apparent parallels. De Gaulle's France and Putin's Russia both made use of anti-American rhetoric and tried to preserve the imperial grandeur of their nations. Both experienced stabilization through the strengthening of presidential power. Both presidents considered loyal cadres extremely important and used administrative pressure to achieve their ends. Because of the style of his rule, the French general with good reason was known as the "republican monarch." And the Russian colonel who became a leader demonstrated the ambition to build a strong presidency as well.

But this exhausts the similarities between current Russian conservatism and French conservatism. De Gaulle stabilized a completely different political reality, which included a structured society and counterbalances. And he did not stop at stabilization but pushed forward ambitious transformation, shaping the Fifth Republic. De Gaulle had a strong prime minister and could not have functioned without a vibrant multiparty system and an effective parliament. But he did not create a system, as Putin was doing, by replacing institutions with loyalists. For Russia to have Gaullism, it would need not only a de Gaulle but traditions, like France's, of fighting for liberty and the people's dignity.

It would be a mistake, however, to view the rise of conservatism in 2000–2001 in Russia as exclusively the consequence of Putin's policies and his pressure on society. Putin was not a politician who would use force to form public moods. At first, it had seemed that he was an authoritarian who wanted to break Russia by coercion. But it soon became clear that in many ways the president just followed events. And he definitely did not want schisms and tried to avoid blatant conflicts whenever possible. He had fallen into a stream of expectations and went with the flow. He may still have been considering his future course. In any case, he was waiting—or rather, drifting—and often yielded when faced with resistance.

Judging by his actions—or better, inaction—Putin's vision of the future at the moment might have fitted into the conservative model. But most of the time he followed the lead of those of his voters who demanded strong rule from him. Even though he must have understood the realities of the postindustrial world, inside the country he consciously used a language that all understood, the language of great-powerhood. Thus, by his behavior and rhetoric, the president reinforced the charged atmosphere roiling with frustrations and doctored memories of past glories and became the hostage of the mood he had helped create.

The new revival of the Russian conservatism was supported not only by the political elites close to the Kremlin and the bureaucracy but also by the intellectual community that sided with the president. While Putin contemplated which agenda to choose for Russia, as he doubted and tried to keep in the centrist niche while starting slowly to build bridges to the West, the Russian intellectual establishment began discussions on who loved Russia more and who was Russia's best patriot.

The spring of 2001 was the climax of the "Love Russia" campaign. I doubt such a discussion would have taken place in a Russia where society and its elites had reached agreement on which pattern of development they wanted to follow and saw that this pattern would lead to Russia's integration into the Western community. The fierce discussion on patriotism and Russian uniqueness, replete with mutual recriminations, confirmed that Russia had not resolved the basic issue of its future and had not yet settled on its perceptions of the world.

The division of Russians into Westerners and great-power advocates was not a new one for Russian political life. It continued the arguments between Westernizers and Slavophiles begun in the nineteenth century. That these arguments were renewed after the Yeltsin reforms showed yet again that the ruling class and intellectuals in Russia were unsure how to think about Russian needs and aspirations, how to understand Russia's new identity, how to define a new future and so sought refuge in the past.

Those who considered themselves "patriots of Russia" attacked the "patriots of NATO" or "patriots of the United States." Russian patriots wanted Russia to be a great nation, supported a military solution to the Chechnya problem, and severely disapproved of any criticism of Kremlin policies on freedom of the press or the Chechen war. The patriots demanded a symmetrical retaliatory response to the United States and the West in case of new NATO enlargement or abrogation by the United States of the Anti–Ballistic Missile Treaty, which Russia regarded as the cornerstone of its own and world security. They dismissed all criticism of Putin and his policies as the desire "to discredit a president of Russia who is inconvenient for the United States and who wants to restore the country's great-power status."[3]

Intellectuals who opposed Russia's great-power ambitions were classed among the patriots of the West. It was interesting to watch new adherents joining the camp of the Russian patriots—it's always safer inside the regime's camp than outside it. All the new patriots were convinced that Putin had made his choice and that it was anti-Western. It would be a blow for them when the president went in an opposite direction.

The division of the political scene into patriots of Russia and patriots of the West signaled a return to the Soviet days, when enemies of the homeland were sought and that search was an important way to consolidate autocratic rule. Specialists on "real" patriotism tried to deny others the right to their vision of what was good for Russia. There were signs that even the Kremlin people felt embarrassed by the unexpected ultrapatriotic surge within the political and intellectual community.

The patriots shrugged off questions they couldn't answer, especially about where Russia would find the financial means to confront NATO and the United States. Why did Russia need a powerful nuclear arsenal when people were living on paltry wages? Why did Russia require military might and influence on the countries around it when it could not solve elementary problems of its own national life? Patriots of Russia could not answer these questions because they had not thought along these lines.

Who were these new "patriots"? Quite often, they were successful "new Russians," who drove Mercedeses and wore Versace-designed clothes. For them, an anti-Western stance was a form of camouflage, especially if their wealth came from ill-gotten gains. No one knew which way the authorities would turn. What if they started nationalizing? What if Putin started looking for the source of their wealth? It was better to be more patriotic (anyway, it couldn't hurt).

For others, anti-Western feeling stemmed from ordinary envy and the realization that Russia would not achieve Western levels of material well-being in their lifetime. It would lessen the sting to simply wall off the West and call it a hostile force. The hopelessness and dreariness of life, the lack of success and inadequacy when faced with new challenges, made some people see an insistence on Russia's uniqueness and a refusal to join Europe as something that could assuage their sense of inferiority and restore their self-esteem.

It was true that Putin sometimes played on these sentiments, continuing to appeal to his base, which included a lot of traditional great-power supporters. He even said once: "Either Russia will be great or it will not be at all." In fact, he placed a dilemma before society: either Russia remains a superpower or it vanishes completely. At that point, some groups within society understood greatness as first of all military might, not as wealth or economic power. The formulation of the issue excluded the evolution of Russia in the direction of a normal state that is concerned with the needs of its people.

As a pragmatist, Putin did not push this theme too much, and to counter it he spoke about the need for Russia to move "into Europe." He must not have wanted—and perhaps even feared—a return to the past. But, at least in early 2001, he also was not ready for a more determined movement into the future. All his turns and zigzags prevented people from drawing any firm conclusions about his true views, or at least his mindset. He remained a political sphinx; it was hard to read anything in his inscrutable face; it was difficult to decide which of his actions was a strategic one. Perhaps he was simply changing his position as circumstances dictated.

The anti-Western appeals and searches for an enemy in the West did not find mass support among ordinary Russian people. Despite the nationalistic rhetoric of the elites, 8 percent of those polled at the end of 2000 had very good feelings about the United States, 62 percent had basically good feelings, 16 percent had basically bad ones, and 6 percent had very bad ones (8 percent had no opinion).[4] The people could not be roused to seek an external enemy. Average Russians were much more tolerant and more pragmatic, and also less hysterical, than intellectuals and politicians. Artificial provocations by some forces around the Kremlin attempting to return to "uniqueness" did not last long. But the vacillating mood among certain political and social groups in Russia proved how unstable people's sentiments still were and how easily they could be manipulated.

This was the climate in which the final round of the struggle for NTV—the well-known and well-respected television station owned by Vladimir Gusinsky—took place. The state-owned monopoly Gazprom, which had obtained 46 percent of NTV's shares, took control of the station on April 3, 2001. Putin must have decided to put an end to the affair. At this point, I admit, he could not stop his persecution of NTV and Gusinsky, for that would have been seen as weakness. The fate of weak leaders in Russia is bleak: They are inevitably failures. And their fate is to be quickly replaced.

The only political party that openly supported NTV was Yabloko. Two rallies to protest the takeover of the station, organized by Yabloko and the Union of Independent Journalists, were held in Moscow. Most of those attending were young people.[5] A new generation in Russia had independent views and no longer feared the regime. Despite the rallies, however, NTV passed into the hands of Gazprom. Thus ended Russia's history of independent television.[6]

The intentional destruction of one of the best broadcasting companies in Russia and the cynicism with which it was done elicited a sharp reaction in the West. The *Washington Post*, in an April 1 editorial, called on Western governments to respond strongly to Putin's attack on freedom of the press. "The Bush administration and the government of the European Union, Canada and Japan now face an important challenge: to ensure that Mr. Putin suffers some consequence from his grossly anti-democratic behavior. To avoid action after so many warnings to Moscow would be a serious blow to Western credibility." The newspaper called for expelling Russia from the Group of Eight. But the disapproval of the West no longer worked on Moscow.

The conflict between the authorities and NTV showed that the regime could switch to authoritarian methods to achieve its goals. But another thing was made clear as well: Society's general support of the authorities at this moment was limited. Those who supported the journalists showed that there was opposition in Russia, albeit divided and unorganized. For the first time after a long hiatus, people rallied to a cause, and it was a sign that the new Russia had survived the surge of conservatism and was still breathing.

The NTV story had a sequel. The remainder of Gusinsky's media empire—the magazine *Itogi* and the newspaper *Segodnya*—were also liquidated (and then in June Gazprom tried to take over the popular radio station Ekho Moskvy). The same pattern was followed: One of the owners of each publication shut it down and purged the unacceptable journalists. Journalists who refused to follow the new rules found themselves on the street.[7] Just as in the case of NTV, part of the former team was rehired, and they began publishing a new *Itogi*, but with content that had not a hint of criticism of the president. On the surface, everything was fine—property rights prevailed, and the notorious oligarch had been punished. But in fact this was the final liquidation of a group that dared to resist the Kremlin.

The unsophisticated viewer or reader might even think that nothing special had occurred. NTV continued to exist, albeit without its former stars. *Itogi* was still published, without the old writers and editors, however. "Why make such a fuss?" the naïve might ask. Apparently, the authorities were counting on such naïveté—that people would assume the contents were the same as long as the sign was still hanging over the door. The construction of wax dummies speeded up. Russia has a long history of Potemkin villages.

As he destroyed irritants, Putin continued building his superpresidential regime. In early 2001, he decided to renew the power bloc. Secretary of the Security Council Sergei Ivanov, Putin's closest ally, was named minister of defense. Boris Gryzlov, the leader of the Unity faction and also Putin's man, became the new minister of the interior.

With these appointments, Putin attempted to create his own base in the power ministries—an important step in freeing himself from the embrace of Yeltsin's political Family. The new leader continued strengthening his position by bringing in loyalists. But he was unable to find trustworthy people to place as political commissars at the head of the other agencies. The problem was not that there were no good human resources in Russia; there just weren't enough people the president trusted. But even in this round of replacements, Putin could not rid himself completely of the old ruling group. He was forced to move former minister of the interior Petr Rushailo, who in his day had had close ties to the Yeltsin court and pretensions to the role of successor, to the post of secretary of the Security Council. In other words, the still-cautious Putin could not fully break with the past, which he very clearly wanted to do.

Once a political stage that was comfortable for the president had been constructed, it would seem there was nothing to distract the Kremlin from resuming reforms. Putin's team instead got involved in intrigues. Some members of his entourage decided that despite its loyalty the Duma must be disbanded so that a totally obedient parliament with a constitutional majority faithful to the Kremlin could be installed. With this majority, the Constitution could be amended—in particular, to extend the presidential term to seven years. With the liquidation of the current Duma, the Kremlin could also get rid of parties it did not need, including Yabloko and the Luzhkov–Primakov Fatherland, and weaken the Communists.

To execute the plan, early in 2001 the Kremlin forced its parliamentary faction, Unity, into an absurd action: supporting the Communist-initiated vote of no confidence in its own cabinet. However, the scheme was never carried out. Even the tractable members of the propresidential movement were not willing to give up their prestigious positions and the comforts of Moscow life voluntarily and return to their homes in the provinces. It also became clear that preterm elections to replace them would damage Putin's image, because he was associated in the public mind with stability. Thus the Kremlin team created a crisis and then lost face extricating itself from it.

The threat to disband the Duma, however, could be used again at any point. An axe hung over the deputies that could be brought into action if the Duma started acting up. This story was a repeat of the tempests of the Yeltsin years. But in Yeltsin's time, when Berezovsky was doing the plotting, the intrigues were much subtler.

The Kremlin's political "technologists" did not stop with the notion of disbanding the Duma, for they had acquired a taste for political engineering. Their success in creating Putin's presidency and a loyal political cadre was pushing them toward more ambitious schemes; their few failures had not put them off. Judging by the actions that soon followed, the ruling team decided to create from above everything that existed in Western society—parties, trade unions, youth movements, the press, and clubs for intellectuals. What was important for them was that nothing arise spontaneously and without the Kremlin's knowledge or permission. Anything that had the slightest connection to politics had to have Kremlin approval. And everything that did not pass inspection was shunted off to the periphery.

The new team's invention was that the shutting down was done not by force or pressure but often through the courts. The Russian judiciary continued to be amazingly flexible and understanding—that is to say, it understood what the executive branch wanted. Judges received their salaries and apartments from the authorities, and being dependent on the executive branch, they became the instruments for purging politicians and business-people the authorities did not want around. That the rules of the game continued undefined in Russia made it possible to turn almost anyone into a defendant, rendering him tractable and free of excessive ambition or criticism.

In other words, Russia was undergoing the full-scale formation of a managerial system in which all social groups and political forces must take the place the Kremlin intended for them. Apparently, the Kremlin technologists had an image of Russia as a gigantic corporation made up of well-managed divisions, headed by a manager-president. The question was whether this outwardly docile but at its core unruly and even anarchic society could be disciplined without blatant force. Was Russia ready to become an obedient corporation? Even if the idea was put into action, could a corporation that was managed from the top break through into the future—which required freedom, enterprise, and personal liberty?

In the meantime, the construction of the new system went full speed ahead and with apparent success for the time being—the remaining political actors occupied the niches earmarked for them. Thus, under pressure from the Kremlin, the oligarchs joined the Russian Union of Entrepreneurs and Industrialists (RUEI). Arkady Volsky, an old apparatchik who survived under every regime, headed the union. The RUEI had been the lobby of a very dogmatic part of the Soviet directors of the state-owned enterprises that had not learned to become accommodated to the market and instead hoped for state, or "regulated," capitalism. The oligarchs joining that kind of union was an unexpected step—crossing the former "red" directors with the oligarchs was tantamount to crossing eels with hedgehogs. But the Kremlin managed to create a hybrid: Arkady Volsky, Anatoly Chubais, Vladimir Potanin, and Mikhail Khodorkovsky, pretending to be happy, sat together at the RUEI. The regime achieved its goal of getting all the industrialists and oligarchs in one place and under its control.

Putin's supporters insisted that the liquidation of Gusinsky's empire and Berezovsky's forced expulsion from Russia meant that the regime was cleansed of oligarchy. But life showed that all oligarchs had not been "equally distanced," as advertised. The oligarchic groups obedient to the Kremlin began growing stronger. New empires formed, such as that of the young and energetic Oleg Deripaska, who first established a monopoly in aluminum production and then started taking over enterprises producing other metals and energy, crowding out the old oligarchs. Deripaska enjoyed Putin's special favor. The president even visited the young businessman's properties to ski—a sign of particular closeness.

The Deripaska phenomenon highlighted a new tendency in Russia's economic development. Until recently, all the major financial-industrial groups had formed on the vertical principle within one branch of industry. But now groups were becoming horizontally integrated, reaching to different economic areas and giving rise to Russian versions of giant South Korean *chaebols*. There was a positive element here. Whereas the former oligarchs had taken money abroad, the new ones began investing in production.

But the new consolidation of regime and capital set off alarms. The new oligarchs all had to be personally loyal to the president; Putin's accent on "equally distancing" all the oligarchs from power was nothing but a myth. The Kremlin continued its deal making with big business. Representatives of the secret services, *siloviki*, played a substantive role in some of the new economic groups of influence. Besides, as the South Korean experience showed, sooner or later the existence of gigantic corporations under state patronage leads to the monopolization of the economy by the few clans and to the degradation of the state itself, with the regime subordinated to the interests of the oligarchic elites.

The next step in the regime's plans was the construction of a new party system. The creation of a ruling coalition was announced, to be made up of yesterday's rivals—Putin's Unity (Edinstvo) on one side and the Luzhkov–Primakov Fatherland (Otechestvo) on the other. One of the puns at the time was that the new acronym for Edinstvo and Otechestvo would be "Ediot." Newspapers joked that "the bear has put on a cap," a reference to the emblem of Unity and Mayor Luzhkov's favorite headgear.

In their day, Yeltsin and his people had tried to create pet party systems. They failed because they were not persistent and because life in Russia was on the boil then and not everyone cared to be subordinated to the center. The docile parties of the Yeltsin era tended to lose elections. Under Putin, the Kremlin parties had every chance of winning. That was another index of how the situation had seemingly changed.

The movers behind the party merger did not hide that they were doing the Kremlin's bidding. The Russian state apparatus wanted to end the schism in its ranks. Neither Luzhkov nor Primakov nor their followers wanted to be perceived as the opposition. The Russian bureaucracy was never in opposition to the center of power. Moreover, many Russians could not even imagine the ruling class breaking into two parts that would take turns in power. The bureaucracy was used to living in a society where the opposition never gained power and the regime was monolithic. Nor were ordinary people accustomed to the idea of the opposition taking power.

That Luzhkov gave up his independence and joined the presidential coalition meant that the last opponents of the federal center had realized that it was pointless to fight Putin and remain outside the Kremlin fold. "The new era has begun. Better stop dueling with the Kremlin," many people thought, watching authorities from the distance.

With the merger of the progovernment factions, Putin got a stable, powerful majority in the Duma that could pass whatever legislation he wanted. This simplified the management of politics. Instead of numerous parties that he had to support and to negotiate with, the president could give orders to a single structure. At first, Unity and Fatherland did not seem eager to unite. It was no wonder, for many functionaries lost their positions in the merger. But in the end the Kremlin won, and after lengthy deal making, the new Edinaya Rossiya (United Russia) movement was formed. Actually, this merger did not enlarge the Kremlin's electoral base, because some of the opposition-minded members of Fatherland stayed out of the new movement.

At the same time, the Kremlin-controlled faction was formed in the Federation Council, and senators rushed to join it. It could have been no other way, for without membership in the Kremlin bloc there could be no possibility of entrée into the offices of executive power. And without that access, no problems in the regions could be solved.

With solid majorities in the Duma and the Federation Council, the Kremlin had the obedient parliament that had existed only in Yeltsin's dreams. Amazingly, after almost fifteen years of parliamentary struggle, the country found itself back in a previous historical period, when the executive branch considered the parliament an extension of itself; the Soviet tradition of unanimity had been restored.

However, neither Putin nor Kasyanov or the other members of the government joined the Kremlin party. Because it lacked representation in the executive branch, the new party majority could not be detrimental. That majority could be disbanded or traded for another, also created by the Kremlin.

The movers behind the tame ruling bloc maintained that Russia was following the same path as Japan with its Liberal Democratic Party, which spent dozens of years in power. The Japanese Liberal Democrats, however, formed a cabinet, whereas the Russian "parties of power" were never even asked for advice on that matter.[8]

The party field was being put in order. The Union of Right Forces (SPS), which consisted of numerous small parties and groups, decided to transform itself into a party with a membership. The transformation was mandatory, according to the new law on parties, if the umbrella group wanted to compete in the next election. The process of forming a new liberal party created mixed emotions. The pressure from Chubais was too evident, because he tried to control the critical impetus and create an organization that would not slide into opposing the Kremlin. Boris Nemtsov's candidacy for leader of the new party was approved by the presidential team, which had to tie Nemtsov's hands. In other words, the authorities were openly supporting one of the elements of the future party system that, as was assumed, would then support the authorities. Those who were too oppositionist did not join the new party of officially supported chosen liberals.[9] Observers philosophized: "The Russian liberal likes power, being near power. Opposition behavior, which cuts you off from receptions at the Kremlin and dooms you to riding the trolley-bus to see your voters, was natural for the left, the human rights activists, but not at all for the right, which considers poverty a greater sin than cooperation with the Kremlin."[10] Besides, both sides needed the collaboration; the liberals needed the Kremlin to protect them from the hostile populist majority, and the Kremlin needed the liberals to give it a reformist image.

The construction of a "managed democracy" continued unabated. Although the Kremlin's struggle for control over television had had its flare-ups and conflicts, the taming of the press was done without particular fuss. Almost of their own accord, all the sizable general-interest publications (with the exception of two or three national papers) swore fealty to the new ruling team and created no problems for it.

With the active participation of the Ministry of the Press and personal help from Minister Mikhail Lesen, notorious for taking part in the attack on NTV, the Media Union was founded—led, naturally, by people close to the Kremlin. Now it could be said that the Union of Independent Journalists, which permitted itself critical remarks about the authorities and even organized protest rallies, no longer had the right to represent Russian journalists.

Next came pressure on the analyst and expert community. Kremlin advisers wanted a change in the intellectual elites. The analysts who were known for their critical attitude toward the regime and who did not show the appropriate respect for the president were not allowed on the air. Their articles were rarely published. They were not invited to official conferences and receptions and were not given access to information. The rebels had a choice: change their tone or their profession.

The representatives of the Kremlin administration thought about the new generation and created a youth movement called Walking Together. The movement had no program except to support Putin. Participants were rewarded with tickets to clubs, theaters, and sports events, and with trips to the capital. This was a hired youth regiment required to do nothing but obey and be present at events—at least for the time being. On May 7, 2001, the young Putinists were dressed in T-shirts with Putin's picture on the front and brought to a rally in Moscow. Muscovites gawked at the thousands of young people filling up Vasilyevsky Spusk, the square around the Kremlin. Walking Together members applauded and shouted in delight when their organizers asked them to turn to the West—with their rear ends. Some ordinary people out for a stroll found this unnerving.

The creation of tame political and public organizations was one of the favorite pastimes of the Russian state. Sometimes it reached absurd levels. In the summer of 2001, Gazprom, the most zealous liquidator of the independent media, including NTV, tried to organize a conference on freedom in the mass media. As a screen, prominent liberals were invited, Nemtsov in particular. That the attempt to convene the conference failed was a promising sign, warning the regime that imitation games can meet resistance both in the West and in Russia. But generally, the president's lieutenants had reason to be extremely pleased—they had created their own mechanism of power.

The Kremlin, satisfied with its shaping of the political scene, moved on to a more complex undertaking: Putin decided to create his own civil society with all its concomitant structures. The irony is that the idea for creating civil society came to the Kremlin politicians only after oligarch Boris Berezovsky, now Putin's chief antagonist, began financing and supporting the creation of independent organizations in Russia.

If anyone in 2001 rebuked the regime for not caring about the people, the authorities could respond: Of course we care, we are actively in dialogue with society—the one we ourselves have created. On June 12, representatives of public organizations were invited to the Kremlin. Some had been completely unknown before that. There were bookkeeping societies;

associations of cosmonauts, gardeners, and settlers; sports unions; Kremlin political technologists; and of course, young members of Walking Together. There were no guests who could spoil the president's mood with questions about Chechnya, human rights, or freedom of the press. Putin spoke at length with the chosen, and the gathering resembled nothing so much as the socializing of former communist leaders with select tame organizations.

The authorities decided to create a civil chamber under the president that would represent the new society. A grand congress of public and social organizations—the Civil Forum—was planned to inaugurate the chamber. The ideologues of the new "civil society" under the aegis of Putin explained their brainchild this way: For "Russia to enter world structures," society had to be formed the way British lawns are grown—"water and mow, mow and water." The Kremlin, of course, had to do the watering and mowing. The presidential staff even came up with a slogan: "For a great country, a great society." Quite a few politicians supported the creation of this civil society under the president—especially because the Kremlin was footing the bill.

Now it could confidently be said that at least outwardly the new Russian reality differed from Yeltsin's Russia. Back then, there were all kinds of parties, clubs, and movements. Anyone could create and register something without approval from on high. Of course, at some point the regime stopped reacting to all those spontaneous movements. Now the wild plants were being weeded out and replaced by hothouse plants tended by official gardeners. The removal of public organizations proceeded with outward civility.

In any case, it would be hard to accuse the Kremlin of authoritarian designs—after all, the president was meeting with representatives of civil society. People who did not know Russian reality would applaud. Not everyone asked the questions: Why was the Kremlin avoiding dialogue with human rights activists and organizations that had already earned their reputation in society? On what basis was acceptance into the Kremlin-approved "civil society" determined? Why did people and groups hurry to join these artificial unions?

The same questions applied to the new Media Union, which all the Russian newspapers and television channels hurried to join. Here the answer was simple: Those who joined the journalism group received benefits and financing from the state. But members of the Media Union could no longer freely criticize the regime. You paid for the benefits with your freedom.

The face of Russian "modernity" was gradually coming into focus. Outwardly, the same personalities continued walking down the scene: KGB officers, oligarchs, liberals, Communists, great-power advocates, and members of the intelligentsia. But this bland crowd was obediently moving along the outline of a carefully drawn circle. Of course, at any moment they might reverse movement. That could happen if the circling actors felt a weakening in centrifugal force from the authorities. This "pluralism" was based not on convictions or principles but on instincts and fears, and being amorphous and blurred, it was therefore unstable and unpredictable.

Chapter 7

THE LONG-AWAITED BREAKTHROUGH

❧

Putin renews market reforms. Fighting bulldogs under the carpet.
Moscow and Washington work it out. The Russian president
chooses the West. Disturbing signs.

A t last the moment had come when Vladimir Putin felt confident.
It was obvious in his manner, his gait, and his gaze, which had lost
their former strain. The president no longer seemed stiff and
reserved; he began speaking off the cuff. He stopped avoiding public
appearances. The time had come for Russia's leader to show why he wanted a concentration of power. He was ready to respond to the accusations
of hesitation and vacillation as well.

On April 3, 2001, the president addressed the Federation Assembly.
Society had been waiting for this speech, hoping it would clarify his future
policies. Putin spoke like a dynamic senior manager rather than a
monarch. He would address the parliament many more times, and his
annual speech would eventually become routine, as it had with Yeltsin. But
his 2001 address will be remembered, because in it he spoke as an energetic advocate of the market and declared his determination to renew economic reforms that had stalled under Yeltsin. He promised for the first
time to put an end to "status rent"—the bureaucracy taking bribes for the
opportunity to lobby—and to reform the state apparatus. The liberals
could finally heave a sigh of relief—after sitting on the fence and wavering
for so long, Putin had turned his face toward them. The only disconcerting
thing was that he said nothing about rights and freedoms, as if there were
no problems in that area in Russia.

Putin's speech, ground-breaking as it was, needed action to make it live. And here the Russian leader stunned the skeptics, me included. He gave the Duma a package of draft laws that encompassed judicial reform, a land code, pension reform, changes in tax legislation and the regulation of business, and a new labor code. What he did in the spring of 2001 looked like a revolution. Even the democrats felt that passage of the liberal legislation could neutralize the negative impression that Putin's avid construction of his pragmatically authoritarian regime had created.

The president scored another breakthrough as well—he dismissed the head of Russia's most powerful "natural monopoly," Gazprom, and put in his own man. The state-owned giant Gazprom kept the country afloat with its exports of natural gas, earning almost a quarter of budget revenues. The chairman of its board, Rem Vyakhirev (who replaced Victor Chernomyrdin in 1992 when the latter became prime minister), had been all powerful; he could kick open any door in the cabinet offices, and not only in Russia. But Vyakhirev was forced to leave without a struggle. The Kremlin let him know that if he did not, interest would be taken in his son, other relatives, and friends, who were getting rich in Gazprom subsidiaries.

Putin installed his own man from Saint Petersburg, Alexei Miller, at Gazprom. The president needed a loyalist at the head of the gas empire to enable him to control its enormous resources. Putin's power was incomplete without Gazprom. It was unclear at the moment whether the president would limit his intervention to naming the new top administrator or whether he would begin a reform of the monopoly and its secretive and dubious business practices. Sooner or later, he would have to realize that the way to raise the value of Gazprom stock, attract Western capital, and pay off the company's $10 billion foreign debt was to restructure the gas empire and ensure its transparency.

In the spring of 2001, the president also decided to reform another "natural monopoly," RAO UES, the Russian electric utility, which was headed by one of the leading liberals, Anatoly Chubais. There were fears, however, that the energetic and determined Chubais would simply privatize the lucrative pieces of the energy system and give the rest back to the state—exactly as his comrades in arms had done, and not just once, during Yeltsin-era privatization in the 1990s. The moment Chubais and his team produced the reform plan, it immediately provoked sharp criticism from a variety of quarters, including Putin economic adviser Andrei Illarionov and Yabloko Party leader Grigory Yavlinsky.

Chubais, however, was accustomed to clashes and it only increased his adrenaline; he was an experienced and tough fighter. The struggle that was beginning around RAO UES restructuring proved that even Russian liberals had conflicting views on a new stage of market reform. The president had to take sides in this struggle, and with his longing for consensus, he obviously did not like the idea.

The important news was that the ruling team had declared its direction and the use Putin planned to make of his omnipotence: He would modernize the economy. After bowing left and right at the same time, he had made up his mind by the spring of 2001. People close to the Kremlin were talking about a combination of mild authoritarianism and market liberalism as a remedy for Russian problems. Yeltsin had not managed to succeed with that mix. Putin was going to repeat the experiment. We would find out where Yeltsin had gone wrong; was it just that his authoritarianism turned into chaotic rule, or did the combination of authoritarianism and the market no longer work in Russia? Russia would have to pay yet again if the new experiment failed.

When the deputies began studying the president's draft laws, the optimism of the democrats and liberals dimmed. Putin's drafts hedged on transformation. The judicial reform revealed the spirit of the whole package. On one hand, it took the positive step of weakening the role of the prosecutor general's office and distributing some of its powers to the courts. But on the other it increased the dependence of the courts on the executive branch, which fit the basic tendency of Russian politics: the strengthening of the autocratic presidency.[1]

The same could be said of the measures intended to make the life of Russian businesspeople easier, the laws on "deregulation of the economy." They significantly reduced the number of licenses that businesses had been required to obtain, and therefore the opportunity for bureaucrats to extract bribes and interfere with the market. The proposed legislation, however, seemed to deal mostly with corruption among minor clerks; as observers joked, bribery was put under the control of higher administrators. Such measures increased the dependency of the lower echelons of the bureaucracy on the higher ones. And the top was given immeasurable power.

Russia had about 400,000 federal bureaucrats and more than 1 million regional ones. All of them occupied themselves somehow, whether doing useful work, make-work, or downright criminal work. Limiting the number of business licenses was unlikely to change the rule of the bureaucracy. What Russia needed was a wide-ranging reform of the state apparatus, including a staff reduction, strict definition of new responsibilities, a long-overdue pay increase to lessen the temptation of bribery, ideas for changing bureaucrats' motivations, and efforts to attract better personnel. But the Kremlin was not yet prepared to go that far. That kind of administrative reform would undermine the foundation of the traditional Russian state and the "Russian System" of power given primacy by Putin. He couldn't saw off the limb he was sitting on.

After reading the president's proposed reform legislation, one could feel that it was designed not only to preserve the political weight of the higher echelon of the state apparatus but also to help oligarchic businesses—and not all big businesses, but primarily those involving natural resources, first of all oil, gas, and aluminum. There were no visible efforts to expand Russian high technology. Small businesses did not sense any particular concern on the part of the Kremlin for their plight. As Putin himself admitted, the number of small and medium-sized enterprises in Russia had fallen—every fourth business was on the verge of bankruptcy or liquidation. Many small businesspeople could not take the pressure from bureaucrats, demands for bribes, unreasonable requirements, and harassment by police and security services or the criminal underworld, so they chose to close their business and work for hire.[2]

Despite the incompleteness of Putin's initiatives, they meant movement after several years of stagnation. And there was no guarantee that the president would have succeeded with more radical reforms. The first obstacle would have been placed in the way by his own base: the bureaucrats and people from the power agencies on whom he still depended, as well as by the tycoons, bent on preserving preferential treatment for their holdings and avoiding competition. At the moment, he was not ready to rock the boat.

Putin's policy seemed to be successful. In the summer of 2001, presidential authority was continuing to gain in power and clout. It looked as if this would be the year of triumph for the leader and his team. He had managed to move simultaneously in two directions: on one hand strengthening his position and consolidating his social support, and on the other hand restarting economic reform. His stabilizer role allowed him to keep moderate and conservative groups in his orbit. His activity as a reformer gave him the chance to regain the wavering trust of the liberally oriented portion of society.

The more experienced Yeltsin had managed to unite these disparate social groups only in extreme situations, and then not for long: when the question of Russia's independence and its break with the Gorbachev center was being decided in 1991, and when Yeltsin became the symbol of parting with the communist past in 1996. Putin had managed to maintain his influence and popularity for two years, a record for mercurial Russia. In October 2001, 75 percent of those polled supported the Russian president; at the same time, only 19 percent trusted him. People still supported the president simply because they did not see any worthy leader around.

But suddenly the smooth course of events was interrupted again. That was always the case in postcommunist Russia, where—unlike in the USSR, known for its staid, closed, and nontransparent nature—stability was continually disrupted by clashes of interests that exploded in public scandals or vicious political fights. Thus, in October 2001, minister of transportation Victor Aksyonenko—one of the highest state officials, a man who had recently had pretensions to the role of Yeltsin's heir—was called in to the prosecutor general's office.

At the same time, the prosecutor's office began investigating the Ministry of Emergency Situations, headed by Putin's friend Sergei Shoigu. These events shook the elites; the prosecutor's office was going after the sacred cows. The prosecutors could not risk doing that without approval from the Kremlin. It was perceived as a sign that the president himself was looking for a way to get rid of the most corrupted members of the old ruling group and at the same time demonstrate his unbiased, impersonal position.

The subsequent desperate struggle among the factions in the Putin entourage showed that the "apparatchik wars," which had temporarily stilled after Putin's election, had resumed. This was a struggle not only for control over the president but for dominance in economics and politics. The battle involved many interest groups. But in numerous squabbles, the conflict between the Putinists (called the Praetorians)[3] and the old Yeltsin "Family"[4] was gradually coming to the fore. Both sides had been waiting too long before deciding on an open clash.

The Putinists were grouped under the banner of cleansing Russia and its politics of oligarchs and corruption and strengthening the state. Their message found support among the millions of Russians who were disoriented, humiliated by poverty, and worried about their future and, most important, who regarded the small band of Russian millionaires with envy and hatred. It was these very feelings that had once moved impoverished Russia to follow the Bolsheviks. Many Russians were unworried by the fact that, under the aegis of a crusade against the oligarchs, they were also gradually being stripped of freedoms they had been accorded under Yeltsin and were being told what to do and what not to do. Many did not even know that Putin's people from the security services and other power ministries, having tasted power, now wanted total control of the Kremlin, not for the sake of battling evil and rot but for the sake of absolute power.

The second group—the Yeltsinites—had achieved everything they could beyond their wildest imaginings. During the Yeltsin era, when there were no limitations on them, they were their own law. They privatized the state and the president along with it. They did much to discredit democracy and the concept of liberalism. They were the ones who kindled social envy and a desire for revenge in the Russian people.

Now, in their struggle with the power ministries and security services, the Yeltsin-era elites raised the banner of freedom and defense of democracy. They really did try to preserve a certain pluralism, realizing that if the siloviki destroyed a free press, political parties, and the parliament, eventually the tycoons' turn would come, whether loyal to the president or not. Or Praetorians might come for them even sooner. Yeltsin's circle had to fight. But they couldn't fight only for their saved or stolen millions—they had to fight for democracy. Neither side was angelic. It just so happened that at that historical moment in Russia, the political interests of the Yeltsin political entourage and the old oligarchs coincided with the interests of the democrats.

In the meantime, Putin's Praetorians were trying to put their own people in the posts of chief of presidential staff and prime minister. The attacks on Aksyonenko and Shoigu were tests to see how hard the members of the Yeltsin circle would resist.

Putin calmly observed the resumption of court squabbling but tried to avoid interfering openly. He was in no hurry to throw Yeltsinites to his Praetorians to be dismembered. In the end, he forced Aksyonenko to resign—there was too much compromising information on him. Besides, he had to nab a few bad guys to show that he was fixing problems, first of all fighting corruption, and he had to deliver something to his people who wanted scalps. But he left the other Yeltsinites, including chief of the presidential staff Alexander Voloshin, in their positions. It was true that they were foreign bodies among the Putin loyalists. It's unlikely that the president, with his acute dislike and distrust of oligarchs and other people who were responsible for Russia's decay, was impressed by the members of the Yeltsin group. And there was another reason why he would loathe these people: Who would like to have around the people who created one's political personality and who might anticipate reciprocity, and still want to have clout?

The president allowed the conflict among the two coteries to continue because he did not want to become hostage to whichever faction triumphed, driving the others out. He realized that the presence of several clans in the Kremlin allowed him to remain above the fray. Besides, he knew that his people, however loyal to him they might be, were still inexperienced. "Who will do the job?" he would exclaim whenever one of the Praetorians was too adamant about freeing him from the old ruling group.

The president's tolerance of the old guard also might have had one further explanation. The Yeltsinites represented economic liberalism, which also was Putin's ideology. Thus Putin again took up the survival tactics practiced by his predecessor. It said a lot about the system both had operated, which began to dictate its own laws, and one of them was this: The survival of personified leadership depended on the nonstop clan infighting that enabled a leader to play arbiter.

In due time, there was a new twist to the Kremlin struggle: The prosecutor's office began an investigation of Gazprom's subsidiaries, in particular Sibur, whose managers were subsequently put behind bars. That turn of events shocked both the successful bureaucrats of the Yeltsin era and the oligarchs. The president sent a message that he would continue his attack on the dubious winners of the previous era, even if they were politically neutral. It was hardly his own initiative—he was inclined to wait and observe calmly—but apparently he yielded to his entourage, which insisted on giving a lesson or two to the arrogant businesspeople.

The prosecutor's office was once more a major player, resembling a loose cannon firing at everything in its path. But the seeming independence of prosecutor general Vladimir Ustinov, who had become a hero in the Russian media, was deceptive. The prosecutor's motive for starting its investigations of the big shots was blatantly political. Ustinov's office investigated people who either were disloyal to the Kremlin in some way or could threaten the president in the future, or who were not ready to cooperate with the new ruling team—who, in other words, had not fit into Putin's regime framework, or who had forgotten to share with the state. Meanwhile, the oligarchs who came to Moscow with the Praetorians were above suspicion—for instance, Saint Petersburg banker Sergei Pugachev, who appeared out of nowhere and whose sources of wealth were murky.

The new stage of the "fighting bulldogs under the carpet" at the Kremlin was inevitable given the logic of the Russian System, even though it was rationalized by Putin. In the absence of independent institutions, the vacuum was filled by groups of influence, and the struggle among them for political clout and property was the major substance of politics in Russia. The victory of one side in the tug-of-war meant only a brief respite, for the next round would start with the birth of a new group of influence. The clan struggle was not something unnatural—it takes place in all societies. The problem in Russia was that neither the rule of law nor independent institutions constrained the clan wars.

Another circumstance that increased the tension was the Kremlin's attack in the fall of 2001 on the non-state-owned TV-6, where journalists from NTV had found refuge after their company was shut down in the spring, and which had begun turning a profit. There was a sense of déjà vu, of watching the sequel in the battle between the Kremlin and independent television. Once again, a legal pretext (annulled a few months later) was used to go after the company. The assault on TV-6 confirmed once more the Russian justice system's lack of independence. The executive branch easily manipulated the courts, and on a larger scale than in Yeltsin's day. One judge after another made decisions that suited the executive departments.

The servility of the court system was clear to see in the fall 2001 presidential election in Yakutia, which presented a picture of open manipulation. The Kremlin wanted to be rid of compromised former Yakutia president Mikhail Nikolayev and to install its own man as head of the diamond-rich republic. It would have been hard to accomplish that democratically, because Nikolayev had created a sultanistic regime, co-opting and bribing all major forces in the republic. The Kremlin put into motion the proven practice of pressure, with the courts as an integral element.

Getting rid of Nikolayev could have gone smoothly, but the judges in Yakutia got so confused that they couldn't understand whose side they were supposed to be on—that of their republican boss or the Kremlin. The legal proceedings turned into theater of the absurd, with the court changing its decisions several times, alternately permitting Nikolayev to run and banning him from running. The Yakutian elections were a sorry sight, revealing the cynicism of the emboldened bureaucracy that did not even try, as in the past, to create the appearance of legality.

Regional elections in Russia descended during Putin's presidency into blatant deal making and arm twisting without any democratic camouflage. It was now difficult to call a new regime an "elected democracy" when many regional elections turned into poorly disguised appointments from above. The drama of the situation was that occasionally—as in the case of Yakutia—free elections, without the Kremlin's intervention, would have secured the feudal rule of regional elites or families of the regional barons. The choice was between the regional autocrats and the federal bureaucrats. The latter were usually more civilized and pragmatic than the local princelings. Thus, one has to admit that in some cases following democratic rules might have preserved fraudulent and crooked administrations, or strengthened traditional forces resisting any change or reform effort.

But manipulations in getting rid of them hardly could help to promote "clean hands" rules of the game and liberal principles.

The events of 2001, with their fistfights and shaky balance of forces within the Kremlin, proved that the new reality in Russia was not stable—it continued vibrating, transmuting from one state to another. That was good, because if the regime and its base solidified completely, there would be no opportunity for change in the near future. As it was, volatility meant hope for evolution, which could mean either a harshening or a softening of the regime, movement toward either more defined authoritarianism or democracy. In any case, movement was better than stagnation and rot.

The zigzags of domestic politics were accompanied by twists in foreign policy. In early 2001, Russia's relations with creditor nations—especially with its main creditor, Germany—worsened after Moscow's announcement that Russia would not pay its debts to the Paris Club. That statement was followed instantly by a warning from German first deputy finance minister Caio Koch-Weser, who demanded that Russia be expelled from the prestigious Group of Eight.

Berlin's harsh tone had an immediate effect: Moscow promised to pay its debts. The confusion over debt payments demonstrated not only the inexperience of the Russian team but also an irresponsibility on the part of the prime minister and liberals responsible for economic policy. Russia's president also had to learn how to deal with foreign policy issues, and especially with the issue of Russian debt.

Very serious problems soon emerged in Russia–United States relations.[5] The Kremlin's hopes that the Bush administration would be a more congenial partner than the Clinton administration were not justified. More than once, Moscow would wax nostalgic about the Clinton era and former deputy secretary of state Strobe Talbott, the architect of U.S. policy toward Russia during the 1990s, for whom Russia was a foreign policy priority and Russia's transformation a key goal. Under Bush, Washington's course had changed in a fundamental way. Without fully formulating its foreign policy doctrine, the new Republican administration led Moscow to understand that Russia was no longer a major issue for the

United States and that Washington would maintain a policy of "selective engagement" with it. The new administration intentionally held itself aloof, as if to say, "Don't call us, we'll call you when we need you."

In short, President Bush offered Moscow a cold shoulder by ignoring it. The Republican team was not going to ingratiate itself with the Kremlin or indulge Russian imperial nostalgia. Washington apparently did not have time for political philanthropy and could not understand how Russia could be important without having something substantial to deliver. Russia was brushed off. During the administration's first months, the White House ordered a review of previous assistance programs for Russia and all other aspects of Russian policy. It seemed that U.S. assistance to Russia and American cooperation with Russia would be dramatically cut back.

Moscow was caught off-guard by Washington's shock-therapy-style policy. The sharp turn from engagement to disengagement produced first consternation, then dismay, especially among Russian elites who had hitched their star to the Republican administration. Clearly, the Russian political class needed to assess more realistically the country's position in the world and its agenda for relations with the United States—but a cold shower from Washington could hardly bring that about. Besides, a condescending attitude and even open ignoring of Moscow by some members of the U.S. administration only activated bitter feelings among the Russian political class. The Russia–United States bilateral relationship had frozen.

On May 1, 2001, in a speech at the National Defense University, President Bush declared that the Cold War was over and "today's Russia is not our enemy." Therefore, the security regime of mutual nuclear deterrence based on the threat of nuclear retaliation was outmoded. Bush called for moving beyond the 1972 Anti–Ballistic Missile (ABM) agreements, which Russia regarded as the major element of the system of its own and world security.

Bush's logic made sense. The Cold War *was* over, and a security system based on a bipolar view of the world—that is, on distrust and the idea of mutually assured destruction—definitely needed to be reviewed. One of the poles of that order, the Soviet Union, no longer existed, and former rivals—the United States and Russia—were no longer locked in a hostile rivalry. New threats had emerged, and Cold War deterrence was not enough to deal with them. The U.S. leader was right; a new framework of security was needed to counter the challenges of the new world. Bush proposed that the United States and Russia should work together "to develop a new foundation for world peace and security." Americans wanted a clear break with the past, and they wanted to move beyond the constraints of the old security system.

However, the way Washington was dealing with the security issue was not reassuring for Russians. First, Moscow was not ready for such a sharp rejection of the old security order. Second, Moscow had doubts that Washington considered Russia a genuine partner for a new security framework. The White House was planning to withdraw from the old security architecture without waiting for a new cooperative security system to be built. And even more important, in Moscow's eyes, the United States was dismantling the basis of Russia's global role. The Russian political class was not yet ready for that surgery. Even Russian liberals and pro-Western political forces seemed to be confused and to view Washington's security agenda with suspicion.

Washington's logic was not without flaws. If the Cold War was over, the reasoning went in Moscow, why keep its other symbols, like NATO, or the Jackson-Vanik amendment, which made United States–Russia trade dependent on levels of Jewish emigration?

No doubt, U.S. allies in Europe would eventually accept, albeit grudgingly, the American way of solving the problem, but it was trickier for Russia. Moscow was not prepared to abandon the nuclear agreements that were the last evidence and proof of its status as a great power. Along with hurt pride and other emotions that count in politics, Russians had concerns that the U.S. withdrawal from the ABM agreements would start a new nuclear weapons race that they had no chance to win.

The Kremlin began desperately looking for an adequate response. It was not so much a question of guaranteeing Russia's strategic interests (few in Moscow thought that the proposed U.S. missile defense was a real threat to their country's security) as of saving face. Making a tough answer to the United States was out of the question; Putin did not want to seriously exacerbate friction between the two countries. That fact was already a new phenomenon in the Kremlin's stance. Yeltsin would have gone ballistic under the circumstances, breaking the china and resorting to harsh rhetoric or even a demonstration of Russian might. Putin remained calm.

But once Washington began formulating new rules without paying attention to Russia's complexes and anxieties, the Russian president was cornered: He knew too well the sentiments of his country's political class, and he did not want to be accused of weakness.

There was an ironic angle to the story as well: It appeared that Russia could have been important for the United States only if it had been dangerous. Having drawn this conclusion, some Russian elites escalated their scare-mongering, militant rhetoric—trying, if not to intimidate Washington, at least to attract its attention and force it to return to its cautious approach to Russia. As for Americans, they decided to go ahead without paying attention to the political neuroses and obsessions of Russian elites.

In an effort to maintain its international stature, the Kremlin played on every possible field simultaneously. Russian diplomacy attempted to fashion a new, energetic European strategy. Russia turned to China and reactivated contacts with former allies such as Cuba and Vietnam. Finally, the Kremlin rediscovered its neighbors—the new independent states established after the breakup of the Soviet Union, and the countries of Central and Eastern Europe.

One could get the impression that Putin launched hectic diplomatic activity to reclaim Russia's world influence as a counterbalance to U.S. hegemony. At least, most members of the Russian ruling team understood Putin's campaign as the means to constrain American primacy. Apparently, at first it was one of the Russian president's goals as well—but not the only one.

Soon Moscow's decision to broaden its foreign policy agenda and to revive its previous contacts and ties acquired new and constructive dimension. The Kremlin team understood that Russia's immediate interests lay first of all in its neighborhood and in Europe. Thus Russia's growing engagement with the world was to a greater degree dictated by the growing pragmatism and commercialization of its foreign policy—that is, by the attempt to base foreign policy on economic interests rather than on nostalgia for the lost imperium or a desire to counterbalance U.S. hegemony.

Continuing to move in all directions at once, Putin invited President

Mohammad Khatami of Iran to Moscow. Russia signed a wide-ranging agreement with Iran on arms shipments and for Russian help in completing the construction of a nuclear power plant in Bushehr. Many read the pact as an open message to Washington: If you ignore Russia, we will be friends with Iran and other rogue nations. However, there was much more of an economic subtext in relations between Russia and Iran—Iran was one of the few countries that still bought Russian arms and nuclear technology, which helped keep the Russian military-industrial complex and atomic energy branch alive and created jobs for thousands of people. But the timing of the Khatami visit and the nature of the deal between Moscow and Iran gave ground to the conclusion that at least partially it was viewed by the Kremlin's team as retaliation for the U.S. decision to abrogate the ABM agreements and growing U.S. neglect of Russia.

Naturally, Washington considered the new agreements between Moscow and Iran a threat. "It is not wise to invest in regimes that do not follow international standards of behavior," U.S. secretary of state Colin Powell declared.[6] Washington's scolding was hardly the right reaction to Russian policy. By behaving like a stern teacher, the United States only increased resentment and even hostility within the Russian political establishment, which did not want to be taught how to behave and where its real interests lay. As some American pundits advised, economic incentives offered by the United States to compensate Russia for the economic losses it would suffer from ending its military cooperation with Iran would be a more constructive way of dealing with the issue. In any case, it was clear that even after Putin's pro-Western shift, the Russian foreign policy agenda could not be brought into conformity with U.S. plans and aspirations.

The majority of Russian analysts concluded that Moscow was doing the right thing by intensifying its relations with Iran. Representatives of various schools of political opinion, such as Andranik Migranyan in the March 5 *Nezavisimaya gazeta*, counseled Putin to answer Washington sharply and maintain an independent policy. Because the United States respects only strength, they said, if Russia bows to pressure from the White House and accepts Bush's rules of the game, no one will take Russia into account anymore.

But could Russia really resist U.S. pressure? How wise was it for

Moscow to support countries of dubious reputation and to create a belt filled with arms around Russia? Where were the guarantees that Iran, and any other country to which Moscow sold arms, including China, would not turn its back on Russia? And might not Tehran or Beijing use cooperation with Russia as a card in a complicated game of their own with the United States? The Russian political class avoided these questions—it was used to living day by day and it was still thinking in emotional terms. It was also true that in pressuring and ignoring Moscow, the new team in Washington did not facilitate Russia's search for new answers, and this policy only strengthened the position of Russian hawks.

Quite a few Russian politicians and observers suspected that the Republicans were intentionally trying to cool relations with Moscow to open up space for maneuvering on issues of national missile defense and NATO enlargement and to gain a free hand with their global goals—sour moods in Moscow were the best pretext for going ahead alone. Russians got the impression that Bush decided to withdraw from all treaties with Russia and build a new world order independently without wasting time on deals and bargains. Dismissive gestures by some of the members of the Bush team, such as defense secretary Donald Rumsfeld, were fuel on the fire to Russian nationalists and a source of dismay for pro-Western liberal groups.

Meanwhile, President Putin appeared to be more level-headed than the majority of Russian elites. Even if he did not feel comfortable with the U.S. decision to alter the post–Cold War security environment without listening to Moscow's objections, he must have reconciled himself to a new role for Russia. Though he had been uncertain at the beginning, when he was playing with different foreign policy goals, he was now more intent on shaping foreign policy priorities on the basis of Russia's limited resources.

In fact, he was the first Russian leader to think about Russia's ambitions in the context of capabilities. But he was operating in the same security and foreign policy community, with the traditional horizons and mentality. Moreover, he obviously was using outbursts of bitterness among his political class when he was buying time or hesitating as to his next step, or trying to get concessions from his U.S. partners. But he never allowed himself to fall into a hostile mood; he was always calm, poised, and patiently waiting for an occasion to begin mending fences with the Americans.

The Kremlin kept trying to set up a meeting of the two leaders. Not a trace was left of recent attempts to show strength in relations with Washington. In the spring of 2001, the ruling team in Russia was more and more energetically looking for ways to defrost the dialogue with the White House. But relations with Washington were a psychological trap for Moscow. On one hand, the United States–Russia relationship was the only thing that gave Moscow a sense of its significance. On the other, this relationship made the Kremlin feel even more acutely that Russia could no longer claim the status of an equal partner.

Bush, who had met with leaders of much smaller countries, seemingly avoided a meeting with Putin. It looked like Washington really had no intention of returning to the politics of bilateral summits. Besides, the U.S. leader had a concrete reason not to rush into a meeting with Putin. On February 18, 2001, a spy scandal had broken that involved a highly placed FBI agent, Robert Hanssen, who had been working for Russia and before that the Soviet Union for fifteen years (and who would plead guilty in July to fifteen counts of espionage and conspiracy).

As revenge, on March 22, the U.S. Department of State expelled 50 Russian diplomats suspected of espionage. Moscow as a reciprocal gesture announced a "symmetrical" expulsion of 50 American diplomats. A cold wind again blew through both capitals. High officials on both sides of the ocean began rehearsing aggressive rhetoric that had not been heard since the early 1980s. "Spying?" asked Robert Kaiser, a leading *Washington Post* columnist, commenting on the spy scandal in the March 24 issue. "We caught the FBI agent working for them because a Russian agent apparently working for us turned him in. . . . We are still in the grip of Cold War reflexes and assumptions. Who's to blame for this nuttiness? That's probably a futile question. This tango requires the usual number of dancers." The tango continued.

The Kremlin leader, however, showed no emotion even during the spy scandal, as if it had no connection with Moscow. He avoided anything that would make it impossible to normalize relations with Washington—he never got near the point of no return. And Washington finally (apparently not without pressure from its European allies) realized that it was time to stop ignoring Moscow. Bush agreed to a meeting with Putin in Ljubljana on June 16, 2001, during a European trip. The Kremlin team sighed in relief.

Despite the chill between the two capitals, the meeting of the two leaders was unexpectedly warm. Bush went much further in expressing friendliness toward Putin than either the Americans or Russians had expected. "I looked into that man's eyes and saw that he is direct and trustworthy. We had a very good dialogue. And I saw his soul," Bush said at a press conference after meeting the Russian president. Bush even invited Putin to his Texas ranch.

Ljubljana was a turning point. The Russian president's approach to relations with the United States was visibly different from that of many European politicians—instead of criticizing, Putin played down differences and the irritant issues, always keeping in mind his goal of normalizing relations with Washington, which he considered crucial for Russia and its dialogue with the West. Bush clearly appreciated that. The first meeting of the two leaders was the beginning of their personal rapport. Condoleezza Rice, Bush's national security adviser and one of his most trusted consultants, helped to build trust between the two, and she became the major force behind shaping a new Republican policy toward Moscow.

By the summer of 2001, the Republican administration had begun to promote the same kind of personal relations and close ties with the Russian president for which Clinton's opponents had roundly criticized him. That change in the wind only proved that without personal rapport and understanding between the leaders it would hardly be possible to build a constructive relationship between the nations, especially when one of the leaders accumulates all powers in his country and there are no other players to speak with. In any case, the personal chemistry of Bush and Putin helped their countries get out of the post–Cold War freeze.

In the meantime, Moscow continued its policy of playing on every field, and in July it signed a friendship agreement with China. Putin wanted to relegate Russia's and China's mutual suspicion to the past. He needed good relations with Russia's most powerful neighbor. Many observers, though, saw Moscow's treaty with Beijing as another response to U.S. hegemony. "Now Russia and China seem to be trying . . . to curb American power," an article in the July 16 *Economist* suggested. It was hardly so. Both Moscow and Beijing tried to use their rapprochement as an extra card in pursuing their relations with the West and the United States. But Putin did not see his dialogue with Beijing as an instrument with which to promote multipolarity, as Primakov had just two years before. Putin's dialogue with China was more pragmatically oriented toward achievable goals and economic priorities. For Putin, Beijing was neither a major partner nor a potential ally in the anti-Western game.

In August, Russia received a visit from North Korean dictator Kim Jong Il. Kim crossed the country in an armored train and was embraced by Putin in a warm welcome at the Kremlin (these train trips of Kim's would become a tradition—in 2002 he would come to Russia again). Outwardly, Moscow seemed to be returning to its old allies, which made Russian liberals uneasy. But in fact the negotiations with Kim had another purpose; Putin wanted to restore Russian influence over North Korea and become the intermediary between it and the rest of the world.

This was a fundamentally important shift. Russia, far from trying to form anti-Western fronts, now was trying to create the basis for a more profitable dialogue with the West, striving to be a partner that had something substantial to offer. Putin was suggesting a new role for Russia in the world: The imperial bully would become a mediator between the West and the states that created problems for the West. Thus Russia's diplomacy under its new leader had undergone serious evolution. At the beginning of Putin's rule, it was aiming at constraining the West and first of all U.S. dominance. But it gradually became an instrument in building a more constructive partnership with the West. How durable the change was remained to be seen.

On September 11, 2001, a trial for the West became a test of Russia's ability to determine its new international identity. Putin's reaction to the terrorist attacks on the United States was unambiguous: He was the first foreign leader to call Bush with words of sympathy and support. The hotline between the two capitals established during the Cold War now appeared to be handy when all telephone connections with Washington had been broken.

For the first time, Putin did not hesitate. He took an absolutely correct step from the human and the political points of view. It does not matter what prompted him: intuition, calculation, or emotion. His now-famous phrase "Americans, we are with you!" coming from this outwardly cold man, broke the barrier he had erected between himself and liberal-minded Russians. With his telephone call, he took a forthright stand as a pro-Western leader.

With those words and his readiness to become the United States's ally with no strings attached, Putin brought about a new phase in relations between Russia and the United States. Moreover, at that moment, he as a leader made his existential choice in favor of the West. Russia (and the USSR) had made a pro-Western choice during World War II, but that did not prevent them from entering a Cold War era. In 2001, in joining an alliance against terrorism formed by the United States, Russia for the first time in its history recognized the hegemony of another state and voluntarily chose to play junior partner. True, nobody, even Putin, at the moment would say whether this change in Russia's role was final and whether it would be accepted by the Russian ruling class—what was happening was too extraordinary, too breathtaking to believe!

What was no less significant was that Putin did not ask for any payoff. Unlike previous Soviet and Russian rulers, who engaged in horse-trading over every compromise they struck with the West, there was no request for a quid pro quo. Moscow did not bargain this time. Putin understood that being with the West at that moment of truth was in Russia's national interest. Irrespective of what would happen in the future, this pro-Western shift would acquire a logic of its own and its own momentum.

Putin's pro-Western turn was not a game, or a tactical maneuver; it was conscious and deliberate. His measured and calculated behavior during the cooling of relations with Washington argues the case. He must have understood that any hesitation, or wait-and-see tactics, would have strengthened mistrust between Russia and the West or even put Russia into the camp of outcast states.

Putin's reaction to the September 11 attacks was also the result of changes in the Russian mentality. Russia—despite the frequently arrogant rhetoric of its ruling class and its unhappiness with Moscow's new role during the 1990s—had been coming to grips with the new global reality and had not once made a serious effort to reverse the pendulum's movement. What is ironic is that it was a former KGB officer who officially acknowledged what Russian society and its elites had known for some time but would not admit even to themselves: that Russia's lingering hegemonic aspirations and global ambitions were an untenable fantasy.

It was true that, when it came to actions, the mood of the Russian political class was still ambivalent. Putin's close entourage showed no particular desire to join the antiterrorist campaign and the war in Afghanistan. Nor were his lieutenants ready to endorse a U.S. presence in Central Asia in preparation for military actions against the Taliban. The reaction of President Putin's comrades in arms just after September 11 was blunt: "[Commonwealth of Independent States] territory will never become a field for Western military operations, and no NATO soldier will ever set foot on Central Asian soil." So said defense minister Sergei Ivanov, one of Putin's closest friends.

Some Russian politicians even blamed the United States and its hegemony as the reason for the terrorist retaliation. The subtext with them was a gloating "Serves you right!" Russian society was shocked by the terrorist attacks, but the majority of Russians were reluctant to endorse Russia's direct participation in the military operations in Afghanistan. Russians—having experienced defeat in Afghanistan in the 1970s and still fighting without success in Chechnya—were not ready to get involved in one more battle.[7]

Putin had real difficulties overcoming the disagreements within Russia's political class—this was the first time he had gone against their advice and taken an independent position. Russia's role in the antiterrorist coalition was decided on at a meeting of the power ministries that Putin called for September 22. The session lasted six hours, interrupted only by a telephone call from Bush. During those hours, President Putin broke the resistance of his generals. It needed a lot of courage and will. In a national television appearance on September 24, Putin with a determined face clarified Moscow's position and, punctuating his words, declared Russia's readiness "to make its contribution to the war on terrorism."

This time Russian cooperation was not just rhetoric. Russia began sharing its intelligence information with the United States; it helped to build bridges between the U.S. military and the Northern Alliance, the main opposition in Afghanistan to the Taliban that Moscow had been supporting for a long time; and it agreed to U.S. use of military airports and bases in Russian allies Kyrgyzstan, Tajikistan, and Uzbekistan. Moscow also continued massive arms shipments to the Northern Alliance, announced other aid for its fighters, and offered Russian airspace for humanitarian relief flights.

A serious test for United States–Russia relations came when the Americans began moving into Central Asia preparatory to their attack on Afghanistan. For the first time in recent history, another great power was in Russia's backyard. Putin's response to the new challenge was calm. It was clear that Washington had informed the Kremlin beforehand and gotten a green light. Outwardly, even the Russian military was restrained in its reaction. The Russian deputy chief of the General Staff, Yuri Baluevsky, commented, "We haven't been enemies in a long time with America. But we are not yet full partners." He added that the presence of the United States in Central Asia was solving problems related to the security of Russia's southern borders. Either the military decided not to oppose the president or they felt that U.S. troops really would help Russia to secure its southern flank.

U.S. secretary of state Colin Powell had high praise for the Russian contribution to the military operation in Afghanistan, stating that Russia had been "a key member" of the international antiterrorist coalition and had played "a crucial role" in the coalition's success "by providing intelligence, bolstering the Northern Alliance, and assisting our entry into Central Asia." That praise was not sheer politeness; the magnitude of Russian assistance surprised even the staunchest skeptics.

There are times when leaders make history. There are also times when history makes leaders. That is what happened in the fall of 2001 in Russia, when the terrorist attacks on the United States forced the Russian president to make a choice that turned a mediocre politician into a leader who amazed the world by proposing a completely new role for Russia. Vladimir Vladimirovich had been moving toward the West for some time. But he needed a catalyst to make him take an open stand.

Putin's speech on September 24 had a second part—on Chechnya. Putin tied the world situation to the situation in Chechnya and delivered an ultimatum to all members of Chechen rebel groups: They had 72 hours to disarm. But if the separatists had been resisting for years, why would they give up the struggle voluntarily now? There was an implication that the president might be prepared to negotiate with moderate separatists. Putin also recognized in his speech that the war had "its prehistory," which implied that he was beginning to reexamine his understanding of the Chechen drama. But even if the Russian leader began to hesitate and try to find a peaceful solution to Chechnya, he did not pursue that option; he was not ready for one more breakthrough.

In the meantime, the Russian president continued his movement toward the West. When he arrived in Germany on September 25, he gave an hour-long speech at the Bundestag, in impeccable German, receiving ovations from the deputies. In essence, he proposed fighting together against Cold War remnants in thinking and politics. "We are still living with the old value system—we speak of partnership, but in fact we have not yet learned to trust one another," he said. "Despite the many sweet words, we continue secretly to oppose one another." He spoke like a European in terms the West could understand, and he said the right things. He also indirectly responded to Bush's call to "go beyond" Cold War arrangements, hinting that the West needed to do its part of the job as well.

It was true that ten years after the collapse of the USSR and the formal conclusion of the Cold War, world leaders continued to use concepts out of the past. The very existence of a NATO without Russia was confirmation of that. Russian observers pointed out that if Western leaders were sincere about closing the Cold War chapter, they should not stop at the abrogation of the old security arrangements with Russia but go further and liquidate NATO—or invite Russia to join the alliance. Otherwise, Russian suspicions about the anti-Russian orientation of the Western security institutions were justified. Russian observers were ignoring the fact that Russian elites and their behavior, not only Western prejudices, often served as the justification for the West to keep its old security framework.

Moscow seemed to have been unexpectedly prodded into a new foreign policy as Putin unfolded his latest round of activity in Brussels at the European Union–Russia summit and in negotiations with NATO leaders in the fall of 2001. Putin announced his desire to form a single economic space with E.U. countries and to take a more active part in European security structures. There was an increasing awareness in Moscow that Europe, long neglected by Yeltsin, was its primary resource for capital and trade.

Russia and Europe had already forged multiple links. Cooperation in the energy field had been the most productive. The European Union continued to be the main destination for Russian energy exports, its countries buying 53 percent of oil exports and 62 percent of natural gas exports. The volume of trade with the Union constituted 48 percent of all Russian trade. The Europeans' growing interest in their own security agenda made Russia a major partner of theirs in the security sphere. In fact, relations between Russia and Europe had a much broader base than those between Russia and the United States. Moreover, Brussels possibly had more leverage than Washington when it came to applying steady pressure on Moscow to implement European standards of democracy, the rule of law, and human rights. It was Brussels that forced the Russian military to at least try to behave in a more civilized way in Chechnya.

Cooperation between Russia and the European Union, however, was not smooth and easy. Russian politicians were increasingly disappointed by the sluggishness and bureaucratization of decision-making processes in Brussels. Russia itself was too slow in bringing its legislation into line with E.U. criteria and has yet to fully realize the potential of its Partnership and Cooperation Agreement with the European Union, which was signed in 1997. As for the E.U. leaders, they had too much on their plates, with Central and Eastern European countries being integrated into the Union, and with Turkey waiting in the wings, reforming its institutions and developing a design for further unity. Europeans had a justified fear of accommodating Russia with its enormous potential and no less enormous problems. At the same time, the E.U. leadership had to answer Russia's challenge, and if Russia was to become a full member of Europe, the

European Union had to consider how to proceed with that puzzle. It was high time to think about forming free trade zones with Russians and moving toward a customs union. Putin was pushing in that direction.

Pundits speculated that growing cooperation between Russia and Europe could lead to an alliance between Europe and Russia on a variety of international issues where their positions differed from that of the United States, for instance on missile defense. But the dreams of some Russian nationalists that this possible rapprochement might acquire an anti-American flavor were hardly grounded in reality, though they might worry Washington. Despite its frustration with Washington, Europe was not ready to freeze its relations with the United States. Putin at that time also did not show an interest in playing off the differences between the Western allies. Paradoxically, on some international issues, including terrorism, Moscow was much closer to Washington than Europe.

Moscow's next step was to restore cooperation with NATO, which had been broken off during the Kosovo crisis in 1999. Putin even risked noting that if NATO were to develop as a political rather than military union, Russia would not object to its new round of enlargement. He even hinted about a possible Russian interest in NATO membership. He hardly believed in such an option—rather, he wanted to see whether NATO was ready to cooperate with Russia and whether Russian elites were ready to relinquish their anti-NATO stance.

In any case, Russia was not prepared to join NATO and thereby give up its sovereignty. In fact, Russia's entry into NATO would mean the end of the alliance as it has been for half a century, and many in the West, especially in Eastern Europe, were not ready for that either. For them, NATO was still a means of "keeping Russia out." But Putin's testing the waters demonstrated how the moods in the Kremlin have changed.

In the eyes of Russians, NATO was losing its previous relevance, especially after it proved not very relevant during the war in Afghanistan. Future relations between NATO and Russia depended not only on Russia's new security thinking but on the ability of the alliance to transform itself. NATO was going through its identity crisis and was looking for a new mission. Russia was in the process of forming its new geopolitical role as well. Their ability to find new forms of dealing with each other might have been one of the ways of handling their identity problems.

There were a lot of questions to answer: Do we trust each other enough? Do we agree on threats the world is facing? Can Russia be directly plugged into NATO's activities, and does it want to be? One NATO insider put the dilemma this way: "Russia has an open door to NATO, but the train is moving!"

Meanwhile, Vladimir Vladimirovich decided that he should seize all opportunities. Hence, the Kremlin was dancing in all directions. The Russian leader might have felt that a Russia–NATO marriage would be a tricky business. That is why he was not very intent to pursue that option more vigorously. He understood the moods of the Russian military too well. There were more realistic and potentially promising goals for Russia. One was joining the World Trade Organization. Moscow began consulting on this issue with Brussels and Washington.

Amazingly, the Kremlin team, so awkward and inexperienced just yesterday, suspicious of all actions by the West, suddenly displayed both great readiness to cooperate and the energy to bring it off. Equally amazing was the change in the mood of the Russian political class. In 2001 and early 2002, almost everyone who was anyone among the Russian elites tried to outdo the rest in great-power sentiments and, especially, anti-Americanism. It had looked as if suspicious and ambitious Russia was returning to its "special path." And then—in a few short months—such an unexpected turn!

Now Russia not only announced that it wanted to be part of Europe and part of the West but made claims to a partnership with the United States, accepting its junior partner role. But the very unexpectedness of the mood shift created ambivalent feelings; if the country and its elites could turn in one direction so quickly, they could turn back just as easily. Russia had yet to learn the political consequences that emotions such as fear, humiliation, suspicion, hurt pride, and a desire for vengeance, even confined to elite circles, might have—and had yet to learn to control those emotions.

Sociologists hurried to test the nation's mood and discovered that a significant portion of ordinary Russians, despite surges of frustrating emotions, were essentially pro-Western. According to polls conducted by Tatyana Kutkovets and Igor Klyamkin at the end of 2001, the vast majority of Russians—87 percent—thought that Russia should orient itself toward Western nations, and only 8 percent (most of them Muslims) preferred an orientation toward Muslim countries. Recent longing to preserve "uniqueness" was forgotten—unexpectedly for observers. When asked, "Partnership with which countries best responds to the interests of people like you?" a strong majority (63 percent) named the countries of Western Europe, 45 percent Belarus, 42 percent the United States, and 40 percent Ukraine. Only 6 percent considered cooperation with Iraq, Iran, and other "states of concern" useful. Cooperation with China was considered desirable by 22 percent.[8]

Some social groups retained exaggerated expectations; 34 percent still considered Russia a superpower no less than the United States. But one saw a breakthrough in Russians' relinquishment of the superpower complex. Forty-three percent considered desirable for Russia the status of France, Germany, or Japan. The vast majority of Russians wanted a country that was not a military power but a "comfortable country, convenient for living, where top priority is given to the interests of people, their well-being, and opportunities."[9] The shift toward the West and its values in Russia was more widespread than many observers had thought. Russians were more ready than they themselves thought to live normal life in a normal country. It seemed that the great-power factor was no longer the only consolidating force in Russia.

Perceptions of Russia as a bastion of anti-Americanism turned out to be mistaken as well. According to polls that the Public Opinion Foundation conducted in October 2001, 35 percent of Russians had a good opinion of Americans, 44 percent were indifferent, 15 percent had a bad opinion, and 5 percent had no opinion. According to VTsIOM polls in November 2001, 65 percent of Russians wanted Russia and the United States to become allies, 13 percent did not care, 12 percent were against the idea, and 10 percent had no opinion.

But suspicions about America's intentions remained. In November, 37 percent of those polled thought the United States was a nation friendly to Russia, 44 percent thought it was not friendly, and 19 percent had no opinion. Yet when questions were posed about specific things, it became clear that Russians did not perceive Americans as the enemy. For instance, in answer to the question, "Would you give blood for Americans wounded in a terrorist act?" 63 percent said yes and only 10 percent said no (25 percent said they could not be blood donors, and 3 percent had no opinion).

There were things to give one pause, however. The majority of those who considered the United States a potential ally based their attitude toward America primarily on the existence of a common enemy of the two countries. That was typical Soviet Russian logic: Against whom will we be friends? If the common enemy were to vanish, what would the two countries have left in common? Russia and the United States could once again find themselves, if not in different camps, then at a distance, at which point mutual suspicions might flare up with renewed vigor. This happened sooner than anyone would have thought.[10]

On November 13, 2001, Putin flew to Washington for a summit meeting. As he was being received in Washington, Kabul was falling and the Taliban were beginning to disintegrate. Few in the Russian delegation understood that the swift collapse of the Taliban regime would undermine the partnership between Russia and the United States—Washington could act independently now. The ousting of the Taliban put a trump card in the hands of those in the U.S. administration who insisted that it waste no more time forming coalitions and cajoling its allies.

As for Putin, his mood was elevated at first. "I have great optimism," he said, beaming before his flight. "If anyone thinks that Russia could become an enemy of the United States again, I think that they don't understand what has happened in the world and what has happened in Russia." He apparently hoped that their personal chemistry would work on Bush and persuade him to retain the old security framework that the Russian leader wanted to preserve at any cost. Putin seemed to believe that his ability to preserve the ABM agreements would be a proof of his leadership strength for the Russian political establishment, and a failure to do this would be perceived as a blow for him personally. Washington, however, made it clear that its withdrawal from the old security concept was inevitable, and initially the Americans had no intention of signing a treaty on reducing offensive weapons, as Moscow insisted. The White House intended to make a clean break with the past without waiting for the Kremlin to become ready to join it in doing so.

It was difficult to get behind the inscrutable mask Putin always wore, but he was evidently frustrated—not because he felt Russia's security threatened but because he had to explain to his political class why he had failed to persuade Americans to preserve old rules of the game in the security area. To give such significance to the ABM agreements and to make Russia–United States relations dependent on them was Moscow's mistake. It was not prudent on the part of Russian diplomacy to waste so much time and energy on an unachievable goal and put the president in an embarrassing situation. But Putin soon demonstrated that he was learning from his mistakes.

Tony Blair sensed that his friend Vladimir needed urgent support, and on November 16, 2001, he sent a four-page letter to Lord George Robertson, NATO's secretary general, in which he proposed the creation of a Russia–NATO Council. The goal was to expand Russian influence on NATO decision making, albeit in strictly negotiated spheres. The proposal looked like moral compensation to the Kremlin for the liquidation of the old security structure. But the idea of raising the status of Russia's cooperation with NATO, even on a limited group of issues, elicited resistance from NATO's new members, Poland, Hungary, and the Czech Republic. That was understandable—they were seeking asylum under NATO's roof from possible Russian hostility, and here they were forced to sit at the same table again.

Most important, Donald Rumsfeld, the U.S. secretary of defense, openly resisted upgrading relations between NATO and Russia. According to the *New York Times*, "Mr. Rumsfeld in November made an eleventh-hour attempt to have the 'NATO at 20' reference removed from the draft communiqué that Secretary Colin Powell and the foreign ministers from NATO's 19 nations were to issue in Brussels." Only Bush's intervention helped preserve the idea of "NATO at Twenty."[11] There, apparently Powell and Rice's line for more active engagement with Russia won—at least for the time being.

In the meantime, on December 13, the United States announced its withdrawal from the ABM Treaty. Putin reacted with restraint and held to his position, characterizing the decision as "mistaken."[12] But at the same time, he acknowledged that the withdrawal did not threaten Russian security. He did not want Russia–United States relations at the mercy of irritants any longer.

Putin's second year in power was drawing to a close. After his initial hesitations and constant looking back, after his courting Russian conservatives, Vladimir Vladimirovich was finally feeling sure enough of himself to go ahead with a modernization agenda. He had proven that he had gotten and strengthened his power not for the sake of just keeping it—he had a mission. He could have been satisfied that he did not waste his time at least in two areas: the economy and foreign policy.

Beginning in 1999, Russia experienced high rates of economic growth; the economy expanded by 8.3 percent in 2000 and by 5.8 percent in 2001. The projected growth for 2002 was 3.6 percent. The Russian gross domestic product increased by 20 percent in 2001, to about 72 percent of the 1990 level. During those years, the problems of non-payment of salaries and pensions and barter were almost completely resolved, and the economy had truly become monetary. After the government introduced a flat 13 percent personal income tax in 2000, revenue collection jumped 50 percent. Putin balanced the budget and kept inflation in check.

For the first time since the Bolshevik Revolution, a new Land Code allowed individuals to buy and sell nonagricultural land. The Russian stock market became the world leader in 2001 with a 77 percent gain, and continued to steam ahead. "Since Putin came to power nearly everything has improved for investors," said Western investors. Barings's Eastern Fund, registered in Dublin, brought investors a return of 34 percent in 2001 and 50 percent over three years. The Credit Suisse First Boston bank was up 36 percent for 2001 and 45 percent in the first half of 2002. It looked as if the gold rush had returned to Russia, as Patrick Collinson suggested in the April 4, 2002, *Guardian*.

In mid-2001, growth rates somewhat declined, mainly because of the world economic recession. But observers predicted that even if oil prices fell to $15 a barrel, Russia would remain stable, losing only its financial reserves. In that case, it would have to turn to the International Monetary Fund in 2003 for help in paying its debts.

But there were other disturbing signs. Foreign investment in 2001 amounted to an insignificant $2.5 billion, somewhat lower than in 2000. Russia attracted less capital than Poland or the Czech Republic. Russian oil companies were not investing in other sectors of the economy. The markets remained risky. The bulk of Russian assets was in the hands of sharks—Russian oligarchs who were not ready for competition or to allow foreign players. There was no working banking system to enable the development of an effective and diversified economy. Above all, the legal system was in the pocket of either executive power or tycoons. "To become 'normal,' Russia must have entrepreneurs and an explosion of small- and medium-size businesses," affirmed an article in the May 13 *Newsweek*, and it was on the mark.

What was even more worrisome were new wage and pension arrears. At the beginning of 2002, wage arrears amounted to 2.7 billion rubles ($90 million). In ten regions, the average wage and pension arrears exceeded ten days. Meanwhile, social stability in Russia could be preserved only if wages and pensions were paid on time.

The Russian economy still was vulnerable. Three major factors contributed to economic stability in Russia: the energy and raw materials sector, the activity of major financial-industrial groups, and modernization "from above" using authoritarian methods. But these three factors also caused problems. The orientation toward raw materials created a lopsided economy heavily dependent on the export of oil and gas. The major conglomerates—the new Russian *chaebols*, which controlled the economy—did not allow medium-sized and small enterprises to develop. And modernization from above was producing immense bureaucratic pressure, which was an obstacle to private initiative and free enterprise, without which an effective market was impossible.

The Russian economist Yevgeny Yasin was right to call for the radical restructuring of the Russian economy; the steps taken by the president so far had not been enough. Yasin proposed several breakthrough areas, including banking reform, the creation of securities markets, reorganization of the "natural monopolies," reduction of state regulation, and expansion of private initiative. The question was whether the Kremlin felt the urgency of pushing for the next stage of reforms. As Yegor Gaidar said in the May 7, 2001, *Yezhenedelny zhurnal*, "The reforms are usually implemented when it is impossible not to initiate them anymore, not when they are needed." At the end of 2001 and beginning of 2002, the general feeling in Moscow was that the level of economic stability that had been achieved was sufficient and that Russia was not ready for more radical restructuring.

Beyond the economic obstacles that continued to hinder further economic recovery, there were more fundamental barriers to a modern market. They derived from the lack of definite separation of political and economic, and public and private, spheres—leading to the merger of business and power, which resulted in nontransparency, corruption, a distortion of economic behavior, and an administrative impact on the economic area. In fact, the key to further economic reforms was not dealing with economic obstacles per se but bringing about change in the political system.

It was not yet clear whether the president and his team were prepared to move from a policy of stabilization to one of structural reform that would radically transform relations between state and society, bureaucracy and business. After restarting economic reform, Putin again vacillated, alternately pressing different pedals. One of the most optimistic foreign observers of Russian market reform, Anders Åslund, said in early 2002 after visiting Russia: "The Soviet bureaucracy is creeping back, extending its multiple regulations. . . . The grand attempt at structural reform has come to an end."

First giving more oxygen to enterprise and private initiative, the Kremlin then pressed another pedal that increased bureaucratic control, blocking the forces of economic freedom and competition and turning the economy back toward arbitrariness. Examples of zigzagging over economic strategy were, on one hand, Russia's attempt to accelerate joining the World Trade Organization and, on the other hand, its turning to protectionist measures. That policy maintained a somewhat shaky equilibrium. But to respond to the new challenges facing Russia, the Kremlin had to turn for support to new social groups interested in more dynamic transformation and in defining a clear vision of the future.

———————— ⤙⤙ ————————

The only sphere in which Russia made a real breakthrough was international relations. In essence, in late 2001 the president started a revolution in Russian foreign policy, moving beyond the country's traditional geopolitical role. Putin made Russia an ally of Western states in the antiterrorist coalition, accepting the asymmetry of the alliance; he agreed to a U.S. presence in the post-Soviet space; and he demonstrated readiness to go beyond the traditional agenda in relations with the West. This was tantamount to rejecting Russia's great-power ambitions. This was a step that shocked even his comrades in arms.

Was the shift due to bewilderment in the Kremlin and lack of alternatives—that is, to forced pragmatism—or was it the product of certain calculations on a new agenda? If Putin's actions were forced, the Kremlin could return to its zigzagging at any moment, and perhaps even pull a U-turn.

The impression observers got was that the Russian president was influenced by a combination of the most contradictory circumstances. These included his understanding of Russia's weakness and its inability to resist pressure from the West and particularly from Washington, his desire to cooperate with the West and use Western resources, and at the same time a lack of understanding of how to promote Russian interests through cooperation with Western countries—of what could be negotiated, how, and when and where Russia could be a partner with the West and where only an ally. Let us add to that, perhaps, Putin's confusion. Events were unfolding too quickly, and he had too many things on the table, which even a much more experienced politician would have had difficulty handling. Often, he went with the flow, unresisting.

With all his concerns, doubts, and suspicions, however, the Russian president understood that his goal of a strong Russia could be achieved only through broader engagement with the West. He could have behaved differently on many occasions. He could have blocked the arrival of the U.S. military in Central Asia and especially in Georgia. But he did not. He could have watched from a distance how the war on terrorism was going in Afghanistan. But he got engaged more actively than some of the American allies. And overall, he could have behaved like the Chinese leaders, observing developments with a demonstratively cold air. But Putin met the Americans halfway. He went even further in his relations with Europe. He began to limit Russia's ambitions before September 11. Thus, despite the resistance of the military, he decided to give up two Russian military bases abroad—in Cuba (Lourdes) and Vietnam (Kamran)—that were symbols of Russia's geopolitical presence.

At the same time, Putin's foreign policy breakthrough still did not have a concrete agenda that would make clear how Moscow planned to cooperate with the West, and who among his entourage would be responsible for his new agenda. Putin started his revolution in foreign policy almost single-handedly, without the support of his team. It had been his personal initiative, his own project. He looked like the Lone Ranger pursuing it while his entourage stood off to the side looking as if they were making bets—would he win or fail? In this case, his authoritarianism allowed him to bring Russia closer to the West.

Unless he gained the support of the political class for that breakthrough, however, and unless he created a new team that included people free from the old mentality and Cold War stereotypes, Putin's new policy was unlikely to be durable and sustainable. Besides, he needed the support of society for such a breakthrough, and he was pulling this one off without explaining his goals to Russians, without trying to form a national consensus. Even liberals and democrats shrugged their shoulders as they watched his foreign policy chess game, wondering what it was that the president was doing: Was this tactics or strategy, a goal or a means?

The Russian turn to the West had caught the Western community unprepared as well. Europe was sincerely interested in a full partnership with Russia. But its inertia and habit of letting the United States lead the way took their toll. Meanwhile, America was preoccupied with its own concerns and obsessions. The West, busy with its problems, seemed not to have the strength or desire to think about how to include Russia in its orbit. People were tired of the constant hassles with Russia, and quite a few who had hailed Russian reform at the start were now thinking, "Maybe those Russians really are different. They'll never mature enough for Western values. Let them live in their Eurasia. At least they'll be useful, protecting the West from China."

Former British ambassador to Moscow Rodric Braithwaite, in his book

Across the Moscow River, wrote: "When the facile optimism was disappointed, Western euphoria faded, and Russophobia returned. . . . The new Russophobia was expressed not by the governments, but in the statements of out-of-office politicians, the publications of academic experts, the sensational writings of journalists, and the products of the entertainment industry. It was fueled by those who argued that the Russian orthodox civilization was doomed to remain apart from the civilization of the West."[13] Unfortunately, the Russian political class did a lot to feed Western criticism and Western suspicions of Russia.

Putin's second year in power was drawing to a close. His sky-high approval ratings seemed to have frozen, being a talisman against defeat. In December 2001, 73 percent of Russians said they approved of the president—a height Yeltsin and Gorbachev would have envied. Forty-two percent of Russians felt that 2001 had passed successfully for Russia, 38 percent thought not, and 20 percent had no opinion. Society was divided in its view of current events of Russia's development; 45 percent thought everything was going in the right direction, and 39 percent saw it going in a "bad" direction. But on the whole, optimism prevailed. Russians were looking at the future in a brighter light.[14] Nobody, however, was sure how sustainable that optimism was.

Chapter 8

ON THE EVE
OF A NEW RACE

The nature of stability. The grudges continue. Putin's foreign policy success.
New uncertainties. Freedom and order.

The year 2002 in Russia was supposed to be the last calm year before a new election fever, which was due in 2003–2004, when parliamentary and then presidential elections had to take place. Before getting an election fever, Russia still had a chance to ponder on major trends and choices, and its president had time to continue his modernization policy. However, this country had always defied any plans and predictions. Russia could plunge into a new race and unruly political fistfight before it knew it.

The beginning of 2002 confirmed Vladimir Putin's political style and the nature of his rule. Having made a pro-Western shift in the foreign arena, on the domestic front he continued his policy of contradictory principles. He was liberal, statist, populist at the same time. He was a consensus guy and authoritarian politician, Russian patriot and pro-Western person simultaneously. Half of the Russian population did not know who their leader was. Everybody still saw what they wanted and imagined the face they would like. It was amazing that Putin had succeeded in playing Everybody's Man for so long—it clearly needed skill and luck.

Thus, contrary to prevailing opinion, Putin announced that capital punishment would be banned in Russia. This was a step toward the European model. He also gave Russian citizens the right to have bank accounts abroad. He supported a new package of liberalization laws introduced by the reformist part of his cabinet. He continued his pro-Western

221

foreign policy, moving further in institutionalizing Russia's relations with the West and building trust with its Western partners.

But at the same time, the Russian president made decisions that were aimed to cajole the traditionalists among the Russian population and elites. He endorsed the law on "counteracting extremism," in which the broad definition of extremism gave the law enforcement agencies the opportunity to view any opposition and even any dissent as a form of extremism. He supported the alternative military service bill pushed through by the General Staff that treated alternative military service as a punishment, and the migration law that toughened the rules for getting Russian citizenship.

Clearly not without the president's knowledge, trials continued in Russia of people accused of espionage for allegedly passing secret information to Western intelligence services. Particular notoriety attached to the case of journalist Grigory Pasko. Pasko made available to the Japanese press information about nuclear pollution from Russian atomic submarines in the Sea of Japan. The journalist was accused of revealing state secrets and was sentenced to four years in labor camps on charges of treason. Despite protests in Russia and abroad, the sentence has not been reviewed.

Putin apparently had not determined how far he could go with his market breakthrough. He did not dare attack the foundations of oligarchic-bureaucratic capitalism. Under the table, sweet deals continued to dominate the playing field. The cabinet continued to spend much of its time and energy coordinating the interests of clans and moguls. The president personally decided the fate of economic laws and institutions. Even the new market legislation was constructed so as to give the leader the opportunity to make economic decisions independent of the parliament.

In some cases, the Kremlin accelerated economic reform. But overall, the market's exclusive dependence on executive power limited economic freedoms and preserved the domineering role of bureaucracy in managing the economy. In fact, the highest level of the executive branch increased its control over the market to an extent comparable to that during Yeltsin's rule.

On the political front, Putin's rule no longer resembled a rigid superpresidential regime, which according to the initial Kremlin plan had to function as a perfectly oiled conveyor belt. The authorities had already understood that such a regime was impossible to implement in Russia without harsh coercion. The Kremlin, however, was not ready to return to coercion and dictatorial ways. Russia would not tolerate that well.

Thus the rule of the second Russian postcommunist president, irrespective of how he personally differed from his predecessor, more and more resembled Yeltsin's electoral monarchy. It also included the fusion of incompatible elements: emphasis on subordination and an inability to cope with the inner resistance; attempts to strengthen a unitary state and acquiescence to feudal regional regimes; a desire to stop bargaining and permanent deal making. It was true that Putin's Kremlin so far had succeeded in implementing stricter rules and achieving more compliance. But under the surface the old spontaneity again was bubbling up. All this proved that if the leader was not ready to reject personified power, in the end, unwittingly, even contrary to his plans, he would be forced to return to Yeltsin's methods of rule—that is, to political barter with vested interests and to an imitation of order.

A hybrid political regime guaranteed calm in Russia; it was the means to link past and present, conservatives and modernizers. It was an instrument to neutralize conflicts, a painkiller that softened the drastic outcomes of Russia's transformation. But there were serious doubts that a hybrid regime could help make the breakthrough to the future.

For the time being, the president seemed to be leaving his political portrait undone. Journalists who tried to determine the character of Putin's leadership wrote about "The Flight of the Two-Headed Eagle" and that "Putin's skis were going in different directions." This was a metaphorical way of showing that the president, while executing pro-Western policies and liberal economic reforms, remained an adherent of the semiauthoritarian model of power, which inevitably meant a suspicious attitude toward the institutions Western civilization had built.[1]

Putin's position was understandable; he was afraid of destroying the fragile balance. He was not prepared to take a risk and make a final decision, betting on one ideology and system of principles, which would mean if not confrontation in society, then at least a violation of the stability that had been created. Moreover, in 2002 the president was already in a rather risky position. His foreign policy had no support, even from his closest entourage. It was true that even the foes of his turn toward the West had quieted down. But any moment, sensing weakness, they could start an attack—and Putin realized this. There were signals that more determined economic reforms could lead to open dissatisfaction in Russian society. Thus, in the spring of 2002, the residents of Voronezh took to the streets to protest housing reforms that led to a sharp increase in rent. This was the first mass protest in Putin's term. It had to have made him think.

Despite the outward stability, there was no guarantee that the political establishment would continue to endorse everything the Kremlin was doing. The elites continued to express their obedience. But the bureaucracy, with the centuries-old habit of sabotage, could block Putin's reforms wherever they touched on its deepest interests.

Putin had already felt the strength of resistance. In early 2001, he tried to get rid of the corrupt governor of Primorye, Yevgeny Nazdratenko. Numerous attempts under Yeltsin to depose Nazdratenko had all come to naught. But after a winter of severe power shortages in Primorye, there were good reasons for removing him. Putin called the governor and persuaded him to resign. I can imagine their conversation: "You must leave, Yevgeny Ivanovich," Putin must have said. "Otherwise we will have to arrest you. And we don't want to create a scandal." Nazdratenko agreed with the reasoning but apparently found a way to blackmail the president. In any case, Putin removed him from Primorye but made him a minister in his cabinet. There were knots the president could not untie. But even after leaving Primorye, Nazdratenko remained its boss. All of Moscow's attempts to support its candidate for governor there failed, and the election was won by a man from Nazdratenko's clan (Sergei Darkin) with criminal ties. That defeat showed Putin he was not omnipotent; having all power resources, he still couldn't force the events to go his way.

Another defeat for the Kremlin took place in the bastion of democratic reform, Nizhny Novgorod, where despite Moscow's direct engagement, a Communist won the elections for governor.

Later in 2002, by applying open pressure and manipulation, Moscow succeeded in getting its candidate elected as Nizhny Novgorod's mayor. But the angered electorate retaliated; nearly one-third of those who voted did so "against everybody." This was proof that Putin's tactics of pressure and deal making were not always successful and that people were getting more and more frustrated with the "imitative democracy."

Also in 2002, the governors began grumbling openly. They were unhappy with having their hands tied and with being required to report to their overseers, the presidential appointees. Quite a few of them were watching the Kremlin with hardly hidden hostility. But the governors knew they had to wait. Presidential elections were approaching. Putin would have to make a bargain with them, because they controlled the regions and the electorate. It was in their power to help him win or lose. They had lost a lot of their privileges, but they still were dangerous and they were no longer intimidated by the Kremlin.

Another pillar of the Putin regime—the security services and the prosecutor general's office—were probably not very pleased with their president either. Putin never did totally become their man. His former colleagues from the security services could not have been thrilled that he made them share influence with the other interest groups. He also had no reason to be happy with the former colleagues he had brought into the Kremlin with him: They appeared to be lousy administrators.

The military also was disillusioned. Its members were not confident about the future and could not understand the president's position on defense policy. The conservative members of the officer corps had trouble with Putin's "Gorbachevism" in foreign policy and what they saw as his constant retreat before the Americans. In the beginning, they kept their grudges to themselves. But gradually, some of them became more vocal, complaining, as did former deputy chief of the General Staff General Leonid Ivashov, about Russia's "geostrategic suicide." The retired generals, including former defense minister Igor Rodionov, began publishing open letters in the newspapers and speaking to the media, accusing Putin of betraying national security interests.

In their turn, the oligarchs did not feel very safe, because the prosecutor's office could send in people to examine their books at any moment. Some tycoons who usually tried to be reticent and keep their dissatisfaction to themselves suddenly came out in the open, showing criticism of the Kremlin. Powerful Russian businesspeople watched the president carefully, not trusting the ruling team and not sure of Putin's intentions.

The left had every reason to be unhappy with the president and his policies. Leftists began talking about Putin's "antipeople regime" in the same spirit that they had attacked Yeltsin's regime. The Communists, for their part, should not have been underestimated—they still influenced a third of the electorate, and because the other political forces were too weak, the Communist Party could become a shelter for other opposition groups.

The political center on which the Kremlin counted, the pro-Putin United Russia, remained amorphous and balanced on a single principle: servility to the leader. In a crisis, with the appearance of a powerful new personality, United Russia could switch to a new leader as easily as Luzhkov and Primakov's Fatherland Party had done. Or even likelier, it would become a burden around Putin's neck. The Kremlin managers understood this and began a game of promoting new rubber-stamp parties (among them the "Party of Life" headed by Federation Council speaker Sergei Mironov, and the left-wing social democratic party created by Duma speaker Gennady Seleznev), preparing for the moment when United Russia had to be scrapped.

The democrats, despite Putin's pro-Western choice, treated him gingerly. Anatoly Chubais, restrained before this, suddenly announced that the regime could evolve in a dangerous direction. In an interview with Robert Cottrell for the February 16, 2002, *Financial Times*, he replied to the interviewer's statement, "Russia is turning into a police state" with: "The fear is not only in the West, it is here, too. We can't just push it aside and say it is stupid. No, it is serious. There are political forces not far from Putin who would support exactly that style of development for Russia."

Chubais had reason to deliver this warning. In January 2002, the last all-national television channel, TV-6, owned by the exiled oligarch Boris Berezovsky, was closed.[2] It was one more victim of the Kremlin's decision to clear the scene of influential opposition instruments on the eve of the 2003 parliamentary elections. The Praetorians in the Kremlin's circle knew the power of television and did not want one of the most popular channels in the hands of their enemy. And from the beginning of the Putin team's tenancy in the Kremlin, the free media had given it indigestion.

Chubais, now realizing what the total victory of the power ministries—*siloviki*—would bring, came to the aid of the journalists who were losing their station a second time. Chubais helped to organize a pool of oligarchs to raise money to buy the shares of a new private television station being created by Yevgeny Kiselev, the former director of TV-6, and his team. Among the shareholders were people from the Yeltsin entourage: Roman Abramovich, Alexander Mamut, Oleg Deripaska, and even Alfred Kokh, who had taken part in the destruction of NTV. Kokh's role in the TV-6 rescue campaign only proved how quickly people in Russia changed camps and loyalties. This action by these businessmen who were close to Yeltsin to save an independent television station was a challenge to Putin's *siloviki* and proof that the Yeltsin echelon had no intention of surrendering without a fight. This was one more vivid clash between two eras—the era of Yeltsin, and the era of Putin and the competing echelons of post-communist *nomenklatura*.

After weighing the pros and cons, Putin endorsed the new broadcasting company with the participation of several oligarchs. He wanted no mutiny on the part of the old Yeltsin group, standing behind the scenes, though that would mean the failure of his own Praetorians who were trying to gain control of the nationwide television channel. But to make absolutely sure that the new channel would behave "reasonably," the Kremlin suggested that former prime minister Yevgeny Primakov and head of the Union of the Industrialists and Entrepreneurs Arkady Volsky, two old apparatchiks, join the board of the broadcasting company. It was a double censorship move by the president; journalists and the oligarchs both had to agree to several levels of subordination. Putin's response demonstrates that he had learned how to create an informal system of checks and balances and neutralize potential enemies. He was following in Yeltsin's footsteps.

In February 2002, the long-silent Yeltsin spoke out as well. Putin's political godfather, speaking of his successor's personnel policies, declared "that it is necessary to surround oneself not so much with loyal people as professional ones." And Yeltsin was much harsher about freedom of the press. "I tolerated all criticism, and today it is difficult to voice even justified criticism," the first Russian president said darkly. In his isolation, the old bear, buffeted by political and personal troubles, still retained his intuition and common sense. He felt that his successor was headed in the wrong direction.

Nor could Putin fully depend on society. His version of a soft Bonapartism guaranteed his power if his administration achieved good economic results and brought at least some normalcy into the lives of ordinary people. But if there were social problems, if corruption and degradation of the state continued, the fickle Russian electorate might begin looking for a new object of its affections. Besides, to have people's steady support the leader had to address them, talk to them, explain his policy to them, ask them to back him. Putin instead preferred a cold and distant style. He offered some of the populist gimmicks, including speaking to selected audiences, but he never really had a dialogue with the nation; he felt awkward, unable to talk to society, or afraid, or did not think it was necessary.

The renewed struggle among the court clans, the muted dissatisfaction among some social groups, the persistent corruption, and the Kremlin's failure to control the regions—all indicated that Russia's calm was an illusion. Moreover, in 2002, sometimes it was not clear whose hands held the power, who bore responsibility for certain decisions, or what the Kremlin's agenda was. Reality was again becoming blurred and hard to predict. The impression was that the presidential regime was being privatized by several groups and used without Putin's knowledge. "Power is making the rounds," skeptics said in Moscow.[3] For now, Russia supported the image of the "virtual Putin" making deals with all strata of society. But the impression persisted that this intentional ambiguity on the domestic front was the result of the Kremlin's weakness and disorientation.

Scholar Peter Reddaway was among the first to notice that the concentration of power resources in Putin's hands did not mean real consolidation of power. "Formally," wrote Reddaway in the January–March 2002 *Post-Soviet Affairs*, Putin had consolidated power "to a very considerable extent. But substantially, he has not. If one reason for this state of affairs were to be highlighted, . . . it would probably be the financial subversion by rich business, or magnates, . . . of key bureaucrats at all levels of government." There were other reasons for unconsolidated power as well: the unruly nature of Russian society, the decentralization of economic wealth, and the existence of patron–client relations.

Once again, the essence of Russia's postcommunist system revealed itself. Lacking independent institutions and definite principles, it could survive only with informal centers of influence to counter the omnipotence of the leader, with intentional ambiguity, constant bickering, and sweet deals. This system could not be consolidated; that is why its outward stability was deceptive, hiding underneath incompatible trends and permanent conflicts. But that forced the leader to constantly monitor the political scene, leaving him no time to think on a macro level; the more he was busy pressing the buttons, the more he was losing his general vision.

On April 18, 2002, the president made his annual address to the nation. This time, there was no response. "The prose of life," a "crisis of the genre," was the indifferent reaction of observers. Some began comparing Putin to Brezhnev, hinting that elements of stagnation had reappeared in Russian life. Such comparisons had to infuriate the leader, whose motto was to be dynamic and active.

Putin seemed to realize that the state machine was beginning to stall again. He grew nervous. He more frequently expressed dissatisfaction with his cabinet. He demanded that the government set "more ambitious goals"—instead of 4 percent economic growth in 2003, he demanded 9 to 11 percent from Prime Minister Kasyanov. He was clearly in a rush—he wanted to get out of the swamp as quickly as possible. But was this growth expectation realistic for Russia while it kept the former sources of growth, among which the main ones were, as in Soviet times, oil and gas? It was unlikely.

Kasyanov replied stubbornly that Russia did not need "big leaps." The prime minister was probably correct—you couldn't speed up the economy by fiat, as in former times. Putin demanded no more leaps from the cabinet, at least during this period.

People unexpectedly began to talk of Kasyanov as a potential rival in the next presidential election. Kasyanov had grown imperceptibly from a "technical prime minister" into a personality. He now had his own opinions. He began arguing with the president. It would be difficult to fire him without serious cause. The entire Yeltsin group stood behind Kasyanov; it seemed to be telling Putin: "If you misbehave, there are other candidates for president." But the structure of power in Russia is such that the prime minister is fully dependent on the president, who can end his political career with the stroke of a pen. Thus, Kasyanov or any other Russian premier could be dealt with. The fact that some elite groups began to look around in search for other potential leaders proved that the establishment was no longer mesmerized by Putin.

Meanwhile, Putin's political team—both parts, the Yeltsinites and the Praetorians—continued their intrigues, as if trying to show their boss that they were constantly busy, worrying about him and strengthening his presidency. One of the most memorable intrigues of that time was with the Communist Party. At the beginning of Putin's rule, the Kremlin had done a deal with the Communists and shared the most important posts in the Duma with them, which had been part of the policy to cajole all political forces. In the spring of 2002, the Kremlin decided to squeeze the Communists out of the parliament. Under Kremlin pressure, the Communists lost their leadership of influential Duma committees. At the same time, the Kremlin tried to create a schism in the Communist Party and initiate the formation of a loyal left-wing party under Duma speaker Seleznev.

Outwardly, this was a victory for liberalism. But only outwardly. The Duma remained managed (obedient to the Kremlin), and the president pushed through with ease all the decisions he needed. The Communists were no obstacle. Then why did the Kremlin want a fight with the Communist Party? At first, one might think that the Kremlin manipulators were trying to get rid of the left-wing opposition and make the political process fully manageable. But in fact, this intrigue had a false bottom— the Kremlin was trying to push Communist leader Gennady Zyuganov toward a more intractable opposition and thereby re-create the situation of previous presidential elections, when Yeltsin and then Putin won because their main opponent Zyuganov seemed like an implacable symbol of the past in the eyes of the vacillating electorate. The Kremlin began to prepare for the election battle of 2004. And the main electoral strategy was not a vision of the new Russia but a repetition of the old election tricks.

What happened as a result? The Communist Party truly was radicalized and its opposition was strengthened, but the party was not weakened. In

Russia, you could predict that it was collaboration with the regime, instead of opposition to it, that could have weakened the Communist Party. The country retained its left-wing and nationalist electorate that did not support the regime. The Communist Party was its only outlet. Its dissatisfaction grew, and a more oppositionist Communist Party could increase its positions. By the end of August, 34 percent of respondents to a poll stated that they would vote for the Communists if the Duma elections were held at that moment (only 29 percent would vote for the "party of power," United Russia). As for the split in the Communist Party, nothing influential came of the separatists loyal to the Kremlin forming their own party.

The Kremlin manipulators did not stop there. They continued squabbling, creating the appearance of activity and the appearance of their being needed. By creating bustle around the president, they forced him to continually be acting as peacemaker and referee. In other words, they were busy with the daily "technology of power," as it's called in Russia. Putin was getting mired in details, superficial and insignificant things. It was not just that his team was always fighting. It was the logic of personified power—it forced the leader to micromanage. The president seemed to realize—he could not be oblivious to this—that the intra-Kremlin squabbles were hampering his initiative and making him hostage to trifles. But he could not escape from the regime's trap, or did not wish to—in any case, not until the presidential elections. That was understandable—why rock the boat, when keeping the current situation would guarantee preservation of power and cautious modernization?

Putin's foreign policy in the first half of 2002 presented a contrast with domestic politics that was becoming more and more bogged down in the court intrigues and attempts to keep stability. On the international scene, the Russian leader continued to demonstrate a strong desire to make Russia a systemic element of the Western community. The president, as if believing that he couldn't achieve much inside the country before the elections, began to pursue his international goals with redoubled energy. It was no longer meddle and muddle. His pro-Western orientation was now beyond doubt. The Kremlin was changing the very substance of

Russian foreign policy, making it a projection not of military ambitions but of the country's economic interests.

Putin also proved that relations with the United States were crucial for his agenda. This relationship underwent an amazing evolution after a rocky start in early 2001. A year later, the world was watching the personal chemistry between Bush and Putin, which would have been unthinkable for earlier leaders of the former rival states.

Unexpectedly for many, in the spring and summer of 2002, the United States–Russia relationship looked much better than relations between Washington and Europe or between Moscow and any other nation, including Russia's former allies. The reason was not only the personal rapport between Bush and Putin but also that they had the same understanding of the major world challenge: Both considered terrorism the key threat for international security, and both were thinking in realpolitik terms.

In a *Wall Street Journal* interview on February 11, 2002, Putin confirmed that he and Bush were heading in the same direction. "In what President Bush said and what I said there is something in common, which is the following: we all recognize that terrorism has taken on an international character." Bush's idea of the "axis of evil" apparently impressed the Russian president. He even mentioned that he was the one who had first, before Bush, spoken of the "arc of instability," meaning hotspots of world terrorism. However, the roots of their unanimity were different; the "arc" was Putin's excuse for a military decision in Chechnya that he was sure was an important piece in the global terrorist chain.

It was true that the Russian president seemed not to like two things in the U.S. leader's conception of the problem: that the "axis of evil" included former Soviet allies, and that the United States was trying to solve the problem of the axis in a unilateral way. But the impression at that moment was that Putin endorsed the idea of the terrorist axis.

The Russian reaction was in sharp contrast to European criticism of the U.S. foreign policy agenda. French prime minister Lionel Jospin couldn't hide his emotions: "The problems of the world cannot be reduced simply to the struggle against terrorism, however vital that struggle may be."[4] The rest of Europe was adopting the same line; on the issue of terrorism, Europeans and Americans were drifting apart. And that emphasized even more suddenly the United States–Russia consensus.

When American journalists asked Putin directly whether Russia would support the United States if Washington began military action in Iraq, he first expressed his desire that the problem be resolved within the framework of the United Nations, and then added: "But that does not mean that Russia in the future would not, under certain conditions, work together with the U.S. and solve the problem of terrorism in a framework of the coalition." Translation: Putin wanted to avoid a repetition of the Yugoslav syndrome, which led Russia to support Yugoslav president Slobodan Milosevic almost up to the moment of his abdication and, after suffering defeat, jump onto the Western bandwagon just as it was pulling out. Moscow did not want to endure a new humiliating failure.

At the beginning of 2002, the Russian leader seemed to be giving a message that next time Moscow was prepared to go along with the United States—especially if Russian economic interests were taken care of. One might assume that at that moment Putin could have supported U.S. action in Iraq even without waiting for the Europeans. This was really a breathtaking change in Russia–United States relations. It was true, though, that observers soon would understand that Putin might backtrack if he felt he had gone too far and his position was not endorsed by Russian elites or his stance was not met with the reciprocity he had hoped for.

The ambiguity of the Kremlin's position, which would have quite unexpected outcomes, would become apparent later. But in the spring of 2002, Bush and Putin were the only two world leaders who openly and without hesitation endorsed the war on terrorism as the top priority in the field of international relations. These leaders of two completely different countries, these politicians with different principles and backgrounds, unexpectedly found themselves thinking alike. It was astounding, puzzling, . . . and worrisome. Cooperation based on a common enemy never survives the enemy. Will it be different this time? Will the United States and Russia find other areas of cooperation as well?

Relations between the United States and Russia continued to improve. The Bush administration, contrary to its initial inclinations, preserved all of the Clinton-era security and economic assistance programs and even increased some. It promoted a dialogue between the United States and Russia to encourage private investment in the Russian economy. It also asked Congress to graduate Russia permanently from the

Jackson-Vanik amendment, thus removing a Cold War–era obstacle to normal trade relations.

At the beginning of 2002, U.S. officials viewed United States–Russia relations as the best in history. The White House continued to praise Russia as "a key member" of the international antiterrorist coalition. Moreover, Washington, working on the security agenda with Russia, made it possible to perceive Russia as a great power—which massaged the complexes of the Russian establishment.

In Russia, however, the initial euphoria of mutual rapprochement gradually began to vanish, and voices of disappointment became louder. Even pro-Western Russians were complaining that Russia had agreed to all the concessions to the United States that it had regarded as unthinkable several years ago: endorsement of a U.S. military presence in Central Asia and, later, a U.S. presence in Georgia; acquiescence to NATO enlargement and Anti–Ballistic Missile Treaty abrogation; and contributions to the antiterrorist campaign, for which it so far had received no substantial "deliverables" from the United States. The incredible happened: Putin was openly criticized in Russia and accused of acting like Gorbachev—giving a lot and getting little or nothing back. The fact that Russian elites were waiting for U.S. "deliverables" proved that they still viewed their endorsement of U.S. policy and their partnership with the United States as some kind of deviation or as a concession to the United States, but not as a strategic course for Russia.

For its acquiescence to the U.S. security measures, Moscow hoped for compensation in the economic field and upgraded cooperation in the security area—first of all, those in joint defense and relations with NATO. Unlike Yeltsin, who could be satisfied with symbolic gestures, Putin wanted more substance in ties with the West, above all with the United States.[5] It appeared, however, that such compensation was hard to come by. Even the repeal of the notorious Jackson-Vanik amendment seemed to be a difficult process. Moreover, the spring of 2002 saw the steel–poultry war, which cast a shadow over United States–Russia relations.[6]

"Long-term marriage between Moscow and Washington is impossible," was the verdict of Russian analysts. What the White House called a coalition, most Russian observers called "just light flirting."[7] The overwhelming elite skepticism concerning perspectives of the Russian–American dialogue was rooted in both—suspicion of the U.S. intentions concerning Russia and doubt in Russia's fast revival. Some American observers, especially in the Democratic Party, also were rather pessimistic, criticizing Bush's approach to relations with Russia. "We wanted full Russian cooperation in the war against terror and we have received it," wrote Leon Fuerth, a former adviser to Al Gore. But in return "we wanted to take such nuclear reductions as suited us, we offered a reinvented version of what already exists (the NATO–Russia Council), we imposed tariffs on Russian steel." "Solid partnerships are not built on winner-take-all rules, they require a search for win-win outcomes," was Fuerth's conclusion.[8]

Americans who wanted to justify limited engagement argued that Russia does not have the capacity at this point to engage in a truly mutually beneficial partnership with the United States. There are several responses to such a view. As the one remaining superpower, the United States has asymmetrical relations with all its closest allies; reciprocity is impossible when one side has such enormous weight. In addition, Russia had already shown that it could hold up its end of the bargain in the antiterrorist campaign—and that was the proof that Russia was learning, albeit somewhat grudgingly, a new part: that of a responsible partner.

However, concerns about the nature and sustainability of the United States–Russia relationship had their point. The relationship was constrained not only by the vestiges of the past and the asymmetry of American and Russian capabilities. With the exception of the antiterrorist struggle, there was nothing substantial on the plate. Elites in both countries still could not go beyond discussing irritants—arms reduction, Iran and Iraq, nuclear proliferation. And relations were hampered by a lack of a new concept of international relations and tainted by remaining mistrust between both elites. Influential forces within the Bush administration viewed Russia as a nuisance that should be shrugged off.

Robert Legvold, analyzing U.S. policy toward Russia, wrote at the end of 2001: "Nothing suggests that Washington or the American public is in a mood to embrace an ambitious policy toward Russia. The inertia leading the United States to disengage from the Russia problem in the last years of the Clinton administration, therefore, seems likely to continue. The Bush administration inherited a policy of benign neglect: Russia is acknowledged, the lines of communication are opened, and various cooperative projects are proffered as a sign of good intentions, but little effort is made to address the hard problems at the core of the relations."[9] This conclusion continued to be true in 2002.

As for Russian politicians, they still watched Washington with suspicion and often hostility, anticipating double standards and unilateralism. The policy community in Moscow continued to have problems translating rapprochement policy into a practical agenda. Most Russian politicians were trying to channel the Russian–American relationship into the non-stop nuclear arms control talks that would allow Moscow to imitate a superpower and would secure a niche for its foreign policy and security establishment totally unable to function in the new environment.

The Bush–Putin summit in Moscow on May 24, 2002, had to prove to what extent both sides were ready to turn their tactical alliance into a more meaningful partnership. Putin had delivered everything he could at the moment. The ball was in the American court. Putin badly needed from Bush the nuclear reduction treaty. Moscow considered this treaty a compensatory gesture for abrogation of the Anti–Ballistic Missile Treaty. Putin also expected Washington to repeal the Jackson-Vanik amendment and give Russia market-economy status. In this case, he could prove to the Russian political class that he was not a Gorbachev II who was only weakening Russia's positions without reciprocity.

Bush had to overcome his aversion to treaties and his pledge to stop making symbolic gestures and help his new buddy Putin. The Americans proved that they understood Putin's difficulties at home; they met him halfway. Bush agreed to sign a legally binding document on the reduction of offensive nuclear weapons. In the clash in Washington between those who regarded Russia as too weak to matter and those who favored cooperation, the latter won—at least at that time.

On May 24, the Strategic Offensive Reduction Treaty was signed. It was the shortest nuclear treaty in history and the most far-reaching. It stipulated that both countries would cut their strategic arsenal from 6,000 to between 1,700 and 2,200 warheads by December 2012—the steepest nuclear reduction so far. There was no real verification procedure, no legal enforcement, and no performance mechanism. "The Treaty of Moscow," as it was called, was based on trust, and it had to both manage the Russian–American relationship in a period of the likely introduction by the United States of ballistic missile defenses and also prevent the proliferation of nuclear weapons. Both the U.S. Congress and Russian Duma had to ratify the treaty. The Russian parliament, controlled by the Kremlin, did not present a problem. But nobody was sure how Congress would react.

Ironically, both sides viewed this treaty in a different way. Americans considered it the confirmation of the end of the Cold War era based on bipolarity, while Russians looked at it as proof that nuclear parity still mattered. And this difference in approaches could become a source of future frustrations.

The Treaty of Moscow was not the only outcome of the May summit: The leaders signed a joint declaration on the new strategic relations that set a basis for joint dealing with new challenges and created a framework for new cooperation on security. This was an attempt to build a new concept of the relationship, laying out common interests.

But Moscow was thinking in practical terms, and from that point of view, the Bush–Putin summit did not justify Russian hopes. Bush did not bring any resolution on doing away with the Jackson-Vanik amendment, nor recognition of Russia's market-economy status. Putin was disappointed, even upset, and that was clear in his behavior. But he restrained himself and did not stress his unhappiness with the Americans. "We are not thrilled that this did not happen," he noted in passing on May 26.

Even though not all the Kremlin hopes for the Moscow summit came to pass, ordinary Russians' attitude toward the United States was again amazingly warm. In May 2002, according to a VTsIOM poll, 69 percent spoke of the importance of the Bush–Putin summit (24 percent doubted its importance). Thirty-five percent felt that Russia had to try to join NATO (47 percent thought otherwise).

Personal relations between Bush and Putin—at least outwardly—were so friendly that some observers began speaking of the "Bush–Putin axis." *Le Monde* wrote on May 18: "Europeans, caught between two fires during the Cold War, should be happy for the new climate between America and Russia. However, we must think—will we be given the role of extras in view of the appearance of the Bush–Putin axis?"

But relations between Russia and the United States looked so good and cloudless only in comparison with the noticeable cooling of relations between the United States and Europe. So far, this was a relationship of allies against a common enemy, not a partnership based on recognition of the same values. This meant that new distancing, and even freezing, between Moscow and Washington was quite possible. The question was whether this cooling would be caused by different visions of national interests of the respective states within a single ideology, as in the relationship between the United States and Europe, or by a retention of conflicting views of society and the world order.

There was a feeling among realistically thinking circles on both sides of the ocean that not only the May 2002 summit but the whole pattern of the United States–Russia relationship was "less a form of power politics than of psychotherapy," as Charles Krauthammer put it in the *Washington Post* on May 31. But sometimes sessions of psychotherapy are useful before world politics can acquire new form and new substance and, most important, before political elites find new roles for their respective states.

In analyzing the new U.S. policy toward Russia, James Goldgeier and Michael McFaul wrote in the October 2002 issue of *Current History*: "Bush's policy represents continuation of Clinton's strategy. . . . The approaches of Bill Clinton and George W. Bush differ in one important way. Bush does not believe that Russia's internal transformation must precede Russia's external integration into the Western clubs."[10] Goldgeier and McFaul called the new policy "integration without transformation." The fact that the Bush administration—at least outwardly—did not try to teach Moscow democracy really can explain why the Russian leader so easily formed a personal bond with Bush. In his turn, the U.S. president, rejecting previous "romanticism"—the attempt to promote democracy in Russia—was quite successful in achieving his major security goals. But the question remained: To what extent were these security gains durable without Russia's further transformation?

Whatever the future development of Russian–American relations, one positive aspect was without doubt: Both sides during the previous decade had gained mutual experience of ungrounded expectations and exaggerated frustrations that forced them this time to be more realistic. "In sharp contrast to the earlier period, however, there was now little euphoria. The sense of possibilities was now tempered by knowledge of the failed hopes of the early 1990s, of the rough road the two countries had traveled later in that decade, and of the challenges that lay ahead," Thomas Graham wrote in his book *Russia's Decline and Uncertain Recovery*, describing new stages of the United States–Russia relationship.[11] That experience could help both Moscow and Washington—to avoid old bumps on the road and to deal with new bumps.

Further events followed with kaleidoscopic speed. On May 29, 2002, the E.U. delegation headed by Romano Prodi arrived in Moscow and brought Putin a long-awaited present: The European Union recognized Russia's market-economy status (the decision was formalized in November 2002). This step sped up Washington's decision to do the same. In June, Bush called Putin in the Kremlin and gave him the good news himself. Recognition of Russia as a market economy created a better climate for Russian trade. Russia lost about $1.5 billion annually because of restrictions on its products on international markets. Now Russian companies would have wider access to Western markets.

The E.U. and U.S. recognition of Russia's status improved its chances of joining the World Trade Organization, which the Kremlin wanted badly. As Mike Moore, the organization's director general, said, "I believe there are in Washington, Brussels, and Moscow people, the horsepower, firepower, and will power to make this accession possible." Encouraged, Putin began talking of the creation of a "single economic space" with the European Union. However, the European reaction to the Russian president's initiative was reserved. The European Union set numerous conditions: first of all, bringing Russian legislation into correspondence with international standards; and second, raising tariffs on energy to correspond to world prices (low domestic prices were an annual energy subsidy for Russian enterprises, estimated to be $5 billion). Russia also had to open its markets.

The last two demands were hard to meet for Moscow. Both Russian and foreign economists warned that Russia's noncompetitive industry could not stand a wide opening of the market, and its collapse could provoke uncontrolled social consequences. "It might be that the forcing pace of change ultimately proved counterproductive," warned economist Padma Desai in the *Financial Times* on July 11. The Kremlin had to walk a tightrope, on the one hand, gradually opening markets, and on the other, preventing negative consequences of these steps for stability. This task required not only thoughtful leadership but also a broad social dialogue.

There remained, however, a deep divide in the relations between Moscow and the European Union—the problem of Kaliningrad, the Russian city on the Baltic Sea, the former capital of East Prussia. Kaliningrad had to be cut off from Russia by the pending entry of Poland and Lithuania into the European Union and to be turned into a Russian "exclave" within the union. Putin tried to get a visa-free regime between Kaliningrad and Russia. But the European Union was not ready to change its Schengen rules, which formed a visa-free zone for E.U. members, citing concerns about illegal Russian migrants to Lithuania and, from there, further to the west. Negotiations were at an impasse, creating a strain in relations between Brussels and Moscow. The Kremlin, however, could not afford to endanger its European policy and had to reach a compromise with the European Union on Kaliningrad.

The next development came on May 28, when the first NATO summit with the participation of Russia was held at the military barracks outside Rome, where the NATO–Russia Council was formed. Putin sat between the leaders of Spain and Portugal, ordered alphabetically by country. In his opening remarks at the inaugural meeting of the council, the NATO secretary general, Lord George Robertson, said: "The leaders of twenty of the world's most powerful nations assembled, not to carve up the world, but to unite it." Putin was also positive, saying: "We've come a long way from confrontation to dialogue and from confrontation to cooperation." But at the same time, Putin suggested that Russian cooperation did not represent unconditional support for any action NATO might choose to take.

The new council provided opportunities for NATO–Russia consultation, joint decision making, and even joint action. The list of issues for cooperation included assessment of the terrorist threat, arms control, nonproliferation, theater missile defense, military-to-military cooperation, and civil emergencies. Russia did not get a veto right on NATO actions. The new Russian responsibility within the council also was far from defined.

But the whole structure represented a step forward from the previous arrangement—the Permanent Joint Council, where Russia had a much narrower role. The NATO–Russia Council could become a platform for dialogue between the former foes; everything depended on the political will from both sides. NATO and Russia were making a second try to forge a partnership. A new failure might raise a question: To what extent was it a result of the leadership problem, the tactics issue, and to what extent was it the outcome of the systemic incompatibility of NATO and Russia?

Then came the June Group of Eight meeting in Kananaskis, Canada. Here Putin was completely self-confident. He felt he was an equal. Russia was already in the front seat and not asking for help. The Kremlin had proven its desire to become a member of the Western community. In response, the group decided to make Russia a full-fledged member, even though the Russian economy did not warrant such status; it was an acknowledgment of Putin's pro-Western policy. The industrial countries also promised Moscow $20 billion to safeguard and dismantle Russian weapons of mass destruction; this aid was linked to Russia's fulfilling its obligations regarding nonproliferation. As if to endorse a new role for Russia, the Group of Eight leaders agreed that in 2006, Russia would assume the presidency and host the group's annual summit.

In solidifying his pro-Western turn, the Russian president made an attempt to show that his politics remained multivectored. He tried to demonstrate Moscow's interest in relations with other nations as well. In May, after the summit with Bush and the creation of the Russia–NATO Council, defense minister Sergei Ivanov went to China to assure Beijing that Russia's turn to the West was not aimed against China. Besides security considerations, Moscow had material interests in good relations with China. In the past decade alone, the trade turnover with China had grown to about $10 billion. China bought modern jets and the famous S-300 missile complex from Russia. In 2001, trade between China and Russia grew by $1 billion. Moscow was definitely interested in a dialogue with Beijing.

In the summer, Moscow initiated meetings within the Shanghai Cooperation Organization. Putin had consultations with members of the

Euro-Asiatic Economic Union and members of the Treaty of Collective Security of the Commonwealth of Independent States, and individual meetings with the presidents of Ukraine and Belarus. The Kremlin seemed to be trying to prove that its Western orientation did not mean forgetting Russia's previous ties.

All these steps evinced the formation of a Putin Doctrine for foreign policy. The essence of the doctrine was a pro-Western orientation, a priority for economic interests in foreign policy, and a normalization of relations between Moscow and its neighbors, especially former allies of the USSR. Putin's multivectored approach, however, differed sharply from Primakov's multipolarity—Putin demonstrated that the West is the priority for him.

But these are just the contours of the doctrine. Putin's foreign policy remained insufficiently structured and vulnerable. Most seriously, a significant group of elites continued to resist the president's orientation toward the West. The Ministry of Foreign Affairs and the Ministry of Defense remained bastions of conservatism. The weakly defined distinctions between these institutions and other foreign policy players, along with their lack of clear areas of responsibility, did not make implementing the Kremlin's new foreign doctrine any easier. It was still unclear who made certain foreign policy decisions, how much political support they had, and how the president could guarantee their irreversibility. If the Russian political class was not sure that a decisive pro-Western orientation was necessary, would Putin's successor turn in the other direction? asked Western observers. Their concerns were not without foundation.

The realization of the Putin Doctrine required an understanding of Russia's new role and defining new identity in the world both from elites and from society as a whole. A new philosophy of foreign policy was urgently needed, and new able people were needed to execute it. "Relations between Russia and the West have rarely been better. But what does it mean in practice? And can it last?" wrote the *Economist* on May 16, 2002, and it answered, "The real danger is not that Russia's march to the West goes into reverse, but that it bogs down for lack of ideas and people."

Meanwhile, the Kremlin had not been making any efforts to prove the rightness of its policy before its own society. This was a problem not of weak propaganda but of insufficient democracy. The Kremlin seemed to be saying to the country, "We will have whatever policies we deem necessary. We have no intention of explaining our goals to you."

It was not only very sad but also destructive that Russia's turn toward the West was made in the same old undemocratic way—without any attention to society, without any effort at explanation. The authorities did not believe that people would understand the reasons for the new policy, and they did not trust Russia. The absence of a constructive dialogue between the regime and the nation on foreign policy issues created a niche for critics of the new policy in the ruling class. Until the Putin Doctrine was supported by the public, it could not be considered the final Kremlin line in foreign policy.

In contrast to foreign policy and new international developments, the shallowness of domestic policy was surprising. The major events were over; there was no open confrontation, no political drama. The struggle continued, but it was reduced to rope-pulling among a few interest groups and clans.

Only one event shook up Russian political life in mid-2002: the reappearance of Boris Yeltsin. He had begun showing signs of life, meeting with politicians and making comments through intermediaries. On Russian Independence Day, June 12, he appeared live, giving an expansive interview on Russian television. Amazingly, he looked energetic, physically stronger, much thinner, and clear-minded. It could have been a double. Tsar Boris admitted that he had had five heart attacks during his presidency. "Yes, five," he confirmed with a sneaky look. "But I remain active, mentally, physically, and emotionally." He said that he had lost 20 kilograms (44 pounds) in recent months. He had not only shed weight, but about ten years. Yeltsin said he had begun studying English. "To train the brain," he explained.

Then Yeltsin headed to Minsk for vacation, untiringly giving interviews and making comments about Russian politics. "I meet every day with ministers, with Prime Minister Kasyanov, Putin—all the time. It is like being a guarantor of stability," Yeltsin said with a sly squint. Everyone noticed that he mentioned Putin in passing. Moreover, he was clearly critical of his successor, whom he had recently praised, including in his memoirs. Russians began to joke: The Guarantor of Stability, as he called himself, was trying to lecture the Guarantor of the Constitution, that is, Putin. And Yeltsin was frankly promoting Kasyanov as a presidential candidate. This was a clear challenge to Putin. Yeltsin's return meant one thing—his political Family had no intention of giving up. Bringing out the heavy artillery—Grandpa himself—it decided to prove that it still had influence.

Putin responded to his godfather and predecessor. He was brief, but harsh. At his press conference on June 24, which was supposed to sum up his two years as president, he announced, "Yeltsin is a free individual who can move about, meet with anyone, and express his opinion. We respect his opinion. However, I have my own opinion, and I will do what I think is best for Russia now and in the future." Putin's words meant, "I will not be scared off. I no longer need advisers and guides."

This open dialogue showed that the relationship between Tsar Boris and his heir was not great. Putin was gradually coming out of the shadow of the Yeltsin entourage, and naturally the old ruling team did not like it. Vladimir Vladimirovich was diverging from Yeltsin's line on some cardinal political issues. He went further than Yeltsin in his movement toward the West. He began reviewing the Yeltsin model of relations with the former Soviet republics, rejecting the former paternalism. At the same time, he rejected Yeltsin's attitude toward the press and freedoms. But much more important for the Yeltsin group was something else—Putin was building his own political regime, which presupposed no godfathers and no gratitude for the predecessor. It looked as if Putin was ready to cut the strings that tied him to Yeltsin.

What was amazing, however, was the fact that even as he stood on the threshold of open polemic with the man who had given him power, the new master of the Kremlin still had to put up with a number of appointees and members of the Yeltsin group. Outwardly, it was incomprehensible and illogical. But the explanation was simple: His own people, the ones he had brought from Saint Petersburg, were blatantly weak. And he had not yet managed to form a new team in the two years of his administration.

So far, Putin preferred burning no bridges, avoiding conflict with powerful forces and with the old political Family. He was not a political gladiator. He did not like open political struggle or even polemic. Was he a fighter at all? Was he prepared to fight for his power or his principles? And what were his principles? Only a real threat or crisis would give the answers. And the new regime had not yet faced such an ordeal. The clash with Yeltsin could have been one more step for Putin toward independent leadership, and it was a litmus test for his ability to stand his ground. But it did not say how he would behave in the moment of truth.

Besides the clearing of the air between the old and new leaders of Russia, besides the tension among several clans in Putin's entourage, the summer of 2002 was far from hectic. Russia tried to get a respite from politics. How long can you live in a state of squabbles and conflicts? The country had been under stress since Gorbachev's *perestroika*, in the mid-1980s. For the past seventeen years, Russians had sought answers to existential questions: Where was Russia going? How should it define its identity? What system should be built?

In 2002, the discussion wound down to almost nothing, not because everything had become clear, but because apathy and indifference had overtaken society—the desire for a Grand Design and a definition of life's goal had been lost. And the Putin regime, with its ideology of pragmatism—its focus on details—did not stimulate interest in Russia's strategic problems and in its continuing soul searching. The policy of pragmatism itself looked like a rejection of any far-reaching strategy.

The summer of 2002 was devoted to private life. The exhausting heat, the worst in years, enervated the country and paralyzed the megalopolises, especially Moscow, slowing down traffic and humans. Putin left Moscow and switched to a summer work regimen—he was in his residence in Sochi, by the sea. There he saw his subordinates and received international guests. French president Jacques Chirac made his official visit to Russia in Sochi. Without Putin in Moscow, there was no politics, for only the president was the main political event.

And yet the absence of political movement and a clear agenda was upsetting: Because in Russia a lull was always followed by a new wave of political intrigue or a series of other upsets. Because outward calm hid the vagueness of the future. Because this was the last calm summer before the next elections and new fistfights. And because in Russia a political lull could always be illusory.

Soon events, not at all connected with politics, confirmed that Russia could not yet be considered a quiet and balanced country. First, the southern regions were swallowed up in floods, which literally washed away dozens of towns, killing dozens people and taking heavy financial tolls. But while similar flooding in Europe made world headlines and elicited support for the victims, in Russia, yet another disaster was merely reported in daily news roundups. Russian society was so used to catastrophes that it seemed to be immune and no longer reacted to them. In any case, Russian television devoted more coverage to the streets of Germany underwater than the suffering of their own citizens, left without shelter.

Then came August, which Russians have learned to fear. Too many dramatic events of the past decade had taken place in August: the putsch in 1991; apartment building explosions and the separatist invasion of Dagestan in 1999, which began the second Chechen war; the *Kursk* submarine disaster in 2000. And once again, catastrophe struck. On August 19, a military helicopter crashed in Chechnya with 140 people on board. The next day a residential building in Moscow blew up, killing several people and leaving dozens wounded.

In the next few days, more helicopter and plane crashes and another apartment building explosion followed, as if to strengthen in Russians a feeling of foreboding. Russians no longer believed in accidents and technological causes—they saw conspiracy and criminal intent behind every disaster. But even dramatic mistakes, technological failures, evil fate, and tragic coincidence were proof of the fragility of Russian stability and how defenseless ordinary people were there. Putin's power, just like Yeltsin's, could not stop the never-ending flow of disasters that were in part the consequence and echo of the collapse of the Soviet empire, the continuing decay of outdated infrastructure, but mostly the result of the sloppiness and inefficiency of the new system and of the irresponsible bureaucracy.[12]

The fall of 2002 brought signs that despite the political lull and absence of visible political threats to Russia's stability, hidden trends and unresolved conflicts could pose a challenge for the Kremlin. Russia's postcommunist history had proven that its transformation still could take quite a few unexpected turns. The kaleidoscope of myriad perspectives on events kept turning as Russia's policy positions continued to evolve.

In the foreign policy arena, skeptics seemed to be proven right as Moscow's long romance with the West turned icy. Moscow continued to be offended by the European community's constant criticism of its Chechen war. Soon Russia would get involved in a real clash with Denmark—after Copenhagen refused to extradite Akhmad Zakayev, one of Chechen president Aslan Maskhadov's associates, in October 2002 and became furious with the United Kingdom for doing the same.

The emotional discussion of the Kaliningrad visa regime clouded Russia's otherwise warm relations with the European Union. Finally, after a long-standing dispute with Russia, the union offered special transit arrangements for Kaliningrad residents—"the Kaliningrad pass," a simplified transit document that would be issued free or for a small fee by the consulates of Lithuania and Poland after these countries joined the union. Brussels also promised to look into the feasibility of nonstop, high-speed trains between Kaliningrad and Russia proper. This ended the dispute and simultaneously proved that the union was not ready to accommodate all of Russia's demands. Moscow would have to make an effort to formulate its European policy so as to avoid future conflicts that could emerge as a result of its desire for special treatment by the union.

Russian relations with the United States also came under strain. The Kremlin riled U.S. leaders by resuming trade negotiations with Baghdad and declaring its intention to expand its nuclear assistance to Iran. Putin made the decision to push forward with a project to link the Trans-Siberian railroad with North Korean rail lines. During his fall visit to Beijing, prime minister Kasyanov signed new arms-sales agreements with China worth billions of dollars. Russia not only sold China Sukhoi fighter jets and Kilo-class submarines but also assisted in building a helicopter manufacturing plant and delivered a wide array of nuclear technology.

U.S. dismay was thinly veiled at best. "Lately, Russia isn't just continuing its tradition of schmoozing with rogue states around the world. It's actually stepping up relations with several of them," wrote *Newsweek* on September 2, accusing Moscow of forging its "own axis of friendship" with Iraq, Iran, and North Korea. Russians in return argued that they had gained too little from their pro-Western orientation and were simply pursuing—as was the United States—their own economic interests.

As if to add more fuel to an already fiery atmosphere, in September tension deepened between Russia and Georgia. Putin accused Georgian leader Eduard Shevardnadze of lacking the political will to root out Chechen rebels from Georgia's Pankisi Gorge. On September 11, the anniversary of the terrorism in the United States the year before, Putin delivered an ultimatum to Tbilisi—essentially, "We are preparing to strike established Chechen terrorist bases on your territory whether you like it or not." In justifying his position, Putin quoted Bush's words about the legitimate need for "preventive measures" against countries harboring terrorists. Both the United States and the Council of Europe spoke out against Russia's desire for such aggressive action. For the first time during their honeymoon, Russia and the West seemed to be on a collision course.

This is not the end of the story. In late September, Washington imposed sanctions on three Russian enterprises for allegedly selling military equipment to countries it believes sponsor terrorism. Pundits predicted a new schism between Russia and the West, as well as Moscow's return to nationalistic anti-Americanism. This was hasty and ungrounded, however. The reality was much more complicated. Putin wanted no rupture with the West; clearly, he continued to consider Moscow's relationship with Washington a top priority and its relationship with the West the major prerequisite for Russia's modernization. But by the end of 2002, some global events were not helping Russia strengthen its pro-Western orientation.

U.S. plans for military action and regime change in Iraq at the end of 2002 became a new test for Russian–American realignment. For the first time after September 11, 2001, the foreign policy agendas and economic interests of the United States and Russia openly diverged. The Kremlin feared that a war in Iraq would destabilize the already volatile situation in the region close to Russian borders. In view of the unfinished story in Afghanistan, it was a justified worry. The Russian political establishment and Russian tycoons were even more concerned that a successor regime in Iraq would not honor Iraq's $8 billion debt to Russia, and that the war would imperil Russia's investments in the country, including multi-billion-dollar oil contracts. The apprehension in Moscow was that future

Iraqi oil would bring falling world oil prices, while oil revenues continued to be the major source of Russian economic development.

At first, Russia (together with France and China) did not support the U.S. draft resolution on Iraq suggesting the automatic use of force, and it opposed military action against Saddam Hussein. Moreover, other European states also expressed their concerns over U.S. policy toward Iraq. This European disagreement with Washington allowed Russia to express its unhappiness with the U.S. policy even more strongly. It was true that President Putin, in his usual reticent manner, said that he would not make negotiations over Iraq into the "Eastern bazaar"—he still did not want to engage in horse trading with Washington. But the Russian establishment tried to get guarantees from the United States that, in return for not obstructing U.S. policy, Russian economic interests would be taken care of. In the Iraqi case, Russia's economic interests prevailed over geopolitical aspirations.

In the end, Moscow—despite "some concerns"—supported a new resolution on Iraq demanding that Baghdad make a full declaration of any weapons of mass destruction and allow weapons inspections. This time, Russia stopped trying to save Saddam's regime and chose to stand together with the Western community while at the same time trying to take advantage of disagreements among Western allies.

It was apparent that in the end Moscow and Washington would eventually cooperate in dealing with Iraq and in a post-Saddam situation. But the controversy over Iraq demonstrated that the emergence of new conflicts of interest between Russia and the United States is possible, and that these conflicts could become quite severe if Moscow failed to solve the structural problems of Russia's further development.

Russia seemed to have problems reconciling its economic interests with the new vector of its foreign policy. Moscow had yet to draw the line between tenable and untenable levels of disagreement with Western powers over policy. The criteria were amorphous. Among the Western powers, minor conflicts were normal and did not provoke serious breaches within the Western community. With Russia, it was a more complicated matter. Russia's political class has yet to understand that sometimes short-term financial incentives and benefits obscure longer-range political danger. For example, massive amounts of weaponry sold by Moscow to "states of concern" and to China could increase instability on Russian borders and create situations with which Moscow is not prepared to deal. Besides, cozy relations with these states can endanger partnership with the West. But a different argument should be mentioned as well: Staying friendly with traditional allies can help Russia to become a mediator that one day can help the renegades join the modern nations. The problem: How should a line be drawn between pragmatism and adherence to the past?

The discrepancy between a pro-Western foreign policy and a nondemocratic regime in power in Russia has slowly taken on greater prominence. Putin, relying upon support from conservative circles that were the basis of that regime, realized he could not afford to ignore their interests entirely. Hence, in the fall of 2002, he drove a hard line on Georgia to massage the military and the security community. The irony was that the Kremlin hawks skillfully appropriated Bush's "preemption" strategy to justify action in Georgia. The argument that if Americans can attack potential terrorists in Iraq, Russia can do the same in Georgia became popular, even among Russian liberals. Eventually, Moscow would grudgingly make peace with Tbilisi, albeit not without behind-the-scenes U.S. diplomacy.

Putin faced an inescapable dilemma: to retreat from his pro-Western course and strengthen the authoritarian nature of his rule, giving his Praetorians more influence, or to consolidate momentum along the pro-Western vector, which would require the adoption of more democratic rules of the game at home and would be appreciated by an entirely different—and democratic—audience. Moscow could not sit forever astride two horses running in opposite directions. Operating on two incompatible principles, Russia could never become a true member of the Western club, Putin's ultimate goal. In this situation, every adversarial line Russia took against the West could be perceived as a red flag, warning of hidden anti-Western sentiment among Russia's policy makers.

Moscow's search for its new niche on the international stage and for a dignified role in the club of industrial nations is not over. The outcome will depend not only on the internal struggle between the conservatives and pro-Western modernizers. It will also depend on the debate with the Western community—the United States and Europe—on the future world order and its new threats and challenges.

In the meantime, Russia moved inexorably toward new parliamentary and presidential elections. And that meant that the political break was coming to an end and the public was beginning to think about the successes and failures of Putin's first term and what lay ahead. A new period of animation and political struggle was coming for the country.

Those who have already tried to take a snapshot of the Putin presidency got a slippery and contradictory image that had no less conflict and half shadows than in the Yeltsin years. The seemingly clear, schematic, logical Vladimir Vladimirovich consistently ended up the hostage of group interests, the Yeltsin legacy, Russian history, the daily grind, and his own prejudices and fears. In the two years of his administration, he desperately tried to stop the momentum of Russia's decay. He succeeded in achieving a great degree of stability: The state began functioning; the bureaucracy started, albeit halfheartedly, working; and people were overcoming their helplessness.

But the project Vladimir Vladimirovich wanted to realize—building a strong, modern Russia—could end up being unviable, despite his wishes and to his surprise. A strong Russia designed on the basis of the traditional state and personified power most likely would have become one more unattainable utopian vision. Of course, in the historical context, even actions that shatter final illusions can be beneficial. It all depends on how strong the public's faith is in nonviable constructs and how sturdy are the roots of conservatism. But if society, or at least a significant part of it, is prepared to move on, yet time and energy are spent on getting elites to realize the obvious, how do we characterize that kind of leadership and regime?

Vladimir Putin's presidency can be seen as an important step in Russia's development that should have shown how much Russia wanted to preserve the vestiges of its traditionalism. Putin had reached the point where he and his team had to admit that the Russian System was incompatible with the twenty-first century. It required very little more prudence for him to see it or more courage to acknowledge it.

Meanwhile, in 2002 the Kremlin was still attempting to solve problems using methods traditional for old Russia. The most dramatic for Russia and its president was the problem of Chechnya. The situation appeared to be stabilizing. Large-scale military actions had ended. An administration of Chechens loyal to the Kremlin had been formed with Akhmad Kadyrov at the head. Money was flowing into the region, and restoration work had begun. But in essence, the guerrilla war in Chechnya continued. Casualties on both sides continued to grow.

Former minister of the interior Anatoly Kulikov, who knows the situation well, announced that in the course of the two wars in Chechnya Russia had lost as many men as in the war in Afghanistan in 1979–1989, that is, about 15,000. According to official sources in Moscow, in the second Chechen war—from 1999 until August 2002—4,249 Russians were killed and 12,285 were wounded (and military data gave the number of separatists killed at about 13,000). But human rights activists maintained that the losses on the Russian side were much higher. "The number for the military death toll should be multiplied by three or four," said the representative of the Committee of Soldiers' Mothers, campaigning for service members' rights. Moscow did not even try to establish the civilian casualties in the Northern Caucasus.

In the fall of 2002, the Russian public no longer believed in a military solution to the Chechen problem. Only 17 percent of those polled by VTsIOM supported a military variant for Chechnya. More than two-thirds supported a peaceful solution. For the president who had entered the Kremlin on the wave of the "antiterrorist operation" in the Northern Caucasus, this was evidence of a fiasco. Besides, this was also a trap. For now, the Kremlin had to think not only about what to do with Chechnya but also about how to preserve the legitimacy of the team that had come to power endorsing antiterrorist operations. The Kremlin was now in a situation where the problem of saving face was turning into a question of survival.

What could be the way out of this seeming dead end? By October 2002, more and more politicians and pundits in Russia—among them even the always-cautious former prime minister Primakov—were coming to the conclusion that the only answer was negotiations with the leaders of the Chechen opposition, particularly Maskhadov, to end military action and reach a peaceful resolution. In rejecting negotiations with Maskhadov, Moscow could lose a chance to come to terms with the generation of

Chechen leaders still willing to talk to Moscow. The new generation of separatists, who grew up during the war with Russia and who think only of the holy jihad against Russians, wants only bloody revenge. These thoughts gradually began to dominate public disputes in Russia.

Viable peaceful options for Chechnya discussed that fall in Russia stipulated Russia's recognition of broad Chechen autonomy or the division of Chechnya into two parts—one part loyal to Russia, which would be part of the Russian Federation as one of its subjects and where the Chechens who wished to remain in Russia would move; and the other part an independent Chechnya. In this case, enormous international assistance would be needed to help the Chechens pursue their own statehood. Was this statehood possible in principle? The previous attempts to do this in 1991–1994 and 1994–1999 had ended in disaster—in the emergence on the territory of Chechnya of lawless lands ruled by warlords who had been engaged in criminal activity, drug trafficking, and kidnapping. How to prevent it happening again when the peace was restored was a task not only for Russia but for the international community as well. The internationalization of the Chechnya problem sooner or later would become inevitable.

Moreover, the new European geopolitical context—with the enlargement of NATO and of the European Union—could stimulate a breakthrough vision of the Chechen conflict. The new framework for European security might offer a chance for joint Russian–European efforts to stabilize the situations in both the Balkans and the Caucasus. The constructive participation of Russian peacekeepers in the Balkans might allow joint Russia–NATO or Russia–European Union rapid-reaction or peacekeeping forces to help solve the Chechnya problem. In any case, the new European context and Russia's movement toward the West not only allowed but demanded nonconventional thinking.

If Moscow finally agreed on dividing Chechnya into two parts, a constitutional way to solve the problem would require referendums on the territory of Chechnya and the Russian Federation. Weary of the endless fighting, Chechnya and Russia might vote for a bipartite Chechnya. But the political will of the Kremlin was needed for negotiations. And first of all, the Russian president needed all his courage to admit that his war in Chechnya was lost and now his goal was not to win but to achieve peace. A peaceful resolution in Chechnya would have meant a new approach from the Kremlin toward Russian statehood and power—a new policy in Chechnya might become a step in finally overcoming the old Russian System. But the Kremlin was not yet ready for that step. And soon the possibility of a peaceful solution for Chechnya became even less possible.

On October 23, 2002, a group of Chechen fighters seized a theater in downtown Moscow and took more than 800 people hostage. The fighters placed explosives around the building, promising to blow up themselves together with their captives. They had only one demand: an end to the war in the Northern Caucasus. Thus brutal war came to the Russian capital.

President Putin rejected any negotiations with the terrorists. For the Kremlin to start negotiations would mean acknowledging that the war with the Chechens was lost, and this war was an important legitimization of Putin's ascendancy to power. No, Vladimitr Putin was not ready for defeat—especially when he was facing the elections. Instead, he ordered special services to storm the theater building. This ruthless rescue operation, in which an unknown gas was used, killed about 120 hostages. Many more—about 600 hostages—found themselves in hospitals suffering from the mysterious gas cocktail.

Initial relief at the success of the special forces in freeing the captives soon gave way to frustration and apprehension. No doubt, the leader and the government had to make a difficult decision, and they had little choice. But the rescue operation was done in a typically Soviet style, reminiscent of the old days. The attack had been launched without making sure that there was enough antidote to treat the hostages for gas poisoning. The rescued people were dying from poisoning, and the state was refusing to say what type of gas it had used—in fact, all the hostages who died, with the exception of two who had been shot, died from the poisoning. And relatives were not given immediate access to the victims, who were virtually imprisoned.

"This is a disgrace, a throwback to the worst of Soviet military secrecy and disregard for human life. The greatest failure is the old Russian nemesis: the failure to be honest," wrote the *Times* of London on October

28, 2002. Meanwhile, the authorities—just as in the days of the Chernobyl nuclear power plant explosion and the *Kursk* submarine disaster—were lying and trying to deliberately hide the truth and escape any responsibility.

The disastrous handling of this hostage crisis—it was as if the government had learned nothing from the previous numerous tragedies—proved that the authorities were much more concerned with their own image and prestige than with the lives of ordinary Russians. Protecting the president's reputation and demonstrating the strength of the state were the imperatives—as if a state that can't guarantee people's security can be considered viable. It was true that Putin, in his brief television address to the nation after the crisis was over, apologized for the loss of life. Yet in his speech, he could not avoid emphasizing the most important aspects for him and for the authorities: "We proved that you can't bring Russia to her knees." That was what really worried the Kremlin.

The Kremlin was not ready to think about the domestic roots of the terrorist problem. Instead, it equated the struggle with the Chechen separatists with the U.S. struggle against Osama bin Laden and interpreted the hostage crisis as the activity of an international terrorism network. Nobody wanted to acknowledge that the Chechnya problem had not been solved. Besides, President Putin, apparently following Bush's preemptive strategy, said in his speech that he would grant the military broader power to deal with what he called "suspected terrorists," and "would take appropriate measures against these terrorists, wherever they may be."

After vacillating for some time as to what to do about Chechnya, the Kremlin's hawks apparently tried to persuade Putin to start a tough offensive—as if several years of war had not been enough to demonstrate that military measures were futile. This step could only have played into the hands of the terrorists and further radicalized the Chechen population. This meant that Russia had to prepare for more hostage taking and suffering by ordinary citizens.

Negotiations with the Chechens now really looked well-nigh impossible because the hostage crisis discredited the only potential Russian partner for negotiations: Maskhadov, who had failed to distance himself from the terrorists. His legitimacy in the eyes of both Russians and the West had suffered a devastating blow. Even the democrats were skeptical as to the possibility of peace talks with the Chechen president. The fragile hope for talks had been destroyed.

Opinion polls conducted by VTsIOM from October 25 to 28 showed that the public mood had changed with regard to Chechnya. Now 46 percent of respondents were in favor of a "military solution," and only 44 percent supported the idea of negotiations (in July, 61 percent were for holding talks). The Russian president's actions during the hostage crisis were supported by 85 percent of those polled. Half of those who did not usually approve of his actions had in this case supported him. The president could be satisfied: The crisis and high death toll had not damaged his popularity. He was definitely a lucky politician. The tragedy had breathed new life into the myth of his strong and effective presidency.

In the aftermath of the hostage crisis, Moscow declared its intention of toughening its policy in the Northern Caucasus. It was, however, difficult to toughen it further; all types of weapons and scorched-earth tactics had been used already, without much result. How could this policy become even harsher?

What was clear was that the Praetorians around Putin had decided to use the crisis to make the regime more authoritarian. Manipulated from above, military hysteria and xenophobia had created the ground for an increased role for the security services and more macho rule. Frightened Duma deputies immediately endorsed restrictions concerning media activity, and they were apparently ready to endorse anything to please the president.

Putin let his hawks go public with hard-line rhetoric and with attempts to bring the media under total control, which corresponded to his way of thinking. But soon it became clear that he was not ready—yet—to allow his colleagues in the security services to change the existing balance of power and take the dominant upper hand. Besides, society—having supported the president during this new test of his leadership—had been anticipating more than simply tough talk.

After some vacillation and evidently painful deliberation, Putin decided to reject the idea of a harsh campaign in Chechnya—he did not want a new bloodbath; he was not ready for criticism from democrats; and more important, he was eager to preserve good relations with the West. Besides, he should have understood by then that a new offensive would lead him into a new dead end. Instead, he chose another solution: "Chechenization" of the conflict. That meant that all responsibility for further developments would be shared by Chechens loyal to the Kremlin, who would get not only an endorsement from Moscow but also democratic legitimacy. On December 12, 2002, the anniversary of the Russian Constitution, the president signed a decree calling for a referendum on a constitution and presidential and parliamentary elections in Chechnya. He did not set a time frame, but it was assumed in Moscow that the referendum would be held in March 2003 and that elections would follow in December 2003, at the time of Russia's parliamentary elections. This plan had to be a political solution for Chechnya.

Critics of the plan argued that the referendum and elections would be meaningless given the situation—with fighting continuing and half the Chechen population having fled the republic. Besides, these steps could hardly put an end to the hostilities, and in any case, everybody understood that the results of the elections would be falsified. During the first Chechen war (1994–1996), the same pattern of pacifying Chechnya had been followed, without much success. But at the moment, the Kremlin was not ready for a different option. All other options seemed hardly viable—so Chechen limbo continued.

Moscow faced many domestic problems on the eve of the elections. There was the need to digest and start implementing the laws passed in the first term. The ruling team had to find the time and means to secure social services that had been left untended. Health, education, culture, science, pensioners, invalids, the homeless and orphans, neglected small towns—all these issues waited patiently for the Kremlin's attention. Even ten terms in office would not be enough for President Putin to solve all the problems of the land—especially if Moscow continued behaving the way it had in his first term, through a system of micromanaging and constant pushing of buttons, of manual drive. For example, after the building explosion in Moscow in August 2002, the firefighters, police, and rescue workers who arrived on the scene had to wait two hours for the arrival of minister of emergency situations Sergei Shoigu and only then set to work clearing rubble and looking for victims. Waiting for orders from above has been the major organizing principle of the Putin regime.

The president and his team may not have liked manual drive much, either—it's the most reliable way to have a heart attack. But this is the style of management dictated by the logic of a superpresidency, whereby the leader is the only full-fledged political actor. Everyone else is part of the crowd of extras. Putin's ministers, representatives, officials, and he himself were constantly on the road around the country, fighting fires and floods, turning electricity back on, paying salaries, finding housing, organizing the elections of needed people, settling local conflicts. They were exhausting themselves, but the number of problems kept growing. Local authorities, deprived of powers and money, cowed and cautious, or cynical and gloating, waited for instructions from the center that they were not necessarily planning to obey.

The authorities faced a dilemma: Should they continue working like a squad of firefighters and first-aid workers, putting out the hottest conflicts and dealing with the avalanches most dangerous for general stability, leaving the rest for later? Or should they try to find solutions that would let Russia know that a truly new era was coming, that is, give society confidence and possibilities to decide its own future? This decision demanded that the authorities reexamine the still-reigning vision in the Kremlin *of freedom and order.*

The Yeltsin period gave Russia quite a few freedoms. Never had Russia been so free. But freedom in the absence of orderly habits, with a weak legal culture and egotistical elites, led to chaos and illegality, a disregard for all taboos and restrictions. Russia—frightened by the unfamiliar freedoms and not knowing how to deal with them—swung the pendulum back toward order in 1999. Putin came to power with that idea, and that idea was supported by the country.

But order can be legal or it can be bureaucratic.[13] Putin's Russia followed the path toward bureaucratic order—through reliance on the apparat, administrative methods, subordination, loyalty, and instructions from above. This order could be yet another illusion: Everything seems to work, commands are given, and subordinates report. But the problems are merely pushed more deeply away and with time become explosive. Igor Klyamkin, the Russian researcher, was right when he said that "the problem of transition of the state and society toward the rule of law (overcoming the dominance of the regime over the law) is fundamental."[14] A transition to the rule of law meant that the regime trusted society, giving it the chance to truly participate in government, and was relying not on behind-the-scenes pacts, force, and fear, but on the law and on independent institutions. Without a strategy of participation for society, millions of people could not consciously participate in the restoration of Russia, and the modernization of which the president spoke could not take place.

The question for Putin's Russia is: Could the president trust society? Could he turn to it directly for a mandate, for carte blanche to implement a transformation of a new type—this time, not from above, as it had always been done in Russia, but with the participation of society? In other words, could Putin take the chance?

Sociological data suggest that Russian society in the new century, despite its vacillation and the possibility of its lurching in either direction under the influence of manipulation by the elites, is much readier for the new project of modernization than many thought, including liberals who did not trust the masses and pinned their hopes on the leader. A poll by Tatyana Kutkovets's group showed that 78 percent of the population of Russia preferred a country that is convenient to live in and where the interests of people are the priority.[15] For the first time, adherents of the Western model are prevailing in Russia.

Of course, we must have no illusions about this society—Russia is still a friable, unstructured country. Its civil society is too weak. But the urban, dynamic, educated strata have already made a choice for individual rights and freedoms and are prepared to accept liberal democracy as a *system*. Yes, these strata have learned to accommodate the reality of the shadow economy and one-man rule. They will survive any regime and in any circumstances—they are amazingly adaptable.

These modernists are not prepared for revolution or resistance; they have gone off into private life—for the time being. But the important point is that they have gotten over the myth of Russia's "special path" and the "Russian idea." They have left the Russian System. They have learned to think in European categories, and taken together, they have achieved an enormous potential for reform.

Thus, with a steady 70 percent approval rating, President Putin has the opportunity to get society's mandate to implement more modernization. But he has not yet decided to fight his way out of the spider web in which he has been trapped. The elites and the Kremlin do not yet know how to rule such a society, how to handle its energy and initiative. The elites are afraid of these people who are free of the state, and try to do everything to hamper their becoming organized. Even the liberals in power fear the energy of the free masses—they do not believe in the people either. But the modernists among ordinary Russians have already learned to live outside the system and the traditional state. The question is whether they will organize spontaneously. Or will some of the people in power realize that there is a base for modernization that could be utilized? The modernists in Russian society, going about their private affairs and mostly supporting Putin, are offering their hand to him.

Preparations for the new elections beginning in Russia could be a strong impulse for forming a new strategy of modernization and a new philosophy of reform. President Putin had no trouble winning the last election. His problem is what to bring to the new elections. The Kremlin has not yet solved that problem. The renewed bustle and campaign tricks create the impression that the Russian regime is not prepared to move beyond the familiar—not yet. But in that case, Russia will have to take another lap around the vicious circle.

Chapter 9

AN UNFINISHED STORY: HOW RUSSIA RESPONDS TO ITS CHALLENGES

The West—means and goal. The Faustian bargain. Will Russia be able to reject
the Russian System fully and forever? Stability as a brake.
Will Putin destroy his regime? Russia's hope.

It is January 2003. I am stopping here, not waiting to see how President Vladimir Putin's administration will end. Yet this is not because it will probably be a long wait until the end of his rule. I have the sense (a gut feeling) that I can halt and ponder here, because the framework of Putin's Russia is more or less clear.

For the first time, the new Russia is taking on a shape and is no longer a "riddle wrapped in a mystery inside an enigma," as Winston Churchill liked to say and many who have written about Russia have repeated. The fundamental challenges facing Russia have become apparent, as well as the means available to deal with them. We know what is out of the question in Russia and what is still possible. We can see the fork in the road where the country has stopped indecisively, and it might be the last fork before the long journey: The society already knows what it wants but has not yet decided how to organize itself on the basis of new values.

Some post-Soviet people are still stumbling and lingering. But more and more Russians are ready to walk forward without turning back. It took them seventeen years (beginning with Gorbachev's *perestroika* in 1985) to reject quite a few traditions, patterns of life, and a mentality they had been accustomed to—what constituted the Russian System, the form that used to embody Russia. It was nearly two decades—a long time in a human life, but a short period in history, just a flash. Russia most likely will not reverse the clock, simply because the clock has been broken beyond repair. It looks as if Russia is finally turning in one definite direction. It is not clear, however, how long it will take the country to throw off the last waverings and what price it will have to pay for its final break with the past. Authoritarian rule and attempts to play a great-power role and to pursue "uniqueness" are the major leftovers from the Soviet and pre-Soviet legacies.

On the positive side of the balance sheet, we see that Russian society after years of coming to grips with the new reality has realized that it cannot modernize itself without help from the outside, relying only on its inner resources, and that a breakthrough to the twenty-first century is impossible without the help of the West (I mean "the West" not in the geographical sense, but rather the whole civilization ordered around the concept of liberal democracy). Though Russia under Yeltsin attempted to get the financial assistance and economic support of Western countries, nurturing hope for a new Marshall Plan, under Putin more and more Russians have come to understand that only integration into Western society can help their country become a modern state. For them, the West is not only a means of modernization and a mine of resources that Russia lacks but also a goal in itself—an altogether new phenomenon in Russian thinking. Yet Russia still has to turn Westernization into concrete political decisions, economic mechanisms—into everyday life.

For the first time, fatalistic Russia came to understand that destiny is not a matter of chance but of choice, and not a thing to anticipate or long for but a task to pursue. Yet every time Russians try to implement liberal and democratic reforms, they are confronted by their remaining fears and superstitions, by stereotypes and norms that for centuries have been the way of Russia's survival. And now, reaching the final fork, quite a few Russians halt again, seeing the dilemma: stability based on the leader ruling through personified power and the limited freedoms to which so many have been accustomed, or dismantling the last elements of the Russian System. Even liberals who support the superpresidency are not ready to shake off the past.

Russians at the start of the new century have, I hope, rejected claims for Russia as a pole of an alternative civilization. But if the society is to move toward the West, it will have to discover what forms that motion can take and what routes it can follow. Russians must guard against fresh illusions and unreasonable expectations, as well as learn how to handle the inevitable frustrations and pain. Dialogue and even cooperation with the West during the 1990s did not preclude stumbling around in new delusions and neuroses, envy of flourishing nations, and self-pity, as well as unexpected outbursts of bitterness. Finally, Russians must overcome the major new temptation to pursue what seems the easiest road: imitating the market and democracy in their surface aspects while underneath preserving patron–client relations, the rule of the few, and governance without accountability.

In the meantime, the alliance that Russia concluded with the West in 2001 contains not only the possibility of real partnership and Russia's integration into the West but the threat of a new Russian alienation. If there were a new misunderstanding or clash of interests with the West, Russia would not revert to its previous hostility toward Western civilization but rather descend to a murky zone of disenchantment with everybody and everything—including Russia itself.

So far, the alliance Russia struck with the West has taken the form of a Faustian bargain. The essence of the bargain is simple: The West is including Russia in the implementation of some of its geopolitical interests—the war on terrorism, strengthening the security agenda, promoting an energy dialogue—while shutting its eyes to how far Russia still is from being a liberal democracy. Moreover, the West continues to view Russia's leadership as the major guarantee of its cozy relations with the West, thus endorsing Russian rule through personified power. In its turn, Russia is solving the problem of external resources for its modernization while retaining the old rules of the game domestically.

The Faustian bargain has its supporters both in the industrial democracies and in Russia. In the West, supporters include those who don't care about Russia, don't see its possible impact on the world, those who continue to view Russia as a hostile country, an embodiment of evil, and those who prefer to see Russia where it is now—at the perimeter of Western civilization, as a curtain dividing the West from rising China.

In Russia, the Faustian bargain is supported by the advocates of authoritarianism and Russia's "uniqueness." Paradoxically, the current alliance between Russia and the West is an ideal means for preserving Russia's bureaucratic, quasi-authoritarian regime.

The inclusion of Russia in the Western orbit on the basis of certain coinciding geopolitical interests could be situational and merely temporary. Only a commonality of values would guarantee the genuine integration of Russia into the Western community. Russia would have to fully embrace liberal democratic principles, rejecting attempts to tailor democratic institutions to the needs of personified power and the bureaucratic state. Only then could Russia join in a "constructive partnership" with the West.

That partnership at first would inevitably have aspects of benevolent asymmetry, at least in the economic field. A serious challenge for Russia is to give up the notion of military parity with the United States, recognize its current limited capabilities, and channel its resources into building an affluent society—this time satisfying its people, not its vanity. Cutting excessive global ambitions now would not preclude the possibility of Russia's emergence in the future as an economically prosperous regional and, perhaps, world power. But for the sake of its future, Russia—and the West—will have to end the imitation game, which is humiliating for all participants and destructive for Russia.

Is the Russian public prepared to reject attempts to combine the incompatible: Westernization with Soviet-style superpower ambitions, democracy with personified power, the market with the regulatory role of the bureaucracy, inclusion in Europe with curbs on a free press? Is it ready to reject great-power status based on military might? The data cited in this book suggest that by the late 1990s many Russians had matured enough to want to be integrated into a system of liberal values. Only a portion of the population—about 24 percent—has retained its open allegiance to the traditional Russian state based on military might, imperial aspirations, and one-man rule. And 22 percent of Russians are trying to combine elements of the traditional Russian System with liberalism.

Russia has in fact rejected key components of its previous identity—messianism and expansionism, Russian Orthodoxy as the state religion, and anti-Westernism as the official ideology. Recent polls indicate that 33 percent of the Russian population fully supports the liberal democratic agenda, with another 37 percent more and more inclined to accept the Western alternative. All that demonstrates that Russia has an enormous reformist potential.

But while quite a growing number of Russians can throw away the crutches imposed by the political regime and walk independently, many in the political class are not ready to give up their attempts to regulate, to reject patrimonialism, to leave behind the shadow networks, and to overcome nostalgia for the imperialist past—and finally to support the rule of law. Those who consider themselves elites have been afraid to let go of the controls. They have no experience living in a free society. They are terrified of competition and have a fear of their own people and of any alternatives. They lean heavily on the police, the security services, the army, and the state apparatus, which they look on as their safety net and guarantors of their survival. Their own helplessness, inadequate education, and lack of experience living in a culture of consensus and dialogue drive them to destroy the new sprouts around them, keeping potential rivals down. It is the political class in Russia, obsessed with self-preservation, that tries to reanimate the archaic elements of the public subconscious and heighten suspicion of the West, fear of openness, and nostalgia for lost empire. Superpower status and authoritarianism are the last bastions of those who do not know how to live and rule in a new way.

In the fall of 2001, Vladimir Putin forced the ruling class to accept his pro-Western shift. Cowardly and opportunistic elites followed the leader, as is usual in Russia. But to move presidential choice into the realm of concrete decisions, a new bureaucracy is needed, one that would leave provincial backwaters and servility behind and think in the imperatives of the modern competitive age. Unfortunately, you could count such bureaucrats in Russia on the fingers of both hands. That is why the president has so few to rely on as he tries to channel Russia's relations with NATO in a new direction, to gain Russia membership in the World Trade Organization, and to move closer to Europe and toward more constructive relations with the United States. He has to make policy on his own, which is what he did in 2001–2002.

Thus the Kremlin's choice in favor of the West is not solidified. It is not supported so far by the national consensus. It has not become Russia's ideology and its elites' key mission. It is based on the wishes and desires of the leader and his understanding of the weakness of other options, and the interests of some advanced social groups. The choice still lacks content, a deeper substance. Moreover, the leader has not gone beyond the Faustian bargain. He remains the classic Russian modernizer, operating within the limits of the triad of autocracy, Western resources, and a market economy. Both President Putin and Russian elites hope to join the West on their own terms—that is, while preserving at least some elements of the Russian System. Seventeen years is not long enough to become accustomed to another tradition—to live, to work, to walk without a leash. Some have learned to do it; others are still afraid or reluctant.

The West, for its part, has not yet decided how much it needs Russia. Western governments are still not prepared to integrate Russia into their space. This is understandable, for no one knows what it would do to Western civilization to bring in a weak (at the moment) giant, with all its complexes and pretensions, its murky past, still-vague desires, and huge ambitions, its enormous potential coupled with the vestiges of Soviet and pre-Soviet legacies.

Yes, there is an understanding, especially in Europe, that fundamental issues confronting the world community cannot be resolved without Russia. But Europe seems bothered that Russia is on a different level of development from itself. Europe is creating policy of a new kind—fashioning transnational governance, liquidating some functions of the nation-state, and destroying borders between countries. Russia continues building a traditional state with all its attributes and has been trying to lace civil society into a tight corset. I wonder how Russian modernism and European postmodernity can coexist. It may not be realistic to anticipate easy integration of entities with radically different views about the very substance of future development.

Besides, broad political groupings in the West are currently out of sympathy with Russia. Western liberals resent Russia's global aspirations,

Moscow's Chechen war, the Kremlin's desire to stifle pluralism and free-dom, every Russian leader's attempt to rule in a monarchic manner. Western conservatives, however, are prepared to engage Moscow in dia-logue, but within the framework of realpolitik, avoiding mention of Russia's domestic problems and regarding the country as innately alien and incorrigible. Thus, unlike during the Gorbachev and early Yeltsin periods, there are no influential forces in the West prepared to more fully engage with Russia and to strive to influence Russian progress toward liberal democracy.

Even those in the West who favor embracing Russia are still undecid-ed about whether they should wait for Russia to complete its transforma-tion into a democracy or start integrating without waiting for the out-comes of Russia's transformation. Western political circles hesitate, and many have almost reached the conclusion that it is better to wait. They still have to absorb eastern Germany into western Germany, to incorporate Central and Eastern Europe, and the Baltic states—and there is neither time for new worries nor money. Liberal democracies outside Europe have even less incentive to think about a sustainable marriage with Russia.

But Russia can transform itself only if it is part of the dialogue. The impulses from the outside world might even become the crucial factor needed for change. Russia's integration into the community of industrial nations should not necessarily mean membership in NATO, the European Union, the World Trade Organization, and so on. Integration is a multi-stage process, and various forms of cooperation are possible—cooperation in strictly defined areas, adaptation, affiliation, mutual dependence, strong bilateral relations. Russia's setting its heart on full membership in Western international institutions could bring new disappointments to both sides if Russia is unable or unwilling to meet the requirements of that member-ship and these institutions do not seek palliatives like "special status" for Russia.

This time, Russians must avoid illusions that integration with the West will solve their problems. United Europe is still evolving and trying to find the optimal pattern for its common destiny. Western democracies contin-ue to search for solutions to their domestic and international problems—growing unemployment, mass disenchantment with democratic institu-tions, the rise of the extreme right.

What does Russia have to offer, critics ask, besides headaches, a bureaucracy that needs neutralizing as badly as it needs modernizing, and practice dealing with the whims and tantrums of politicians? Until quite recently, Russia was the center of attention because of its nuclear warheads. Once it became clear that Russia would not fight a war with the West, interest in it cooled. Yet Russia remains a microcosm in which a series of challenges to the West come together. All these challenges—strengthening European, Asian, and world security; combating terrorism and crime; building effective world markets; diversifying energy resources—require Russian cooperation. And that is hardly the end of the list.

As for Russia itself, its search for its new identity depends on when the political class realizes that the bureaucratic, quasi-authoritarian regime must be dropped. In the 1990s, the country rejected society's total subordination to the regime. The authorities began—at least to some degree—to depend on ordinary Russians and the election process. But the essence of the political regime remains the power of the leader who has taken all the levers in his hands and could rule unchecked, with no accountability. That power gives substance to the Russian System, preventing its final burial and generating attempts to save its leftovers disguised by a democratic shell.

The Russian ruling class wants to appear civilized in the eyes of the world, and so it tries to re-create in Russia the entire system of Western institutions, leaving out what it does not like and what really matters: definite rules of the game and uncertain results. What Russian political elites want is just the opposite: uncertain rules that can be changed at will, and predictable, certain results guaranteeing that they remain in power. Not only Putin and his team but also a part of Russian society have decided that a democracy managed from above by a small group of people is perhaps not just the best but the only form of government possible—at least at this stage.

Russia must decide, on the basis of painful experience, whether Russian-style "democracy," or rather imitative democracy, is an effective tool for modernizing the country. In two years, Putin's regime has created opportunities for stabilization and moderate reform, for ordering politics to some extent, and for strengthening the state. These achievements practically guarantee Putin's reelection in 2004. A substantial portion of society is quite satisfied with what it has, fearing the options and alternatives.

The probability of serious crises in Russia in the next few years—if the basic tendencies of development hold and the president escapes fatal blunders—is very small or, rather, small. The regime has no serious foes. Nor is there a large gap between expectations and fulfillment, if only because society's expectations are so low, basically reduced to the wish that things not get any worse. Very little is needed to retain stability in Russia aside from paying salaries and pensions regularly. As long as oil prices remain at about $15 a barrel, the Kremlin has no cause for worry. At least it hasn't had, as yet!

Yet in the longer run, stability based on the absence of alternatives, on low expectations, and on oil prices must be detrimental. The multiparty system, the government, the parliament, and the power of regional bosses all depend on loyalty to the leader, who in turn depends on his ratings. But let us imagine what could happen if the president's ratings plunged: It would shake the entire system or even trigger its collapse. A system built on shadowy deals and one-man rule is much more vulnerable than a system formed on the foundation of strong and viable institutions. Russia still must come to this conclusion, and this is the major challenge it is facing.

A combination of mild authoritarianism and economic liberalization is perfectly adequate for dragging a peasant country onto the road of industrialization. To meet postindustrial challenges, however, to move toward a high-technology society, a new type of regime is needed, one that makes room for social initiatives, local self-government, and individual freedom.

Issues that need answers have been accumulating. How could a dialogue with the West coexist with the desire to "seal up" society, depriving it of the freedoms to which it grew accustomed during the Yeltsin years? How could Moscow get out of the Chechen war and stabilize the Northern Caucasus? How could the Kremlin keep stability from again turning into stagnation? And how could Russians achieve a new breakthrough while avoiding chaos and disintegration? Questions, questions, very difficult questions . . .

So far, the Kremlin's policy has been creating traps for Russia and for the presidency that might turn out to be disastrous for the current regime. On one hand, the policy permits the natural, albeit slow, growth of the middle class, of the new Russian generation ready to live and compete in the modern world. On the other hand, it hinders political pluralism and the competition for power in the country. Sooner or later, conflict would be inevitable between the new social groups that strive for parliamentary democracy, local self-government, freedoms, and decentralization of power and those that support the current regime of the bureaucracy, the power ministries, and oligarchs. That could lead to a crisis of the political system.

It is difficult to tell what form that conflict would take—a pressure from the bottom, a gradual reform from the top, or a combination of both—or how it would end. The key would be solving the conflict without bloodshed or major social upheaval. No less important is avoiding the growth of marginal nationalist forces, which as old Europe has found, can happen even in stable, mature democracies. That would be Putin's task if reelected, or it would be the task for another leader if Putin proves that he cannot reform Russian politics. In any case, the challenge of changing Russian mechanisms of governance is unavoidable.

Russia's leader is influencing its future, and at some moments he is making the future even if he is often reluctant to take a position or is leading his regiment from behind. Is President Putin capable of comprehending that the rule he has created will not allow him to realize his goal—forming a civilized market economy and a modern state? And if he realizes that, is the founder of bureaucratic semiauthoritarianism prepared to restructure his rule accordingly? There is no point hoping that he might think about these issues while preparing for the parliamentary and presidential elections in 2003 and 2004, since no one implements reforms during elections; that is a time for populism and vote tallying.

Sooner or later, however, the Russian president will have to think about his historical mission. In fact, Putin is definitely thinking about it already. And then he will have to solve a dilemma: whether to stay a stabilizing leader of corrupt capitalism and of a country doomed to living in the waiting room of Western civilization, or to become a transformer and start building a new system that would allow Russia to become a full-fledged liberal democracy and enter the industrial world as an equal.

The first choice would mean a continuation of imitation and the construction of Potemkin villages, that is, the usual pastime of Russia's leaders and political class. It would be a life of pretending: The authorities pretend to rule and the people pretend to obey. That choice would mean slow degradation without a chance for Russia to get on its feet. Avalanchelike collapse, blown to bits by a bomb, unexpected ruin, disintegration—all these theatrical and frightening options are not—thank God!—for Russia. The gloomiest scenario for the country is the slow spreading of rot, which might not always be visible but in the end would lead to the disintegration of the people's will, of the Russian spirit of adventure and political and intellectual courage, and lead to muddling through for years and decades. That is the price of stabilizing current Russian reality.

For Putin personally, this first scenario would end with a repeat of Yeltsin's story—that is, with the "privatization" of the leader and the regime by a band of Kremlin conspirators. Any leader in Russia will be doomed if he has no strong institutions to support him. But in the historical context, the personal destiny of the leader, if he becomes a hostage of his entourage or of circumstances, will not be important or even interesting. He will remain a footnote to history—the leader who squandered his chance.

The second possible path for President Putin—reform of the regime— is riskier, without guarantees of success, and with a likelihood that he might break his neck. If the political steering wheel is not turned wisely, reform could end up in Gorbachevism, with the leader losing control of power and events. Breaking one's neck while undertaking a historic task, however, is not the worst end for a world leader. There is honor in it. But Vladimir Putin could be lucky. If he decided to de-hermeticize the regime and managed to cross thin ice without falling in, he would accomplish what no Russian or Soviet leader ever had: He would begin building a responsible system of governance based not on the irrational and mystic power embodied in the leader but on the rule of law. That would be a new chapter in Russian history. Overcoming the self and finding new impulses or a new destiny is enough to make any nation great and any leader worth remembering.

Is Putin capable of taking that step? It could be tantamount to political suicide for him—to dismantle what he has been creating during his first term. No one in political history has done such a contradictory thing—no one has ever created an authoritarian regime only to consciously destroy it. Could President Vladimir Putin perform the unthinkable?

We may be demanding the impossible from Vladimir the Modernizer. We reproach him for his rule through personified power and his attempts to control the country's fate single-handedly. But at the same time, there is no sign that influential forces have formed in Russian society that could offer enough support for a completely new, democratic regime. Even the liberals are supporting the elected monarchy. Yet we expect the authoritarian leader to democratize "from above" and voluntarily give up power to institutions in Russian society that appear to be embarrassingly happy while snoring quietly. I admit that this seems beyond the limits of realism.

But leadership presupposes vision and the ability to see beyond the present day. The purpose of getting power is to be able to give it away; otherwise, it is not leadership but power grabbing. The rule of the personality in Russia is an atavistic remnant of the past, and it is high time to get rid of it peacefully. If Putin at some point understands that and has the courage and will to solve this problem, he will enter Russian history as Leader-Transformer.

But if there is a transition from autocratic rule to the rule of institutions, the leader has to consider how to prevent the young Russian democracy from succumbing to angry populism and destroying the market, using Bolshevik means to redress injustices by taking from the rich, and returning to suspicion of the West. We admit that it is thanks in great part to Putin's authoritarianism that Russia has revived economic reform and has entered into an alliance with Western countries. Has Russia matured enough to put an end to civilized tsarism? We won't be able to answer this question until Russia begins that transition. But Russia will never mature into a real democracy if it does not start building one.

Leadership is still the basic Russian institution. But sooner or later, Russians themselves will have to decide the country's fate. Sometimes this society's patience, conservatism, and inertness are astonishing. It seems hard to budge, turn, or reform. But Russian passivity and patience can be explained, if only partially, by common sense. There were so many opportunities for Russians to straighten their shoulders, shake off the bureaucratic midges enveloping them, and go on a rampage of destruction—in the Russian manner, without differentiation and with blood. But Russia under Yeltsin and subsequently under Putin, even unhappy and frustrated, has avoided hysteria and madness to this point and is still avoiding the worst. It did not crash, even though its ruling class pushed it to the brink many times. Now there is hope that Russia's most important reform—the transformation of autocracy, splitting power into institutional pieces—will be achieved without bloodshed.

Russia can accomplish its farewell to its dramatic history, and the final systemic vestige of that history, if several factors come together: pressure from society, understanding among the political class that rule through personified power and the irresponsibility of elites are dangerous to its survival, and the intuition of the leader telling him that separation of powers and power sharing will make his rule more stable.

The history of Russia under Yeltsin and Putin has shown that during a time of historic transformations, many things must be regarded in a new light. What seems like an obstacle in normal development may turn out to be a blessing when a transitional society is seeking a new identity. Thus Russia is saved by the fact that a complete consolidation of society and rule is still impossible there. Today's reality, including the bureaucratic, quasi-authoritarian regime, cannot be cast in concrete. Therefore, movement in a more positive direction is possible. Yet we cannot rule out temporal retrograde movement completely. Patients recovering from a virulent disease have occasional setbacks.

The conflicts and the struggle that have revived in Russia despite the Kremlin's attempts to control everything are more good than bad. The conflicts show that the country is alive, and interests are formed though the conflicts. Struggle does not permit the regime to ossify. An even more positive factor is the spontaneity present in the populace and its growing independence: When polled, 45 percent of the population said that the state plays no role in their lives at all.

Of course, it is not good for society and the state to travel on parallel tracks. But it is good that people are coming out from the shadow of the state leviathan and living independently. Soon they will have to build a new kind of statehood, based on different principles, and the product will be their own state serving their interests. In the meantime, Russia retains a certain unruliness and spontaneity that allow society to breathe. When I see how the state apparatus tries to control our lives again, I think: the more spontaneity, the better—for now.

In the final analysis, what happens in Russia in the next ten to fifteen years will depend on the generation that replaces the final echelons of the Soviet *nomenklatura*, diluted by pragmatists. Who will they be, the people who arrive on the scene in 2008 or 2012? They will be people who grew up in the eras of Gorbachev, Yeltsin, and Putin. We know that they are not interested in ideology, that they don't remember Russia's history of totalitarianism very well, and that they are uninhibited and liberated—sometimes too much so. Many of them are cynics or look like cynics.

But the important thing is that they are not cowed—they have never known fear. They don't have slaves' instincts anymore. This is an absolutely new phenomenon for Russia—its future elites will be free of the complexes and phobias that burdened the ruling classes of the country for centuries. It is not yet clear how they see the future of Russia. If Putin creates chances for their education and preserves freedom for this generation, if he gives them the chance to bear responsibility for their actions—which is impossible without freedom—it will be one of his contributions.

For now and for a few years to come, Russian politics will see palace wars, highs and lows. There will be attempts to shape a political system to fit the needs of the political class that is trying to guarantee itself a future in an uncertain situation. Russia will have to pay for the training of its leaders and their teams again and again. Russia has to solve one more problem: the peaceful and legitimate transfer of power from Vladimir Putin to his democratically elected—not appointed, this time—successor.

Russians still have to learn not to never fall, but to rise up again every time they fall. Russia and the West will have to work on their relationship. And they are unlikely to avoid mutual hurts and suspicions. The Russian economy is still unstable and subject to shocks because it is now tied to the world economy and because it is still unstructured.

Unfortunately, we cannot discount the possibility of yet another experiment in Russia—this time, with harsh authoritarianism. It is not clear how the people who are running Russia will act in a crisis or in an attempt to hold onto their power. What if, feeling desperate and cornered, they decide that they can solve problems only by resorting to violence, and kick over the chessboard? The result of that experiment is clear beforehand: It will fail both because the authorities don't have the power to push society back into the cage and because society has grown accustomed to living in freedom, even if it is limited freedom. That certainty is promising.

And so we have reached the end of our ruminations. "Is that all?" the reader may demand, left with unanswered questions. People who are used to clarity and unambivalence will be confused. So, is Russia a democracy or a dictatorship? And who is Putin—a noble knight or an evil demon? Russia still avoids black or white answers. The country will be a hybrid for a long time. Both optimists and pessimists will find arguments to support their point of view on Russia. Both will be right—and wrong.

Will President Putin be able to move from being a Modernizer of the system to its Transformer? As I write, it seems that he has not made a decision. But he will have to act very soon. Inability to act is also a choice.

And what about hope? Is it still delayed disappointment, as it has always been in Russia? It depends on what we have in mind. My hope today is that Russia, for all its setbacks, passions, and tiresome scandals, not only keeps on keeping on but is moving. Even when it is limping, it is moving . . . and, I believe, moving into the future.

NOTES

Chapter 1

1. Russia's oligarchs are the country's biggest businessmen. Their influence over state officials, often gained through blatant corruption, has allowed them to establish and advance their business empires, while degrading government power. The leading oligarchs of the Yeltsin era were Boris Berezovsky, Vladimir Potanin, Petr Aven, Mikhail Khodorkovsky, Mikhail Fridman, Alexander Smolensky, and Vladimir Gusinsky, known as the "seven bankers." In 1996, that group played a major role in Yeltsin's reelection to a second term as president. Its members were rewarded with extensive property (mainly in the field of natural resources) for which they paid almost nothing, in a deal that came to be known as "loans for shares." Under Putin, new oligarchs have emerged, among them Alexei Mordashov, head of the metallurgy conglomerate Severstal, Oleg Deripaska, who privatized Russia's aluminum industry, and Sergei Pugachev, a Saint Petersburg banker who allegedly was close to Putin's team. See Paul Klebnikov, *Godfather of the Kremlin: Boris Berezovsky and the Looting of Russia* (New York: Harcourt Brace, 2000), and David E. Hoffman, *The Oligarchs: Wealth and Power in the New Russia* (New York: Public Affairs, 2002).

2. Thomas E. Graham, *Russia's Decline and Uncertain Recovery* (Washington, D.C.: Carnegie Endowment for International Peace, 2002), p. 26.

3. Lebed was killed in a helicopter crash on April 27, 2002. The first person who attempted to play the role of Russian Pinochet tragically departed from the political scene. Lebed was a well-known author of aphorisms. A couple of them: "Pinochet—this is a Chilean problem. . . . To be exact it is not a problem—this is Chilean luck"; "You can't change horses while crossing the river, but you should change the assholes."

4. Primakov could not stand independent journalists and was suspicious of the press in general. But at the same time, in the dark days for Russia's independent television station NTV and later TV-6, he was one of the few politicians who was not afraid to come to the station and be interviewed by opposition journalists. Later, in 2002,

Primakov helped the team of independent journalists from the old NTV to build a new private channel TVS, becoming a member of its board.

5. Boris Yeltsin, *Prezidentskii marafon* [Presidential marathon] (Moscow: AKT, 2000), p. 246.

6. The president pushed Korzhakov out of his entourage on the eve of the 1996 elections. Korzhakov later wrote his memoirs, *Dawn to Sunset* (Moscow: Interbook, 1997), which revealed unflattering facts about Yeltsin and his family—unverifiable, whether true or not.

7. Roman Abramovich had at a certain point in his entrepreneurial career been under investigation on suspicion of embezzlement. Voloshin, Berezovsky's right-hand man, managed the structures which, so the newspapers said, siphoned funds out of pyramid schemes that had been created by Berezovsky.

8. Former deputy secretary of state Strobe Talbott drew my attention to a certain logic in Yeltsin's appointments as prime minister: young—old—young—old (Gaidar, Chernomyrdin, Kiriyenko, Primakov, Stepashin). Apparently, age had meaning for Yeltsin when he was thinking about breakthrough versus stabilization. For breakthroughs, he sought out young prime ministers; when he thought about stabilization, he turned to middle-aged politicians. Putin, however, did not fit entirely this logic.

9. Subsequently, Stepashin grew close to Putin and was appointed head of the Accounting Chamber. From this post, he initiated an attack on the oligarchs, obviously not without the president's knowledge, turning over materials on the machinations of the big businessmen to the prosecutor general's office.

10. The journalist Sergei Dorenko, a friend of Berezovsky's and one who was privy to much information, described the search process this way: "The name [Putin] was first thought of by Yumashev. It was supported strongly by Voloshin. Putin was received and they came to an agreement. Putin resisted for a long time and expressed unwillingness to be involved in this adventuristic undertaking. He was persuaded." S. Dorenko, "Statista Putina smenit general Shamanov" [Moderate Putin will be replaced by general Shamanov], *Moskovskaya pravda*, March 24, 2001. In turn, Berezovsky later declared more than once that it had been his idea to make Putin Yeltsin's successor.

11. Prosecutor general Skuratov was videotaped relaxing with prostitutes and then blackmailed. He refused to retire voluntarily and tried to prove that Yeltsin was firing him because he was investigating wrongdoing at the Kremlin. Putin unambiguously took Yeltsin's side in the matter, and his agency, the Federal Security Service (FSB), was active in coming up with compromising materials that hurt Skuratov. Later it became clear that some evidence against Skuratov had been forged.

12. The August 19, 1999, *New York Times* carried an article by Raymond Bonner and Timothy O'Brien, "Bank Activity Elicits Suspicion of Ties with Russian Organized Crime." According to Bonner and O'Brien, nearly $4.2 billion from Russia had

passed through Bank of New York accounts in New York City in the course of a year, and the transfers, they said, could be part of money-laundering operations of Russian criminals. Rumors spread alleging that the entire International Monetary Fund tranche given to Russia before the financial collapse of 1998 had been privatized by Russian bureaucrats and oligarchs and transferred to the West through the Bank of New York.

13. Russian officials instantly sprang to the defense of their own. The minister of foreign affairs, Igor Ivanov, declared, "We have no need to justify ourselves, and as for Russia's good name, we have it" (*Rossiiskii delovoi monitor*, September 4, 1999).

14. Mabetex is a construction firm that participated in the restoration of the Kremlin and was also involved in highly publicized corruption scandals with people from the Yeltsin circle, primarily Pavel Borodin, who headed the office of the president's affairs and was personally close to Yeltsin. The Italian newspaper *Corriere della Sera* of August 25, 1999, contained an exposé listing credit cards slips signed by Yeltsin and his daughters that were allegedly found during a police raid on the Mabetex offices in Lugano, Switzerland. The article alleged that Mabetex paid the bills on the Yeltsin family credit cards.

15. Rumors spread that right before the invasion Berezovsky allegedly met in France with Shamil Basayev, one of the Chechen separatist leaders who led the attack by the Chechen separatists on Dagestan, and Alexander Voloshin, the head of Yeltsin's presidential staff. Basayev is one of the most famous of the Chechen warlords, long suspected of having ties to the Russian secret services. See "Vnimanie, snimayu" [Attention, Camera!], *Profil'*, November 27, 2000, pp. 18–20.

16. Human rights activist Sergei Kovalev spoke about this openly, as did Chechen president Aslan Maskhadov, who, by the way, separated himself from the actions of the fighters who attacked Dagestan. In his interview with the Spanish newspaper *La Guardia*, Maskhadov said the following: "As for Dagestan, I can declare with full responsibility that Berezovsky, Voloshin, Magomedov [chair of the State Council of Dagestan], and Putin all knew. We absolutely did not need either Dagestan or the conquest of alien territory. It was all programmed by Moscow. Dagestan was an excuse for war." Cited from *Kommersant-Daily*, February 8, 2000.

17. One of the most suspicious episodes of this drama took place in Ryazan', where officers of the FSB were caught planting gexogen, an explosive used in the explosions in Moscow, in the cellar of the apartment house. The head of the FSB, Nikolai Patrushev, later declared that his people were taking part in "an exercise" (!). The Kremlin prevented any further investigation into what had happened in Ryazan'. See Pavel Voloshin, "Geksogen. FSB. Ryazan," *Novaya gazeta*, March 13–16, 2000.

18. In March 2002, Berezovsky, who had moved to London, organized the screening of a film he had commissioned from French journalists, which attempted to prove that the 1999 apartment building explosions were the work of the Russian security agen-

cies. The Kremlin responded by accusing Berezovsky of being mixed up in the Chechen separatists' invasion of Dagestan. This looked clumsy: If Moscow had proof of Berezovsky's involvement in the invasion of Dagestan, he should have been brought to justice long before. But the question raised in the film financed by Berezovsky and entitled "Assault on Russia" has never been answered.

19. "Zheleznyi Putin" [Iron Putin], *Kommersant-Daily*, March 10, 2000.

Chapter 2

1. The upper house of the parliament—the Federation Council—is formed from the representatives of the regions appointed by the regional authorities.

2. Putin showed support for the SPS in his characteristically restrained manner: He received Sergei Kiriyenko, one of the party's leaders, in the Kremlin and heard him out attentively in front of the television cameras, looking benignly at the thick program of the party that Kiriyenko had placed on a table for him. In farewell, Putin smiled and promised to study the program. That was all. But the very fact of the meeting was interpreted by the leaders of the SPS—and not only them—as a gesture of support from Putin, who did not contradict that interpretation.

3. After the parliamentary elections, Primakov became the leader of the Fatherland and All-Russia faction in the Duma. But he was obviously bored by parliamentary work. After lengthy negotiations with the Kremlin, he was appointed head of the Chamber of Commerce. He had requested the post of speaker of the Federation Council, the upper chamber of the parliament, but Putin gave that to his man from Saint Petersburg, Sergei Mironov.

4. Anatoly Chubais, who was in charge of the SPS election headquarters, described the party's election results as "a complete revolution in the political structure of Russia." On another occasion, he trumpeted: "SPS is tomorrow's power." As usual, he exaggerated.

5. Soon after, Sergei Kiriyenko, who accepted the post of presidential representative in Putin's new superpresidential regime, confirmed the evolutionary tendencies of the leaders of the SPS movement, whose aim was to have at any cost an official post that would give them the opportunity to engage in business. Chubais was already a state oligarch, having become under Yeltsin the director of RAO UES (Unified Electricity System), a "natural monopoly" that managed all of Russia's electricity.

6. According to a VTsIOM poll conducted January 6–10, 2000, 51 percent of Russians expressed satisfaction with Yeltsin's retirement, 27 percent surprise, 11 percent delight, 7 percent confusion, 4 percent each anxiety and regret, and 1 percent outrage; 12 percent had no particular feelings about it, and 1 percent had no opinion.

7. Notably, Yeltsin spoke about resigning even sooner and handing over power to Putin before the parliamentary elections. That might suggest that the ruling Family had already made its decision about the successor. It also suggests that the Kremlin was not very worried about the results of the Duma election, apparently feeling that they could control them. But obviously the failure of the pro-Kremlin movements to get a majority of votes in December 1999 could have led to corrections in the "succession plans."

8. In September 1999, according to VTsIOM, the desire to see Yeltsin retire predominated among Russians. Thus, 65 percent of those polled felt that it would be better for Yeltsin to retire and for new elections to be held, 21 percent felt that Yeltsin should stay on to the end of his term but not get involved in the work of the government, 5 percent felt that Yeltsin should keep all his powers to the end of his term, and 9 percent had no opinion.

9. See the analysis of Yeltsin's rule in Leon Aron, *Yeltsin: A Revolutionary Life* (New York: Saint Martin's Press, 2000); Peter Reddaway and Dmitri Glinsky, *The Tragedy of Russian Reforms* (Washington, D.C.: U.S. Peace Institute, 2001); Michael McFaul, *Russia's Unfinished Revolution* (Ithaca, N.Y.: Cornell University Press, 2000); George Breslauer, *Gorbachev and Yeltsin as Leaders* (New York: Cambridge University Press, 2002); and Lilia Shevtsova, *Yeltsin: Myths and Reality* (Washington, D.C.: Carnegie Endowment for International Peace, 1999), which is also available in a Russian edition, *Rezhim Borisa El'tsina* (a Carnegie Moscow Center publication; Washington, D.C.: Carnegie Endowment for International Peace, 1999).

10. I remember, in a film about Yeltsin shown in 2000, that Yeltsin's daughter Tatyana is watching former Soviet president Mikhail Gorbachev on television and says to her father, "How Gorbachev has aged!" Yet at that time, Yeltsin was a total ruin in comparison with the dynamic, youthful, still attractive Gorby.

11. Guillermo O'Donnell, "Delegative Democracy," *Journal of Democracy*, vol. 5, no. 1 (January 1994), pp. 59–62.

Chapter 3

1. Putin celebrated the New Year as acting president in notable fashion—he and his wife flew to war-torn Chechnya. It was yet another demonstration of his new, mobile leadership style.

2. *Moskovskie novosti*, January 5, 2000.

3. Oligarch Boris Berezovsky said, "Putin is a man who could guarantee the succession of power," explaining that he defined succession as "not allowing a redistribution of property." *Kommersant-Daily*, November 27, 1999.

4. *Nezavisimaya gazeta*, December 30, 1999.

5. *Izvestija*, February 25, 2000.

6. Lev Gudkov and Boris Dubin, "Vse edino: Rossiiskomu obshchestvu stalo zhit' khuzhe, stalo zhit' skuchnee" [All the same: The Russian government began to live worse and its life became more boring], *Itogi*, January 23, 2001.

7. Thus, in April 2000, only 2 percent of those polled felt that positive changes could be expected right after the election, 10 percent felt that such changes would happen after six months, 20 percent after a year, and 22 percent in two to three years; 20 percent felt it would take more than three years, 12 percent doubted there would be such changes under this president, and 14 percent had no opinion. VTsIOM, www.polit.ru, April 14, 2000.

8. VTsIOM, www.polit.ru, March 7, 2000.

9. VTsIOM, www.polit.ru, April 14, 2000.

10. Putin worked for Borodin for a time in the Office of the President's Affairs. After his election, he recommended Borodin for secretary of the Russian–Belarusian Union—a diplomatic position that gave him immunity. By making this recommendation, Putin was demonstrating his gratitude.

11. *Obshchaya gazeta*, February 9, 2000.

12. VTsIOM, www.polit.ru, November 2000.

13. Kasyanov was supported by 325 deputies—a record. The most influential prime minister before him, Yevgeny Primakov, got 317 votes.

14. Putin named as head of the Central Okrug Georgy Poltavchenko, lieutenant general of the tax police and Putin's close friend. The head of the North-West Okrug was to be Victor Cherkesov, an FSB comrade of Putin's in Saint Petersburg and the first deputy director of the FSB. Sergei Kiriyenko, a leader of the SPS faction and former prime minister, was named head of the Povolzhye Okrug. For the Siberian Okrug, Putin tapped Leonid Drachevsky, minister of affairs of the Commonwealth of Independent States. The head named for the North-Caucasus Okrug was General Victor Kazantsev, previously responsible for operations of the "antiterrorist operation" in the Northern Caucasus. The head of the Ural Okrug was to be Lieutenant General Petr Latyshev, deputy minister of internal affairs. For the Far East Okrug, the head was to be General Konstantin Pulikovsky, commander of federal forces in Chechnya in the first Chechen war. On Putin's Federation reform, see Eugene Huskey, "Center–Periphery Struggle: Putin's Reforms," in Archie Brown and Lilia Shevtsova, eds., *Gorbachev, Yeltsin, and Putin: Political Leadership in Transition* (Washington, D.C.: Carnegie Endowment for International Peace, 2001).

15. The first law gave the president the right to demand that the regional bosses obey the laws of the Russian Federation and to punish them by suspending the powers of the

law-breaking governors and replacing them with temporary leaders. Another law gave the same powers to the governors vis-à-vis local leaders. The third law covered new principles for the formation of the Federation Council, among them that governors and heads of local legislatures could no longer preside in the upper chamber and no longer had immunity from prosecution for criminal or administrative wrongdoing. The Federation Council would consist of regional representatives proposed by the regional authorities.

16. Writing in *Kommersant-Daily* on May 20, 2000, Ilya Bulavinov, Nikolai Vardul, and Azer Mursaliev declared, "There is yet another revolution in Russia. And once again from above. Of course, it is not clear whether it will achieve its goals. After all, not only are the disadvantages of the former administration still here, but new ones have appeared."

17. By 2002, the presidential representatives in the *okrugs* had basically fulfilled their positive role—thanks to the pressure on the governors, they had helped bring local laws in line with the Russian Constitution. But then they became an obstacle in the relations between the regions and the center, increasing its bureaucratization. Putin seemed to realize that, but he did not know what to do with his representatives.

18. Chubais's role in this period was contradictory. While trying to curtail Berezovsky and Gusinsky, he continued to support the oligarch Vladimir Potanin, who was close to the liberals at that time.

19. "Diktatura razrushit stranu: Obshchestvu est' chto teryat'" [Society has a lot to lose], *Obshchaya gazeta*, May 25–31, 2000.

Chapter 4

1. I observed this unequal battle close up—in 2000, I was a member of the Public Board of NTV, a consultative organ of the television network, headed by former USSR president Mikhail Gorbachev. The board included several well-known democrats of the first wave: Yuri Afanasyev and Yuri Ryzhov; writer Alexander Gelman; the editor of *Obshchaya gazeta*, Yegor Yakovlev; the editor of *Novaya gazeta*, Dmitry Muratov; and Mikhail Fedotov, a former press minister in the Yeltsin government. The Public Board tried to organize support for the persecuted journalists.

2. The results of another poll conducted by the VTsIOM in July 2002 are worth mentioning. In that survey, 39 percent were attracted to Putin because he was energetic and strong-willed, 19 percent thought he could bring order to the country, 9 percent thought that he was a leader who could lead others, 6 percent considered him an experienced politician, and 5 percent thought him a far-seeing politician. The rest selected other qualities in Putin—that outwardly he was nice, that he understood the

needs of ordinary people, and so on. When the same respondents were asked what they didn't like about Putin, 29 percent of them said that he had ties to the Yeltsin entourage, 12 percent that he had no clear policies, and 10 percent that his actions in Chechnya were solely to boost his popularity. Forty-three percent of respondents could not identify what they did not like about the new president.

3. Berezovsky, attempting to appear to be a defender of democracy, began subsidizing nongovernmental and human rights organizations. He even bailed out the Andrei Sakharov Foundation, named for one of the best-known Soviet dissidents, which was in a perilous financial state. Sakharov's widow, the human rights activist Yelena Bonner, accepted the money, albeit after some vacillation, thereby legitimating Berezovsky's new role.

4. But the intriguer remained faithful to intrigue—in his numerous speeches in that period, Berezovsky left open the possibility of rapprochement with Putin, if the president only called him. Berezovsky always said that there was no alternative to Putin in the presidential elections and that he would support him again.

5. After fleeing to London, Berezovsky created his party, Liberal Russia, which was joined by the well-known liberals and former members of the SPS Sergei Yushenkov and Victor Pokhmelkin. The oligarch took his place among the leadership of the party, which he financed. In April 2002, Berezovsky published "Manifesto of Russian Liberalism," one of the most eloquent attempts to set a liberal agenda for Russia. The former oligarch seemed to understand better than many other liberal politicians what Russia needed to resume its liberal reforms. Boris Berezovsky, "Manifesto of Russian Liberalism," *Nezavisimaya gazeta*, April 11, 2002. In October 2002, Berezovsky was expelled from his own party after trying to make friends with nationalists and communists.

6. *Kommersant-Vlast*, August 20, 2000.

7. When Russians learned from a note found with one of the bodies that some of the crew had remained alive for a time after the accident, 40 percent of those polled expressed outrage at the authorities, 25 percent expressed grief over the deaths, 16 percent said that the people had been lied to, 11 percent expressed sadness, 6 percent expressed no feelings, and 2 percent could not define their reaction to the event.

8. At that time, the Kremlin administration began examining the possibility of ending gubernatorial elections. The idea was fully consonant with the logic of the president's pragmatic authoritarianism, which was built on the lower echelons' dependence on the leader and not on the voters. Besides which, the people in the Kremlin were tired of expending energy and money supporting their candidates in the regions.

9. The president's political engineers began work on new electoral legislation. It proposed introducing proportional elections—following the model the Duma had created—in all the regional parliaments by 2003. That would change the political landscape in the

regions, strengthening the center's control, because, in accordance with the law on parties, regional parties were in fact liquidated. The new laws on parties and on elections were supposed to be a new step in political reform that would establish the role of the Kremlin "party of power" (first it was Unity, later United Russia) and make it the ruling party.

10. In the fall of 2002, the pro-Kremlin party United Russia suggested that the threshold required for the political party to get representation in the Duma be raised from 5 to 7 percent (at the beginning, a 12.5 percent threshold was suggested). It was one more step toward a party system fully controlled from above that would keep the ruling team from having any unpleasant surprises.

11. The "Pristina dash" by Russian parachutists in 1999 during the Kosovo crisis (the purpose of the "dash" was to force NATO to guarantee for Russia a separate sector of responsibility in Kosovo) was organized by the head of the General Staff, Anatoly Kvashnin, and his deputy, Leonid Ivashov, without the knowledge of minister of defense Igor Sergeyev and most likely also without Yeltsin's knowledge. It could have created a real conflict between Russia and NATO.

12. Unbelievable but true: In 2001, almost a million Russian service members continued to guard "mobilization resources" in case of global war; that is, they worked as warehouse guards. The warehouses they protected held enough old-style military topcoats to dress the entire male population of draft age.

13. Thus, in the course of the military reform initiated by Putin, the salary of officers went up by 300 to 500 rubles ($100 to $160), which would hardly have satisfied them.

14. Oleg Odnikolenko, "Skol'ko stoi profi" [How much do professionals cost], *Itogi*, January 22, 2002.

15. Every Russian man of age 18–27 years is required to serve two years in the military. But most get deferments for higher education and other reasons or exemptions for poor health. Others avoid the call-up by paying bribes or just fleeing.

16. In the heat of the 1996 reelection campaign, Yeltsin had pledged to form a fully contract military by 2000. But his promise was quickly disavowed by top officials, who said that such a project was too expensive.

Chapter 5

1. On the second Chechen war, see Gail W. Lapidus, "Putin's War on Terrorism: Lessons from Chechnya," *Post-Soviet Affairs,* vol. 18, no. 1 (January–March 2002), pp. 41–49; Anna Politkovskaya, *A Dirty War: A Russian Reporter in Chechnya* (London: Harvill Press, 2002); and Alexei Malashenko and Dmitri Trenin, *Vremia Iuga: Rossiia v*

Chechnie—Chechnya v Rossii [The time of the South: Russia in Chechnya—Chechnya in Russia] (a Carnegie Moscow Center publication; Washington, D.C.: Carnegie Endowment for International Peace, 2002).

2. And only 17 percent felt that Russia was obligated to compensate Chechnya for war damages, while 73 percent were against it, feeling that Russia had enough of its own problems without the Chechens. Yuri Levada, "Rossiyane ustali ot voiny" [Russians are tired of war], *Obshchaya gazeta*, August 17–23, 2000.

3. Politkovskaya, *A Dirty War*, p. 21.

4. Ruslan Khasbulatov, "Situatsiya v Chechenskoi respublike" [The situation in the Chechen Republic], *Nezavisimaya gazeta*, December 29, 2000.

5. Quite a few Russians in the army, including officers, entered into a deal with Chechen units to sell Chechen oil illegally or to sell arms to the separatists Russia was fighting.

6. In April 2000, 60 percent spoke out in support of military action in Chechnya, but by October the figure was down to 44 percent. In April, 21 percent supported the idea of negotiations with Chechnya, whereas in October it was 47 percent. Yuri Levada, "Chto schitaem po oseni" [What we think in autumn], *NG–Stsenarii*, November 15, 2000.

7. In November, an International Monetary Fund mission came to Moscow and found the economic situation in the country so good that it concluded that Russia did not need new credits and could pay the Paris Club. This was a blow to the government, which had been counting on International Monetary Fund loans.

8. The price of Russian exports rose as much as 38 percent, while the cost of imports fell 14 percent. The index of industrial growth, compared with the same period in 1999, rose 9.6 percent. The growth in oil production continued. Real incomes rose 9.5 percent in ten months compared with the same period the year before. But they did not reach the 80 percent level of pre-crisis 1997. *Vedomosti*, November 27, 2000.

9. *Niezavisimaja gazeta*, November 17, 2000.

10. Polls showed that only 39 percent of Russians supported reinstating the Soviet anthem. The rest preferred other options, including the current anthem with music by Ivan Glinka (20 percent). *Vedomosti*, December 9, 2000.

11. *Komsomolskaya pravda*, December 8, 2000. Yeltsin spoke after Anatoly Chubais drove out to the dacha where Yeltsin was living like a hermit and persuaded him to protest the return to the Soviet symbols. It was obvious that Yeltsin was sincerely upset by Putin's decision to reinstate the old symbols.

12. The only possible path for Russia is to conclude a long-term strategic alliance with Asia, said Alexander Dugin, one of the ideologues of Eurasianism, a form of Russian nationalism. Available at www.strana.ru, November 14, 2000.

13. Strobe Talbott, *The Russia Hand, A Memoir of Presidential Diplomacy* (New York: Random House, 2002).

14. Thomas Graham and Arnold Horelick, *U.S.–Russian Relations at the Turn of the Century*, Report of the U.S. and Russia Working Groups (Washington, D.C.: Carnegie Endowment for International Peace, 2001), p. 9.

15. Talbott, *The Russia Hand*, p. 4.

16. Jim Hoagland, "From Russia with Chutzpah, or How to Alienate a Partner," *International Herald Tribune*, November 23, 2000.

17. U.S. assistance to Russia was significant, but not as large as the Russian leadership expected. Between 1992 and 1999, the United States provided Russia with $7.67 billion in economic assistance (the European Union between 1991 and 2000 provided Russia with $2.28 billion). In addition, Russia got $8.89 billion in commercial financing and insurance from the U.S. government, of the $18.01 billion provided to the newly independent states. In 1999, Washington provided $905 million in official assistance to Russia. (The European Union provided $144 million, including Germany's contribution of $82 million.) Russia became the second largest recipient of American aid, after Israel. Esther Brimmer, Benjamin Schreer, and Christian Tuschoff, *Contemporary Perspectives on European Security*, German Issues No. 27 (Washington, D.C.: American Institute for Contemporary Studies, Johns Hopkins University, 2002). In the 1990s, the United States became the largest outside investor in the Russian economy, accounting for 30 percent of all foreign investments.

18. Yuri Levada, "2000 god—razocharovaniya i nadezhdy" [The year 2000—disappointments and hopes], *Moskovskie novosti*, December 26, 1999–January 2, 2000.

19. *Kommersant-Vlast'*, December 26, 2000.

Chapter 6

1. According to polls, only 15 percent of Russians at that moment wanted Russia to take "the path of European civilization common to the modern world," 18 percent wanted to return to the path followed by the USSR, 60 percent preferred Russia's "own special path," and 7 percent had no opinion. Lev Gudkov and Boris Dubin, "Rossiiskomu obshchestvu stalo zhit' khuzhe, stalo zhit' skuchnee" [Life is worse and less merry for Russian society], *Itogi*, January 23, 2001, p. 14.

2. Gudkov and Dubin, "Rossiiskomu obshchestvu stalo zhit' khuzhe," p. 14.

3. Alexander Tsipko, "Smozhet li Putin pereigrat' Gusinskogo?" [Will Putin be able to outplay Gusinsky?], *Nezavisimaya gazeta*, February 20, 2001, and Vitaly Tretyakov, "Bolshaya stat'ya o Putine i Rossii" [Big article on Putin and Russia], *Nezavisimaya gazeta*, January 31, 2001.

4. Gudkov and Dubin, "Rossiiskomu obshchestvu stalo zhit' khuzhe."

5. At the peak of the crisis with NTV in March 2001, 35 percent of those polled across the country expressed outrage over the events (in Moscow it was much higher—55 percent). In April, three-quarters of Muscovites said they trusted NTV. Almost half those polled in this period thought that the conflict surrounding NTV had been created because of the authorities' desire to liquidate independent television. Another 33 percent were blaming the company. Yuri Levada, "Vlast' sil'na no bespomoshchna" [The regime strong but helpless], *Moskovskie novosti*, April 10–16, 2001.

6. Part of the team from the old NTV, headed by Yevgeny Kiselev, moved to a different channel, TV-6, which by an irony of fate was owned by Boris Berezovsky. This is the drama of the Russian mass media—there were no alternative publicly financed outlets, and media that wanted to be independent of the state had to bow down to the oligarchs.

7. The former teams of *Itogi* and *Segodnya* soon began to publish the new journals *Ezhenedel'ny zhurnal* and *Djelovaya khronika*. But those journals had no previous popularity.

8. In 2002, the Kremlin began discussing the idea of forming the government on the basis of the dominant party, United Russia.

9. A number of active members of the Union of Right Forces (SPS), among them Sergei Yushenkov and Victor Pokhmelkin, created the new Liberal Party, in opposition to the Kremlin, with the active support of oligarch Boris Berezovsky.

10. Vitaly Tretyakov, "Putin, Chubais i SPS" [Putin, Chubais, and the SPS], *Nezavisimaya gazeta*, May 23, 2001.

Chapter 7

1. Now three disciplinary warnings were enough to get a judge fired. The mechanism for holding judges criminally liable was simplified. Ordinary judges and their tenures depended on the chairmen of courts, who were appointed by the executive branch.

2. In Europe, small and medium-sized businesses accounted for 70 percent of gross domestic product, whereas in Russia, they accounted for only 10 percent. *Novye izvestiya*, December 21, 2001.

3. The Putinists were also known as the Northern Alliance, a reference to Afghanistan's Northern Alliance and to the fact that these people had come with Putin from Saint Petersburg, Russia's "northern capital." The Putinists of that period included Nikolai Patrushev, director of the FSB; his deputy, Nikolai Zaostrovtsev; Igor Sechin and Victor Ivanov of the presidential staff; and Victor Cherkesov and Georgy Poltavchenko, presidential representatives in the *okrugs* (new regional jurisdictions).

4. The leader of the Yeltsinites was first head of the presidential staff Alexander Voloshin. Prime Minister Mikhail Kasyanov was part of the group. They were soon joined by former privatization tsar Anatoly Chubais, who would for some time be the new inspiration of the old Yeltsin circle. Several oligarchs, such as Oleg Deripaska and Roman Abramovich, were part of the circle as well.

5. On United States–Russia relations under Bush and Putin, see Angela Stent and Lilia Shevtsova, "America, Russia and Europe: A Realignment?" *Survival*, vol. 44, no. 4 (Winter 2002–2003).

6. Other administration officials were less restrained. The secretary of defense, Donald Rumsfeld, said openly, "Russia is an active proliferator. It has been providing countries with assistance in these areas in a way that complicates the problem for the U.S. and Western Europe." And the deputy secretary of defense, Paul Wolfowitz, was even more frank: "These people seem to be willing to sell anything to anyone for money. I recall Lenin's phrase that the capitalists will sell the very rope from which we will hang them."

7. Right after the terrorist attacks on the United States, 52 percent of Russians polled expressed their support for Americans. A majority of 54 percent, however, thought Russia should remain neutral and not take part in the response to September 11; only 28 percent said Russia should give the West moral support, and 30 percent supported participation in United States–organized military operations aimed at terrorists.

8. Figures in this paragraph and the next are taken from "Rossiia v poiskakh strategicheskoi positsii" [Russia in search of a strategic position], posted on www.liberal.ru, October 2002.

9. "Rossiia v poiskakh."

10. At least a partial flare-up in the Russian public occurred during the Winter Olympic Games in Salt Lake City in February 2002, when the Russians began to lose. Some Russian media outlets tied these losses to a "conspiracy against Russia" with a bias toward the United States. Even Putin did not avoid outrage over "nonobjective judges."

11. Patrick E. Tyler, "In Spat on NATO and Russia, Powell Fends Off Rumsfeld," *New York Times*, December 8, 2001.

12. According to Public Opinion Foundation polls, 43 percent of Russians had negative feelings about the U.S. withdrawal from the ABM Treaty, 31 percent were indifferent, and 8 percent were positive (18 percent had no opinion). And 42 percent of those polled felt that Putin had to take action in response (only 28 percent felt that he should not). Posted on www.fom.ru, December 27, 2001.

13. Rodric Braithwaite, *Across the Moscow River: The World Turned Upside Down* (New Haven, Conn.: Yale University Press, 2002), pp. 338–39.

14. Yuri Levada and Leonid Sledov, "Obshchestvenno-politicheskaia situatsiia v dekabre 2001" [The sociopolitical situation in December 2001], VTsIOM, December 27, 2001.

Chapter 8

1. Putin's constant vacillation increased the frustration of the liberal-minded people in Russia who had strongly endorsed his pro-Western shift. See Andrei Piontkovsky, "My Putin," *Novaya gazeta,* October 10, 2002.

2. Putin proved that he was consequential—he did not forgive and he did not forget his personal enemies as his predecessor sometimes had done. At that time, the president's chief enemy was Boris Berezovsky, who was waging his own vendetta against Putin and who continued to be the owner of TV-6. Having no possibility of reaching Berezovsky in the United Kingdom, where the oligarch found political asylum in 2000, the Kremlin cracked down on TV-6. But even without Berezovsky, independent television in Russia had no future.

3. *Moskovskie novosti,* January 8–21, 2002

4. *Financial Times*, February 10, 2002.

5. Andrew Kuchins, *Summit with Substance: Creating Payoffs in an Unequal Partnership,* Carnegie Endowment Policy Brief 16 (May 2002).

6. In the spring of 2002, the United States withdrew from its steel agreement with Russia, increasing its tariffs, which was a painful blow to Russian producers: It cost Russian producers up to $600 million annually. Moscow reciprocated with a ban on American poultry—"Bush chicken legs" (as Russians called American chickens imported into Russia beginning during George H. W. Bush's presidency)—that affected American farmers in 32 states and cost American producers $800 million a year. In the end, the United States made exemptions on steel imports for its European allies. Those exemptions did not, however, extend to Russia. Meanwhile, Russia lifted its ban on American poultry.

7. *Nezavisimaya gazeta,* April 8, 2002.

8. Leon Fuerth, "On Russia, Think Big," *Washington Post*, May 1, 2002. Katrina Vanden Heuvel and Stephen Cohen criticized Washington policy for "treating Russia not as a real partner but as a helper when it suits U.S. purposes." Katrina Vanden Heuvel and Stephen Cohen, "U.S. Takes Russia for Granted at Its Peril," *Los Angeles Times*, May 1, 2002.

9. Robert Legvold, "Russia's Unformed Foreign Policy," *Foreign Affairs*, vol. 80, no. 5 (2001), p. 72. On United States–Russia relations after September 11, 2001, see Robert

Legvold, "U.S.–Russian Relations Ten Months after September 11," paper presented at the 27th Conference of the Aspen Institute, U.S.–Russia Relations: A New Framework (Washington, D.C., August 15–21, 2002).

10. See *Current History*, October 2002, www.currenthistory.com.

11. Thomas Graham, *Russia's Decline and Uncertain Recovery* (Washington, D.C.: Carnegie Endowment for International Peace, 2002), p. 84.

12. Stephen Kotkin, *Armageddon Averted: The Soviet Collapse, 1970–2000* (New York: Oxford University Press, 2001).

13. On issues of order in Russia, see Richard Rose and Neil Munro, *Elections without Order: Russia's Challenge to Vladimir Putin* (Cambridge: Cambridge University Press, 2002).

14. *Vedomosti*, April 23, 2002.

15. Tatyana Kutkovets and Igor Klyamkin, "Normal'nyje ludi v nienormal'noi stranie" [Normal people in the abnormal country], *Moskovskie novosti*, July 8, 2002.

INDEX

Vlasov, Andrei, 144

Voloshin, Alexander: membership in the Family of, 17, 27, 278n10, 289n4; as Putin's head of staff, 84–85, 89, 111, 193; in Chechen war, 279nn15–16; and suspicions of corruption, 278n7

Volsky, Arkady, 180, 227

Voronezh protests, 224

VTsIOM. *See* All-Russian Center for Public Opinion Research

Vyakhirev, Rem, 188

Walesa, Lech, 61

Walking Together, 183

Washington Post, 176, 202, 238

Western world and Russia: future partnership options and, 261–68; and "integration without transformation," 238–39, 263–64; and preference for multiparty system, 130; and Putin's relationship with the West, 22, 97–98, 205, 208–13; and Russian desires for Western lifestyles, 169–71; and Russia's anti-Westernism, 153–54, 173–76, 212, 225, 234–35, 242, 265; and Western reactions to Putin's media crackdowns, 107, 176–77. *See also* European Union; United States–Russia relationship

Wolfowitz, Paul, 289n5

World Bank, 10, 140. *See also* foreign debt

World Trade Organization, 211, 217, 239, 265–67

Yabloko Party: and approval of Putin's 2001 budget, 140; and economic crisis of 1998, 12–13; and law on parties, 128–29; opposition to Putin by, 52–53, 102, 225; in parliamentary elections of 1999, 47, 50; in presidential elections of 2000, 70, 75; and support for NTV's independence, 176

Yakovlev, Vladimir, 31, 90

Yakovlev, Yegor, 283n1

Yakutia elections, 195

Yasin, Yevgeny, 216–17

Yavlinsky, Grigory, 19, 22, 53, 110, 189; and economic crisis of 1998, 12–13; and presidential elections of 2000, 70, 73, 75. *See also* Yabloko Party

Years in Big-Time Politics (Primakov), 19

Yegorov, Vladimir, 126–27

Yeltsin, Boris, 3–5, 8–9, 273; and autocratic monarchical style, 59–65; and Bank of New York money-laundering scandal, 35, 147, 278–79nn12–14; concerns regarding Primakov, 23–25; concerns regarding Stepashin, 29; contributions to communism's end in Russia, 61–65, 67; democratic traits of, 60–61; and election of Primakov in 1999, 40–42; and failure to enact democratic reforms, 65–67; and family's role in governing, 26–28; and freedom of press, 227; goals as president, 60–61; health of, 9, 25–26, 63, 281n10; immunity granted by Putin, 69; impeachment attempt, 24–25; influence on Putin's presidency of, 80, 87, 89–90, 227; leadership style of, 17–18, 59–65; opinion of Soviet anthem, 145–46, 286n11; personal habits of, 17; reappearance in 2002 of, 243–45; reform goals of, 60–61; retirement of, 54–68, 278n10, 281n7; and role of business oligarchy, 277n1; succession considerations for, 28–30; tolerance of Communist Party by, 41. *See also* Dyachenko, Tatyana; Family, the; *Presidential Marathon* (Yeltsin)

Yezhenedel'ny zhurnal, 217, 288n7

youth movement, 183

Yumashev, Valentin, 17, 19, 26–27, 85, 278n10

Yushenkov, Sergei, 284n5, 288n9

Zakayev, Akhmad, 247

Zaostrovtsev, Nikolai, 288n3

Zhirinovsky, Vladimir, 47, 70, 75

Zyuganov, Gennady, 22; and 2000 presidential elections, 41–42, 49, 70, 73–75; in Communist Party, 63–64, 230. *See also* Communist Party

ABOUT THE
AUTHOR

Lilia Shevtsova is a senior associate in the Russian and Eurasian Program at the Carnegie Endowment, dividing her time between the Endowment offices in Washington and Moscow. She is one of Russia's top political analysts, an award-winning journalist, and a regular commentator for major world television and radio networks.

Ms. Shevtsova has been a visiting professor at the University of California at Berkeley and at Cornell University, and she was a fellow at the Woodrow Wilson International Center for Scholars. She is a member of the executive committee of the International Council for Central and East European Studies, and a member of the board of the Institute for Human Science at Boston University. She also serves on the editorial boards of *Megapolis*, *Journal of Democracy*, *Polis*, and *Demokratizatsiya*.

Ms. Shevtsova is the author of six books, including *Yeltsin's Russia: Myths and Reality* (Carnegie Endowment, 1999) and *Gorbachev, Yeltsin, and Putin: Political Leadership in Russia's Transition*, edited with Archie Brown (Carnegie Endowment, 2001). She holds a doctorate from the Institute of International Relations and the Academy of Sciences in Moscow.

Carnegie Endowment for International Peace

The Carnegie Endowment is a private, nonprofit organization dedicated to advancing cooperation between nations and promoting active international engagement by the United States. Founded in 1910, its work is nonpartisan and dedicated to achieving practical results.

Through research, publishing, convening, and, on occasion, creating new institutions and international networks, Endowment associates shape fresh policy approaches. Their interests span geographic regions and the relations between governments, business, international organizations, and civil society, focusing on the economic, political, and technological forces driving global change. Through its Carnegie Moscow Center, the Endowment helps to develop a tradition of public policy analysis in the states of the former Soviet Union and to improve relations between Russia and the United States. The Endowment publishes *Foreign Policy*, one of the world's leading magazines of international politics and economics.